John K. Andrews, Jr.

Interview... ...

on Bae...

D0371960

CRUEL
AND
USUAL
PUNISHMENT

CRUEL
AND
USUAL
PUNISHMENT

By

NONIE DARWISH

THOMAS NELSON
Since 1798

NASHVILLE   DALLAS   MEXICO CITY   RIO DE JANEIRO   BEIJING

Published in Nashville, Tennessee, by Thomas Nelson. Thomas Nelson is a registered trademark of Thomas Nelson, Inc.

Unless otherwise noted, Scripture quotations are taken from the HOLY BIBLE: NEW INTERNATIONAL VERSION®. © 1973, 1978, 1984 by International Bible Society. Used by permission of Zondervan Publishing House. All rights reserved.

Editoral staff: Thom Chittom and Heather Skelton

Thomas Nelson, Inc., titles may be purchased in bulk for educational, business, fundraising, or sales promotional use. For information, please e-mail SpecialMarkets@ThomasNelson.com.

ISBN 978-1-59555-209-9 (IE)

Library of Congress Cataloging-in-Publication Data

Darwish, Nonie.
    Cruel and usual punishment / by Nonie Darwish.
        p. cm.
    Includes bibliographical references and index.
    ISBN 978-1-59555-161-0
    1. Islamic law—Social aspects. 2. Women—Legal status, laws, etc. (Islamic law)
3. Islam—Controversial literature. I. Title.
KBP173.25.D37 2008
340.5'9—dc22   2008046080

Printed in the United States of America

08 09 10 11 12 QW 6 5 4 3 2 1

To my family

"I take no pleasure in the death of the wicked, but rather that they turn from their ways and live."

— EZEKIEL 33:11

Contents

Introduction

FOR THE FIRST THIRTY YEARS OF MY LIFE, I LIVED as a virtual slave. I was a bird in a cage; a second-class citizen who had to watch what I said even to my close friends. Under Islamic law I had to live in a gender-segregated environment and always be aware that the legal and social penalty for "sin" could end my life. This is what it is to live as a woman under Sharia law. Sharia (the body of Islamic law) is different from law in the West, because it deals with all aspects of day-to-day life, including politics, economics, banking, business law, contract law, marriage, divorce, child rearing and custody, sexuality, sin, crime, and social issues. Among other things, it allows a woman seen without a headdress to be flogged, punishes rape victims, and calls for beheading for adultery. I never questioned or challenged it—or dared to even think about its validity.

During my years in Egypt, the vast majority of Muslim women lived in cramped apartments or unhealthy little mud huts, spending their entire lives working hard under the severe Egyptian sun. Yet they rarely complained or made an effort to change their circumstances.

Whatever came their way, no matter how hard or unjust, they viewed it as "God's will." They struggled, coped, adapted, and bent their lives, denying their most basic human needs to suit Sharia's cruel misogyny. Most women got used to their cages, but even the most opulent palace can still have bars.

None of us tried to examine what Sharia was, ask how it came about, or question why we followed it. "This is Allah's law," we were told. Doubting any word from the Qur'an (Islam's holy book) or Mohammed (the founder of Islam) is *haram*, a sin, and we all knew what awaited those who questioned Allah's law: death. Now that this life is behind me, I feel it is very important to share my experiences with citizens of Western nations and to explain how these brutal Islamic Sharia laws not only control every aspect of the lives of followers of Islam in the Middle East, but also how Sharia law is on the march to Western nations.

◊   ◊   ◊

To escape Sharia marriage laws, I moved to America in 1978, in large part to be able to marry an Egyptian Coptic Christian. Even so, it was necessary for him to convert to Islam in order to protect me from the long arm of Sharia law. My move to America in 1978 liberated me from life under the most oppressive system of laws in the world—the best gift that living in America has given me. To live under Islamic Sharia law is to live in the world's largest maximum-security prison, and I for one don't want to be incarcerated again.

For the next twenty years, I quietly lived the American dream. I raised a family, had a good job, and generally enjoyed the freedoms of a democracy that respects the rights of individuals. One day, trying to impress a close family friend visiting from Egypt, we visited a mosque for Friday prayers. As I listened to the sermon, I was amazed at the radical tone. Even my Egyptian friend was offended and asked to leave. Something was happening in the America I loved, but I pushed it out of my mind and did nothing. Later, in the summer of 2001, I took my American-born children for a visit to Egypt and was struck by how much more radical Egypt had become. I returned to the U.S. on September 10, 2001, and woke to a nightmare the next morning.

When I saw the second plane fly into the Twin Towers, I knew that jihad had come to America, and my life would change forever. I would need to speak out to warn my fellow Americans of what was coming.

For me, what is most troublesome is not the terrorists attacking from the outside, terrible as that is. It is the attack on democracy from within. The radicals and Sharia enforcers are now here in the West and often operate under the radar of Western law and their open systems of government. Demands for Sharia have arrived on the shores of Europe and America by Muslim minorities who demand it as part of their religious rights. Informing the West of the tragedy of Sharia Law and its impact on women, the Muslim family, and society has thus become my objective. I began writing about it and was invited to speak on college campuses across the country. After the publication of my book *Now They Call Me Infidel*, I began traveling around the country speaking out.

Muslim Sharia Goals in the West

In the fall of 2007, I was part of a panel discussion called "Islam and Democracy: Companions or Competitors?" at Mount San Antonio College in Southern California. What happened afterward is indicative of the kind of viewpoints I am hearing from young Muslim students across the country. It is something that we need to be aware of and understand. To ignore this would be at the peril of our democracy.

One of the panelists, the head of the Muslim student organization, fiercely defended Sharia. After the discussion I asked him, "If Sharia is the perfect system that every Muslim should follow, why are you living in America and not in a Muslim Sharia state such as Iran or Saudi Arabia?" His answer was that not one Muslim country applied Sharia as it should and that is why he was in America.

In the heated discussion that followed, another student who believed that Muslim countries failed to bring about the true Sharia state, actually believed that perhaps the United States could be the first country to apply Sharia the proper way, the way it was intended by Allah. Many of the students echoed that belief, and some even expressed a desire to demand the enforcement of Sharia in America.

Here is an important distinction: it is not just that they intend to perfect and correct Sharia in their own countries of origin and then gradually expand this perfected Sharia-driven society outward to the rest of the world. Rather, they want to supplant or transplant a way of life to America and the West—even though they know it has never worked and has left behind a trail of destruction, misery, stagnation, and cultural chaos in Muslim countries. Their intent is nothing less than the wholesale supplanting of Western civilization and constitutional law with their ideal of the perfect Sharia-based society, one that has never existed except in their fantasy of Andalusia Spain under Arab rule.

What they want to do has been done before to countries like Egypt, which was once a superpower but is no longer. History holds some important lessons that the West must not ignore.

My daughter, who was with me that night, was chatting next to me with a different group of Muslim student organization members on the topic of Zionism. I called out to her and said, "Let's go." I was too sad to continue the discussion. As we walked away toward my car, we heard some of the students calling after us, "You and your mother are both Jews and Zionists." Their words saddened me deeply.

Wherever I go to speak on U.S. college campuses, Muslim student organizations are defending Sharia and claiming that it is Americans who need an education about true Islam and Sharia. Even young female Muslim students defend polygamy and are uninterested in my discussion of the tragedy of the stoning and flogging of women going on right now in the name of

Sharia in many areas of the Muslim world. Their reaction is always defensive, and their strategy is always to attack the messengers. I and a few others who speak out are those messengers.

At another event, this time the Islamo-Fascism Awareness Week at George Washington University in Washington DC, in which I participated in October 2007, a young Muslim woman with a tiger-print head scarf, apparently a student, said: "I want the Sharia law imposed in my country." By "my country," I presume that she meant the United States, since her country of origin—I would guess Egypt, by the sound of her accent—already largely applies Sharia not only to the Muslim population but also on the minority Christian population. I was stunned at her choice of the word *imposed,* but she is right: Sharia can only be imposed, and she wants it imposed in America because, wherever she came from, no Muslim country is totally ruled by Sharia.

∘ ∘ ∘

The book is divided into two parts. Part One explains what Sharia is and how it impacts individuals—women, men, and families, showing in effect the *micro* impact of Sharia. Part Two examines the *macro* impact of Sharia, how it affects society, the Muslim world, and the frightening implications for the West. At the end, I lay out a detailed strategy that each nation must adopt lest it suffer the same fate as formerly Christian Egypt.

The purpose of this book is not to spread hatred of a people, but to tell the truth about the wickedness of Islamic Sharia law. Islam is at the gates. Western democracies are underestimating a major threat that will push their futures to a point of no return. The West must either wake up to the danger today or submit unconditionally tomorrow.

A Warning
to the West

WESTERN CIVILIZATION FINDS ITSELF AT A CROSSROADS:
Will democratic nations be "politically tolerant" of radical Islam
inside their own countries, or will they recognize the threat in
time to defend their way of life?

The West must act and act now. If it cannot—or will not—
its citizens will wake up one day and find themselves living in
an Islamic world. The history of Islam is full of similar sce-
narios. About sixty million Christians, eighty million Hindus,
and ten million Buddhists were killed during the jihad conquests. Jews saw a mosque built on top of their temple mount
in their own Holy Land in Jerusalem, and Egypt was a
Byzantine Coptic Christian nation for six hundred years before
Muslim Bedouins invaded this ancient civilization in the seventh century and forced Islam and the Arabic language on its
citizens who suffered an extreme and brutal genocide. Africa
suffered 120 million deaths from jihad in the last fourteen
hundred years.

The numbers of non-Muslim casualties of jihad are still rising
daily. Terrorist attacks on Jews and Christians are a daily occur-
rence in the Muslim world, and now the sword of jihad is
moving toward Europe, America, Australia, Asia, and Africa. No
corner of the world is safe any longer.

Islam has annihilated every culture it has invaded or immigrated into. The annihilation sometimes takes centuries, but once Islam is ascendant, it never fails to cause bloodshed and civil wars. The ensuing war pits the very soul of the original host culture against the forces that want it to become extinct.

The Takeover Program

The following is a straightforward and accurate description of the plan of Islam According to Sayyid Abul Ala Maududi, one of the most influential theologians and Islamic thinkers of the twentieth century:

> Islam wishes to destroy all states and governments anywhere on the face of the earth which are opposed to the ideology and program of Islam regardless of the country or the nation which rules it. The purpose of Islam is to set up a state on the basis of its own ideology and programme, regardless of which nation assumes the role of the standard bearer of Islam or the rule of which nation is undermined in the process of the establishment of an ideological Islamic state. It must be evident to you from this discussion that the objective of Islamic jihad is to eliminate the rule of an un-Islamic system and establish in its stead an Islamic system of state rule. Islam does not intend to confine this revolution to a single state or a few countries; the aim of Islam is to bring about a universal revolution.[1]

Or consider the words of Omar Ahmad, cofounder of the Washington DC-based Council on American-Islamic Relations (CAIR):

> If you choose to live here (in America) . . . you have a responsibility to deliver the message of Islam. . . . Islam isn't in America to be equal to any other faith, but to become dominant. . . . The Koran,

the Muslim book of scripture, should be the highest authority in America, and Islam the only accepted religion on Earth.[2]

I subscribe to Arab TV and hear many Muslim religious leaders tell the world "we will conquer Rome, Britain, and America," and frankly even without "conquering," they can do a lot of long-term harm and create civil unrest through immigration, high birth rates, and proselytizing among vulnerable Western citizens. Kosovo was the last Muslim nation to emerge as a result of a separatist movement from within a larger, non-Muslim nation. The West today might laugh at the word conquer, but if Chechnya or Kosovo-style events begin to happen in Western countries between Muslims and non-Muslims, it will usher in a long, bloody history of demands for yet another separatist movement. If this sounds far-fetched now, tell that to the people of the former Yugoslavia.

Your Money at Work for Sharia

Saudi Arabia, Iran, and other oil-rich Muslim countries are in a race to spread Sharia around the world with financial strings attached. The Saudi government's financial aid to needy Muslim countries and organizations around the world is linked to their compliance and promotion of Sharia law. Formerly moderate Muslim countries such as Bangladesh are becoming more and more radicalized with demands for the enforcement of Sharia law. The same thing is happening in many other formerly moderate Muslim Arab and African countries. With all their investments in financial institutions and companies in the West, Saudi Arabia may also be setting up Europe and the United States for similar pressure in the future.

Indeed, with today's power from petrodollars, Islam is undergoing a huge new expansionist movement. Cultural, economic, financial, religious, political, legal, and violent "terror" jihad is already underway in the West. The same old jihad methods are used, plus some new ones. Many who have their money in Saudi financial investments and the Islamic banking industry have no idea that their money is used to promote Sharia enforcement. Saudi Arabia requires Sharia compliance from many states and organizations in the Middle East that deal with it financially. This could apply indirectly to promote or punish companies that deal with non-Sharia states or reward those who deal only with Sharia states. Islamic bond investments could also punish organizations that deal with Israel. That is why Westerners must know that their investments could be used in promotion of Sharia around the world before investing in Saudi bonds.

The World-wide Goal of Jihad

The ultimate goal of jihad is not to Islamize per se but rather to enforce Sharia. Islamic theologian Sayyid Abul Ala Maududi believed that a Muslim society cannot be Islamic without Sharia law. As he explained in Islamic Law and Its Introduction: "If an Islamic society consciously resolves not to accept the Sharia, and decides to enact its own constitution and laws or borrow them from any other source in disregard of the Sharia, such a society breaks its contract with God and forfeits its right to be called 'Islamic.'"[3]

The ultimate goal of Islam is not simply to convert people to follow the religion of Islam; it is to establish Sharia law over the entire world. It is nothing less than the achievement of totalitarian power and the subjugation of humanity to the most brutal set of laws of enslavement, and to Arabize world culture, laws, and politics.

Islam does not urge Muslims to have a personal relationship with Allah, but instead it seeks to bring back laws of medieval cruelty that take away the dignity of the human spirit and suck dry the very soul of freedom.

Conquering through numbers is more important than faith, and that is why, for example, Muslim Sharia courts cannot tolerate demands to officially leave Islam by changing the religious affiliation on government-issued IDs. In the Muslim State, the value of a Muslim is in his subjugation to Sharia, and it does not matter what is in his or her heart. Muslim leadership is happy with numbers—the power of the huge clan, the huge tribe—millions and billions of Muslims, as long as they make no demands. Remaining a soldier in the Army of Islam is all that matters. That is what counts in the opinion of Muslim leaders. To be a Muslim is to take an oath of submission to the Sharia state, and that oath prevents you from claiming the human rights that are the priority of any true religion. That is why Islam's greatest enemies are Christianity and Judaism and nations that are founded on their values.

Islam is actually anti-religion, and in that it is similar to Communism. What counts is obedience to the State as well as a few ritualistic religious commandments that give Islam the veneer and credibility of religious practice and give Sharia-slaves the illusion that they have a religion.

A Natural Progression

The plan of Islam is clear and follows a natural progression. At the beginning, Muslims are just a few and engage in peaceful proselytizing with rapid mosque building, which is helped by today's petrodollars. Muslims are warned and intimidated from emulating or assimilating in the non-Muslim culture in which they live. Maududi believed that copying the cultural practices of non-Muslims was forbidden in Islam, having "very disastrous consequences upon a nation; it destroys its inner vitality, blurs its vision, befogs its critical faculties, breeds inferiority complexes, and gradually but assuredly saps all the springs of culture and sounds its death-knell. That is why the Holy Prophet has positively and forcefully forbidden the Muslims to assume the culture and mode of life of the non-Muslims."[4]

In regards to non-Muslims, Maududi said that: "Islamic Jihad does not recognize their right to administer State affairs according to a system, which, in the view of Islam, is evil. Furthermore, Islamic Jihad also refuses to admit their right to continue with such practices under an Islamic government which fatally affect the public interest from the viewpoint of Islam."[5]

According to Muslim scriptures, a land that has a mosque built on it becomes Muslim land and must forever remain a mosque. Land acquisition for the purpose of building Islamic institutions is a major priority of the Muslim agenda in the West. When majority non-Muslim citizens start asking questions and becoming skeptical about the calls for jihad and jihadists using the mosques as a base for their activities, Muslim leadership starts claiming discrimination, racism, and misunderstood religion, suggesting that the host country needs an education in what true Islam and its Sharia mean. Islam counts on the natural humanity and basic decency of unsuspecting people and nations to accommodate their immigrant minority Muslim population and bend to their demands.

New Demands

As their numbers increase, Muslims then start demanding to live under Sharia as a religious right from their newly adopted governments. Non-Muslims in their host countries who question, criticize, or try to expose their plans are intimidated, threatened, and even assassinated, such as Theo van Gogh in Holland. All the while, Muslim leaders engage in the usual double-talk. While trying to calm the fears of the indigenous population, they tell their Muslim followers not to assimilate with the non-Muslim larger society and to have larger families.

The threat to non-conforming Muslims in the host country is even greater than for the rest of the indigenous population.

Being in the West does not protect Muslims who are against violent jihad, or worse—those who leave Islam. Secular Muslims who denounce violent jihad, assimilate, and start spilling the beans on the jihadist agenda in the West will receive death threats from followers of the "religion of peace." Some will actually be assassinated. At the very least, these secular Muslims will be subjected to constant intimidation and harassment.

Muslim schools in the West serve as centers of indoctrination, engaging in hate propaganda against the larger non-Muslim population, as did British Muslim schools when they described non-Muslims as "filth" to students.[6] While the West considers this to be egregious hate-mongering, it is simply abiding by what Muslim scriptures say.

Working against the host society's culture and government will go hand-in-hand with claims of the "peaceful intentions" of Muslims, all while blaming the larger population for misunderstanding Islam and Muslims.

"It's a Religion of Peace"

While Islamic terror and fatwa is working on crushing the will of nations, some Muslim leaders tell the West that their fear of Islam is an exaggeration, a misunderstanding, or Islamophobia. Thus they recommend that Americans or Europeans get an education in Islam, telling them there is nothing to fear from Muslim scriptures and to be respectful of Islam; Westerners must ignore the threats in Muslim scriptures, otherwise they are bigoted and Islamophobic. A committed jihadist will look you in the eye and tell you Islam is a religion of peace. According to the Qur'an, Allah said that he has unleashed devils to stir up (confuse) the disbelievers.[7] Also, the following verse from the Qur'an tells Muslims to not befriend non-Muslims but that it is acceptable to use deceptive tactics and pretend to befriend infidels to guard themselves from real or imagined harm:

Let not the believers take for friends or helpers unbelievers rather
than believers: if any do that, in nothing will there be help from
Allah: except by way of precaution, that ye may guard yourselves
from them.[8]

While Sharia is portrayed as comparable with democracy (or
whatever the host country's political system is), Muslim leadership and Muslims in general ally themselves with forces
antagonistic to the political system of the country. In the case of
the United States, Muslims ally themselves with anti-American
far left groups and even U.S. Communist groups. They also concentrate their efforts of indoctrination through the schools,
particularly universities. They have learned that the millions of
dollars Saudi Arabia donates to American institutions of higher
learning go a long way in shaping American attitudes.

More than any other minority in the country, Muslims are
politically inclined and exert a huge effort to penetrate the
political and legal structure from within. Muslim youth are
encouraged to work in Washington DC in order to learn about
the system and how to work within it. On the eve of the election
celebrations for Keith Ellison, the first Muslim congressman,
supporting crowds chanted, "Allahu Akbar," the chant for the
triumph of Islam.[9]

Legal Jihad

The jihad on the West comes from every angle, including the legal
one. Muslims are currently attempting to introduce blasphemy laws
in Western countries.[10] In order to silence critics of Islam, death
threats and intimidation are now coupled with attempts to take legal
action against anyone who commits the blasphemy of insulting
Mohammed or Islam, regardless of whether they reside in London,
New York, or Riyadh. Some of these laws are already effectively
practiced in Europe and Australia, where several Westerners were

sued and lost cases for insulting Islam. The Organization of Islamic Conference (OIC) has been actively attempting to Islamize international human rights laws and apply the Sharia "standard" for blasphemy to all nations.

Even when the number of Muslims is only 1 or 2 percent of the county, they start pushing the envelope very early, making demands from the larger community, such as foot-level faucets for washing feet before praying in public schools, businesses, and airports. Airports in Kansas City, Phoenix, and Indianapolis are among those who have already installed foot baths for Muslim cab drivers. I was totally surprised by such demands in the United States simply because I have never seen foot-level faucets in any public school or business in Egypt! They only exist in mosques. So why are Muslims in America demanding things that do not even exist in the majority of Muslim countries? The answer is simple: Muslims in America are bringing to bear the demands of radical Wahabi Islam from the country that is financing their power structure. These demands are also a way to test how far Americans will go in accommodating the Muslim minority. In sharp contrast, we never see similar demands from Hindus or Buddhists living in America, who practice their religion in peace and harmony within the larger community.

This testing of American tolerance could be seen in a Muslim parade in New York on September 9, 2007, two days before the sixth anniversary of 9/11. Muslims defiantly carried signs reading, "Muslims against Democracy and Western Values," "The Holocaust Is a Hoax," and "Ban the Talmud," and they were selling books on jihad with guns and barbwire on the cover.[11] This comes from the same groups who complain of discrimination and Islamophobia. Do they think this will bring them sympathy and understanding? Extremists are quick to take advantage of America's right of free speech, a privilege not granted in any of the Muslim countries from which they came.

Scare Tactics

It is not difficult to pluck any number of examples of the above practices from the pages of newspapers all over the Western world. Rest assured, as Muslims increase in numbers, levels of intolerance and defiance against the non-Muslim majority will increase. Assassination of critics, for example, will be used to scare opposition. Among the first groups targeted for silencing and assassinations are Muslims who seek reform and speak out against violence. Jews and Christians, along with their places of worship, will increasingly be the object of violence, murder, and destruction. We've already seen killings at Jewish Community Centers, such as the one in Seattle on July 28, 2006.[12]

Jihadists will target a country's main source of wealth for destruction. The Twin Towers represented American capitalism. The tourism industry in Egypt and Lebanon were both targets of Islamists who wanted to change the system by weakening it. Feminists, intellectuals, and leaders of other religions will also be threatened, intimidated, or killed.

Wherever a Muslim immigrant community exists, whether in France, Great Britain, Canada, Australia, or the United States, there is agitation for Sharia "family law" within the Muslim community. It seems innocuous enough to some Western governments because they do not understand that it encompasses far more than simple marriage procedures, inheritance morays, or ways to resolve domestic disputes. Some nations of the West have already given in to this. Sharia family arbitration was allowed to function for fifteen years in Canada, from 1991 to 2006, and operate on a limited scale in Great Britain.[13]

As Islamists gain more political power with the increase in the Muslim population, demands for Sharia will no longer be restricted to laws pertaining to marriage and inheritance, but will include Sharia-mandated corporal punishment and executions, not only for crimes against society but for sins against

Allah. If this is not given to them, vigilante street violence against citizens who do not abide by Sharia will produce an outward compliance with Sharia through fear. Like Egyptian Christian girls, who wear a head scarf so as not to be noticed, non-Muslims will try to blend in by wearing Islamic clothes so as to avoid standing out on the street. We saw this stage in the progression of Islamization in Lebanon, which until recently was predominantly Christian.

Political leaders who refuse to yield to Muslim demands, befriend enemies of Islam, or are perceived as anti-Sharia will be targets for assassination. Today's Lebanese and Iraqi leaders and former Egyptian president Anwar Sadat serve as examples. When finally a country becomes an independent majority Muslim State, Sharia law will be the law of the land over Muslims as well as non-Muslim minorities. All institutions of society will be geared toward promoting Islam and eradicating any other form of religion. Minorities will find life impossible to live unless they convert or leave the homeland of their ancestors. But will the bloodshed in the Islamic state end here? I believe not; the violence and bloodshed inside Islamic states is never ending, even if the Muslim State is 100 percent Muslim.

Any Chance for an Islamic Reformation?

The West has been warned of the Islamist intentions, but so far it is in denial, relying on the hope that Islam will eventually reform. The West presumes it is only logical that Muslims will discover the virtues of Western democracies and find it so wonderful they will want to reform. Yet history proves otherwise. Sharia and jihad have been extremely effective and have served Islam well. The West cannot rely on Muslims to reform their religion on their own since they are themselves hostages to an ideology parading as religion. For Muslims, the wages of reformation is death. From its inception and its founding principles, Islam was terrified and threatened by the mere existence of Judaism and Christianity in and around the Arabian Peninsula, and it is still chasing them out of existence in the fifty-four Muslim countries on earth. So to presume that the ultimate destiny of Islam is reformation and acceptance of other religions displays an ignorance of Islam and the reason it came into being.

While Christian literature is full of repentance, Muslim scriptures, society, and history are devoid of it. In fact those who "repent" of Islam's teachings of cruelty and violence are called apostates and must be killed. On March 15, 2008, two Saudi writers, Abdullah bin Bejad al-Otaibi and Yousef Aba al-Khail, called for a reconsideration of the notion that all non-Muslims are *kuffar* (an Arabic word meaning "rejecter," one who refuses to submit to Allah, an Infidel—the term carries a derogatory meaning). That prompted a top religious figure, Abdul-Rahman al-Barrak, to call for their deaths in a fatwa against the two. Such is the punishment for those who wish to repent when evil is done in the name of Islam.

It is naïve, at best, for the West to count on a collective Islamic repentance and reformation that would bring Muslims to appreciate peace with the West. Since 9/11, there has been no collective Muslim outrage over Islamic terrorism, over the stoning of women in Iran, over the ethnic cleansing in the Muslim world against Christians and Jews, over violence and murder against those perceived to have insulted Islam, or over the kidnapping and murder of Christian missionaries by Muslims. How can a reformation happen when Muslims as a whole do not feel that there is anything wrong with their scriptures that command violence? It is the West that is dreaming of an Islamic reformation simply because it does not want to face the fact that something must be done about the Muslim threat. The longer it waits, the higher the cost. Islam must be contained, and its tumultuous and destructive lifestyle must be prevented from spilling over and becoming a power in the West.

The War on Terror

So far the West has been more reactive than proactive in what it calls a "war on terror," limiting its definition of the threat to bombs or attacks by airplanes or explosives in mass transportation. Whether Western media or governments want to acknowledge this or not, the last thirty or forty years have seen the rise of a militant movement of major proportion throughout the world to Islamize, Arabize, and Wahabize all corners of the globe. Islamic jihad seeks to turn the soul of a nation against its own past in relentless pursuit of the perfect Sharia state. With today's extensive literature on Islam and the ready access to knowledge ushered in by the Information Age, the West has the means to be well informed and has the power to stop such a threat. Today's rise of radical Islam is a challenge to the world, but the West's hands should not be tied; Western nations must realize they still rule in their own lands.

Muslim Fatwa of Death on Non-Muslims

On February 14, 1989, a fatwa requiring the execution of the British writer Salman Rushdie was announced on Radio Tehran by the leader of Iran, Ayatollah Khomeini. Mr. Rushdie is not Iranian, nor does he live within the borders of Iran. So what does this fatwa mean? It is a call on Muslims worldwide, in particular British Muslims, to execute a fatwa using vigilante street justice—which is allowed under Sharia law—on a citizen who does not even live under Iranian Sharia rule. That is the level of power of the Muslim fatwa; it can enact vigilante justice anywhere on earth.

The West was appalled by such barbarity, but what the West does not know is that they all are under a fatwa of death issued by Mohammed in his hadiths (hadith is an Arabic word for "Saying by Mohammed") and in the Qur'an. This fatwa is expressed in hundreds of hadiths and verses commanding Muslims to kill non-Muslims wherever they find them. The Qur'an says:

> Then take them and kill them wherever ye find them. Against such We have given you clear warrant.[14]

> Lo! Those who disbelieve Our revelations, We shall expose them to the Fire. As often as their skins are consumed We shall exchange them for fresh skins that they may taste the torment. Lo! Allah is ever Mighty, Wise.[15]

> Those who believe do battle for the cause of Allah; and those who disbelieve do battle for the cause of idols. So fight the minions of the devil. Lo! the devil's strategy is ever weak.[16]

> I will instill terror into the hearts of the unbelievers (non-Muslims), smite ye above their necks and smite all their fingertips off them. It is not ye who slew them, it was Allah.[17]

> Against them make ready your strength to the utmost of your power, including steeds of war, to strike terror into (the hearts of) the enemies, of Allah and your enemies, and others besides, whom ye may not know, but whom Allah doth know.[18]

> Therefore, when ye meet the Unbelievers (in fight), smite at their necks; at length, when ye have thoroughly subdued them, bind a bond firmly (on them): thereafter (is the time for) either generosity or ransom: Until the war lays down its burdens.[19]

It is clear from the above verses that the commandment to kidnap for ransom and slit throats is issued to Muslims as a whole and not just to select terrorists. We have known about or have seen the videotaped beheading of non-Muslims. All of it has its basis in the Qur'an. And that's why we hear "Allahu

Akbar" chanted while the warriors of Islam slit the throats of "infidels."

Terrorism, beheading, and the killing of non-Muslims are directly linked to Muslim scriptures that order Muslims to kill infidels. What a horrific burden that must be for the good, humane, and peace-loving but committed Muslims. I often wonder how they can psychologically process such intensely violent commandments while at the same time believe that all human beings are basically equal and should be treated with respect?

In my Muslim days, I could not process or feel at peace with those violent commandments. In 1956, when I was eight years old, President Gamal Abdel Nasser of Egypt and several high-ranking government officials came to our home in Cairo to pay condolences after the death of my father who died as a *shahid* (martyr) in the jihad against Israel. I looked out to see the whole neighborhood watching our home, and I wondered what was happening. My mother instructed my siblings and me to stand next to each other to greet the Egyptian president. As we were greeting them, I heard one of them ask us: "Which one of you will avenge your father's blood by killing Jews?" My siblings and I were all speechless. I felt like crying, but held myself back. The question made me feel that if I really loved my father, I must kill Jews in retaliation. We were led to believe it was our destiny to do the jihad against the enemies of Islam, the Jewish people. But I did not want to kill anyone. From that moment, I felt both guilty and ambivalent about everything good and honorable I had been taught about my religion.

Is it any wonder that the good and peace-loving Muslims were silent after 9/11? What can they say? To speak against their religious commandments would be apostasy, and to openly condone that what the terrorists were doing as jihad would make them terror supporters.

When several suicide bombers were captured by the police, they were asked by reporters why they were going to kill people.

Their answer: "We were doing it by the order of Qur'anic instructions by Allah." When Bangladesh terrorist leader Maulana Abdur Rahman and Bangla Bhai were captured by the police, Rahman said: "We have done it to establish Allah's laws in Bangladesh, and we were doing it according to the Qur'an." Showing one copy of the Qur'an in his hand, he continued, "If I am a terrorist, then Qur'an is also a terrorist." Even the twentieth hijacker of 9/11 terrorism, Zacarias Moussaoui, proudly declared in the court: "I wish I could kill more Americans, because my religion Islam demands that I kill infidels."[20]

An Egyptian member of the Islamist group Takfir wal-Hijra, who is also a member of the Egyptian parliament, was reported by the Egyptian magazine Rose El Yusef as saying: "Why should we Muslims be ashamed of terrorism or promoting it especially since it is the Qur'an that orders us to do terrorism?"[21]

Islamic scriptures ignite a flame of eternal conflict and a perpetual declaration of war against all those who do not believe in Allah and Mohammed. According to Qur'an 60:4, "And there hath arisen between us and you hostility and hate forever until ye believe in Allah only."

However, let me be clear: The West must understand that the problem is not individual Muslims as much as it is Muslim scriptures commanding them to kill. And the question is what will the West do to protect its citizens from violent commandments against non-Muslims that appear in the Qur'an, Hadith, and Sharia?

Part I

SHARIA: The Family

One

The Roots
of Sharia

In 2006 Afghani citizen Abdul Rahman was arrested and sentenced to death for converting to Christianity. This occurred not under the Islamic state of the Taliban, but in the newly liberated secular government of Afghanistan. The Constitution of Afghanistan was contradictory. On one hand, it recognized a limited form of freedom of religion. On the other, it allowed Islamic jurisprudence, which mandates the death penalty for apostasy from Islam.

Under international pressure, the government released Rahman under cover of night, citing mental illness concerns so that he could "receive medical treatment overseas." He was spirited out of the country to protect him from Sharia enforcers who had vowed to take matters into their own hands.

Sharia courts hand down such death sentences all over the Islamic world. But, just as often, the courts aren't even involved. Converts from Islam are killed either by their own family or by Islamists on the street even before the government is notified. In Abdul Rahman's case, his family turned him in to the authorities.

When news of Rahman's secret release hit the streets of Kabul, several hundred clerics, students, and other protestors gathered, calling for his execution and shouting, "Death to

Christians!" Afghanistan's deputy attorney general appeased hardliners by saying that Rahman was allowed to go overseas for medical treatment but that the case could be reopened "when he is healthy."

The death penalty for apostasy is the ultimate Sharia club to keep Muslims in line. This was the case in the seventh century, and it is still the case in the twenty-first.

What Is Sharia?

Sharia is the body of Islamic law. It deals with all aspects of day-to-day life, including politics, economics, banking, business law, contract law, marriage, divorce, child rearing and custody, sexuality, sin, crime, and social issues. It makes no distinction between public and private life, treating all aspects of human relations as governable by Allah's law. The Sharia laws are based on the Qur'an and hadiths (sayings and example of the Prophet) as well as centuries of debate, interpretation, and precedent. There are literally thousands of Sharia laws.

There are four Sharia schools: Hanafi (of Imam Abu Hanifa), Shafi'i (of Imam Shafi'i), Maliki (of Imam Malik), and Hanbali (of Imam Hanbal). Hanbali law is the strictest and is followed only in Saudi Arabia. Most of the world's Muslims follow Hanafi law, which is the most liberal.

Muslim countries follow different schools and enforce Sharia to different degrees. Some, such as Saudia Arabia and Iran, enforce full Sharia, which includes three major categories of crimes:

1. *Hudud* crimes are crimes such as murder, apostasy (leaving Islam), theft, adultery, or drinking alcohol. Punishments for such crimes include stoning, beheading, amputation of limbs, and flogging. (Hudud is Arabic for "limits," implying crimes that are beyond the limit,

crossing a border that should not be crossed. It is the most serious category of crimes.)

2. *Qesas* crimes are revenge crimes in which the victim has the right to seek retribution and retaliation. For example, the family of a murder victim can ask for blood money from the murderer instead of a public execution.

3. *Tazir* crimes are the least serious and can carry punishments such as fines, public or private censure, family and clan pressure and support, seizure of property, confinement in the home or place of detention, and flogging.

When it comes to punishment for Hudud crimes, Sharia does not distinguish between crime and sin—that is, "sin" as defined by Islam. So punishments for adultery and murder could be the same: beheading. Countries such as Saudi Arabia and Iran follow all of the Sharia punishments for the above crimes, including the flogging of any woman caught without a head cover or seen with a man who is not her relative. In a recent Saudi case, a woman who had been gang-raped by seven men was sentenced to flogging because she had been seen talking with a man who was not her relative. Her attackers, by the way, saw that infraction as a justification to rape her. Some secular Muslim countries, such as Egypt, are formally Sharia states. Informally, however, Egypt does not follow the Sharia mode of punishments for some Hudud crimes, punishments such as flogging, beheading, and amputation of limbs for theft. In Egypt, death by hanging is the mode of execution.

Before we begin looking at specific Islamic Sharia laws and their effects on individuals and society, we need to understand how they came about. That requires going back to the seventh-century Arabian Peninsula, when Mohammed burst upon the scene, and then to the eighth century, when the laws began to be formulated and written down under the direction of various caliphs, or Islamic heads of state.

Arabian Desert Culture

To fully understand the world of Sharia, we must delve into the historical dynamics and physical environment of the Bedouin tribal culture of the Arabian Peninsula. The harsh desert climate in many ways dictated the way of life for nomadic tribes: their culture, dress, methods of warfare, family structure, and ways of obtaining food and water. We start with the commodity most necessary for survival—water itself; the very word, *Sharia*, means "way to water."

Without rivers or natural sources of fresh water, desert tribes gathered around scattered underground wells. It was their only source of life. With the exception of a few palm trees, there was hardly any agriculture or vegetation in a mostly flat desert and very little shelter from the hot sun and wind. Long before Islam, both men and women had to wear head cover as protection both from the sun and the severe sand storms.

Even though Egypt had a milder climate than Arabia, I remember the spring *khamaseen* sandstorms that were terrible, especially if a person was caught outdoors unprepared. The strong winds carried the desert sand into the air, blinding and striking us with a stinging sensation to uncovered arms, faces, legs, and eyes. It felt like a million mosquitoes attacking the body all at once. Now, one can just imagine how that felt in the open desert of seventh-century Arabia where the landscape offered little protection—no hills, valleys, or trees to break the wind, and no buildings, merely tents. Bedouins clustered in close proximity around a well—their only source for water. This proximity required a highly regulated social environment. In this open, exposed desert, a woman's clothes were her only means of privacy. The female nomad could only protect her privacy and dignity in two places—her tent, which she shared with many others, and within her clothing. The robe and head cover protected her face, eyes, and skin from the harsh environment, but they also gave her much-needed privacy in the dense area around the well. A verse from the Sahih Bukhari hadith collection gives some insight: "The Prophet said to his wives, 'You are allowed to go out to answer the call of nature.'"[1] Women in the exposed desert climate had to walk out in the open field hidden in their tent-like protective clothes to relieve themselves.

Her clothing also represented a woman's boundary in a tribe that allowed little privacy. The head cover that could be wrapped around the face when necessary for protection from sun and sand and the long garment that covered arms and legs were not the creation of Islam, but existed prior to Islam; it was not originally adopted for religious reasons, but rather was an adaptation to the physical environment. Men in the Arabian desert also adapted to the environment by wearing the well-known Arabian male robes and head cover.

The extreme climate and scarcity of resources resulted in a primal struggle for survival and protection. Basic thirst and hunger necessitated a high level of dependency. Absolute obedience and loyalty to the tribe was essential to staying alive. The removal of tribal protection for any reason meant death from the elements or at best, enslavement by a rival tribe. Tribes competed and battled over the limited sources of water, food, and other essential goods. The scarcity of water contributed to a lack of hygienic practices among the Bedouins who had to use sand or rocks for cleansing their bodies. The following hadith by Mohammed reflects this hardship: "Use odd number of stones (minimum three) to clean your private parts."[2] Bedouins often used pre-used or dirty water. In another hadith collection, "Narrated Abu Said al-Khudri: 'I heard that the people asked the Prophet of Allah: Water is brought for you from the well of Budai'ah. It is a well in which dead dogs, menstrual clothes, and excrement of people are thrown. The Messenger of Allah replied: Verily water is pure and is not defiled by anything."' That is probably the reason Islam stressed the necessity of ablution before every prayer.[3] Paradise according to Islam also reflects the scarcity of water in Arabia. In verse 47:15, Allah promises Muslims who go to Paradise gardens with rivers of incorruptible water, milk, wine, and honey, where as non-Muslims will dwell in fire and drink boiling water that will tear their intestines.

The whole tribe relied heavily on their strong young men who were revered fighters in an environment where tribes lived under constant anxiety over finding resources—all that while having to defend themselves from other tribes, who were always ready to do battle over such resources. Waiting patiently in hiding for their prey, attacking and raiding a caravan was honorable—and even a noble—act for the survival of the tribe.

The tribal system rewarded the young males who defended the tribe and brought it wealth. They were rewarded not only with a good share of the booty, but also with brides from within the tribe in addition to the ones won in battle. Women adored them and were happy to be given to them in marriage, even as one of the many wives to serve the heroes of the tribe. The young warriors were given not only great respect but also all the sexual gratification they asked for; the most beautiful and young females of the tribe were at their disposal. Such a reward was not taken by force, but offered as a sign of gratitude for the returning young warriors who survived a ruthless battle for survival.

The gratitude of the tribe— expressed in songs of encouragement and in poetry about their bravery and courage—for the men who returned from battle was immense, and those who died were heroes to be remembered for generations. With them they brought the booty of war—goods, food, and slaves that would keep the tribe alive for some time. Victory in battle brought not only wealth to the tribe but also protection to all the males—such as the older men who would otherwise have been killed by rival tribes—and protection for the females and children who would have been taken as slaves.

War and raiding were glorified in Arab poetry, a major cultural aspect of Arabia. Poems often expressed pride in battle and shedding the blood of the enemy. I have childhood memories of learning old Arab poems describing the Bedouin's pride in his arrows and how they fly to kill the enemy, and when their garments would be stained with blood, its scent to the Bedouin fighter was sweeter than the odor of musk. Many famous Arab poets glorified swords, battles, and the capture of booty while describing their bodies as made of iron. They would boast about drinking the blood of their enemies from their skulls. Female poets expressed pride in fighters who do not hesitate, the one with a brave and stubborn heart.

Arabian desert culture practiced a dual system of justice and ethics: one for their tribe, and another for all others. You had the right to justice only when judged by your own tribe, but you had no rights if you fell in the hands of raiders of the other tribe. Women and children of the defeated tribe became slaves, and men were killed. Justice did not apply to everyone equally. This law of the desert was the major cultural factor that produced Islamic Sharia, a system that gives justice to people depending on who they are and to which tribe they belong. Sharia codified this kind of legal discrimination, creating different sets of laws for Muslim and non-Muslim. Under Sharia, if you are a Muslim, you have one set of laws to protect you; and if you are not, a different set of laws can protect you—if you accept a second-class citizen protected status, called a *dhimmi*—as long as you pay the *jizya* tax. It is a penalty fee a non-Muslim must pay to the Muslim government for protection from being killed for being a non-Muslim. The Western Judeo-Christian Golden Rule that applies to all was and still is alien to Arabia and to the Islamic Sharia laws that Arabian culture produced and still lives by today.

The use of females as reward to the heroes was an institution in the Arab tribal culture and existed long before Mohammed. Acquiring many wives and women slaves was a sign of a man's bravery, manhood, and social status in the tribe. Men who were weak or with physical disabilities, if not wealthy by inheritance, could not have the reward of females and pay their dowry. Having women and sexual gratification was a privilege of the brave warriors that weaker and poorer men could not have. Women, sex, power, violence, the sword, pride, and battle were all linked with one another in the culture of Arabia. Women as well as men were invested in a desert-raiding survival system that brought with it prestige and immense pride. The whole system was based on exhibiting power. Strong tribes were admired, respected, and feared. Others would think twice about attacking them and in fact sought out alliances.

Both male and female not only accepted the nature of their gender roles but also wanted to preserve these roles—power, respect, and sexual rewards for the male; protection from slavery and assurance of survival in a harsh environment for the female. The last thing the Bedouin female thought of was her human rights or her independence. Being one of the gifts to the man who returned triumphant from battle was not something to be ashamed of but was a source of pride, and women of the tribe competed to appease them. This competition was enhanced by polygamy where wives had to compete over a husband's love and approval. A woman's social status was measured by whom she married; she would rather be one of the many wives of the hero rather than the wife of a weaker, poorer male. Females linked their safety and security to their surrender to male power. Arabian women knew well what could happen to them if their heroes were defeated in battle; they would become not only sexual slaves but also slaves and servants of the females of the conquering tribe. Thus, tribal culture produced a female who wanted to please and was thankful and proud of her protector hero. The roles of male supremacy and female submission in Arabian Peninsula culture would come to form the basis of Sharia law governing the relationships of the sexes.

Arabia is one of the few regions in the Middle East that was unattractive to the great conquerors, who were often discouraged by the harsh desert environment and the fierce, warring tribes. For the Arab man, the desert was his curse as well as his protection from slavery. The lack of a conquering history made the Arabian man value his independence and freedom immensely and despise the semi-slave settled lifestyle of the peasant. For centuries, Arabia had remained a culture of the proud independent rebel male hero, with no central authority and no social structure beyond the family and the tribe.

Arabia, in fact, looked with disdain at the settled cultures— Egypt, for example, with its dense population along the Nile River, which provided water for an agrarian style of life. Because of the Nile, Egypt was an old, settled society controlled by a central government. Arabia was also very different from the *Sham* region to the north (today's Syria, Lebanon, Jordan, and Israel). These were also more settled communities with more reliable water resources and fewer struggles for survival.

When Mohammed arose and began attracting followers around 622 CE, there was a huge Byzantine Christian Empire to the northwest, the Persian Zoroastrian Empire to the northeast, and Egypt, a thriving, diverse region with a large majority of Coptic Christians as well as members of other religions, to the southwest. Furthermore, within Arabia itself there were many different groups—Jewish tribes in Yemen and also scattered around northern Arabia, Eastern Christians in northern Arabia, and pagan tribes who worshiped many deities scattered throughout the Peninsula. But it was the earlier monotheistic religions—Judaism and Christianity—that on one hand inspired Mohammed, but on the other hand were seen as rivals to Mohammed's emerging new religion. During the life of Mohammed in the seventh century, the impact of Christianity and Judaism was strongly felt in Arabia, and some tribes were actually converting to Christianity.

Arabia was at a crossroad—undergo major cultural and organizational change represented by Christianity and Judaism, or protect their tribal way of life by rejecting those two foreign religions, religions that were the product of the more-settled cultures that Arabia despised but also envied—envied for having more available water resources, rivers, agriculture, and wealth. The impact of the "treat your neighbor like yourself" culture was threatening to the "raid your neighbor before he raids you" culture.

The Arabian fighter male did not want to lose his privileges. Protecting his tribe and raiding other tribes was a matter of life or death, and it brought him status, glory, booty, slaves, and, most of all, lots of women. The Arab warrior was the king of the desert and wanted to remain that way. The way he saw it, he did not want to exchange this honorable status with that of a peasant in Egypt or a semi-slave to a central government in the north. Arabia's proud culture was not going to surrender and absorb foreign values so different from the existential harsh reality of the Arabian Peninsula.

Christianity also threatened the long-standing desert institution of polygamy and would have required a revolution in the sexual life of the Arabian male. The old settled nations such as Egypt had a far different attitude toward women and marriage. In the Arabian desert, Bedouin women were property and often the spoils of war. Egypt, on the other hand, had a tradition of strong women. The empire had once been ruled by queens who wore lovely dresses yet ruled with the power of men. They were respected and adored by the citizens. Such a thing was alien to Arabia. So was the idea of "one man and one woman joined in holy matrimony," a strange Christian concept to be sure. Jesus had taught a revolutionary notion that a man should leave his family and bond with his one and only wife. This was unthinkable to the tribal Arab culture where a man can bring many wives and concubines to live with him in *his* tribe.

Would the Arabian Bedouin culture undergo major change by accepting foreign religions from settled cultures of the north, or would they reject them but use them as a foundation for their own new religion that better fit the culture and lifestyle of Arabia? Islam became the defensive answer to these new and revolutionary ideas that were going to turn Arabian culture upside down. Within these troubling winds of change, the prophet Mohammed rose to the defense of the culture of the Arabian Peninsula. He also rose to reform and unify warring tribes and assure the desert culture's survival. Mohammed's message was initially a rejection of the pagan religions of Mecca, against which his earliest battles were fought. His message to them was to reject their many deities, destroy their idols, and bow to the one true God, Allah.

Mohammed and the Supremacy of Arabia

During his early revelations, Mohammed spoke favorably about the Jews, the "People of the Book," who themselves had arisen out of nomadic desert tribes and were monotheistic. Arabs and Jews—and by extension Christians—were, after all, both branches of Abraham, the shared patriarch of Nomadic desert tribes. As Mohammed battled the pagan tribes of Mecca, he sought refuge with the Jewish tribes. He had left his own tribe in Mecca and fled to the protection of Medina, which was dominated by powerful Jewish tribes. That in itself was a major violation of the norms of the Arabian tribal culture—to leave one's own and seek refuge with another. From his new base in Medina, he now waged war against his own people of Mecca, gaining power and wealth through the same tribal raiding system into which he had been born, and which he originally wanted to change. However, Mohammed's raiding, plunder, and collection of booty was permitted by Allah even against his own tribe in Mecca, as said in the following hadith:

> Abu Huraira reported that the Messenger of Allah said: "I have been given superiority over the other prophets in six respects: I have been given words, which are concise but comprehensive in meaning; I have been helped by terror (in the hearts of enemies): spoils have been made lawful to me: the earth has been made for me clean and a place of worship; I have been sent to all mankind and the line of prophets is closed with me."[4]

In the early days of his movement, Mohammed learned and borrowed from and was inspired by both Judaism and Christianity. To triumph over those two religions, a good idea was to claim that all three religions sprang from the same source, but that the first two—Judaism and Christianity, which were originally intended to be Islam—were corrupted and that Mohammed was the final prophet. So, Mohammed's plan was for all the Jews and Christians to convert to Islam. With Islam replacing Judaism and Christianity, the Arabian culture and language would dominate, preventing any challenge to the supremacy of the culture of Arabia and its male warrior Bedouin. On that hope, Mohammed forged alliances with the Jewish tribes of Medina as he and his earliest followers lived among them and under their protection. He even instructed his followers to pray facing Jerusalem.

When Mohammed declared himself to be the last and final prophet, the awaited messiah to the Jews, he expected them to convert to his new religion. But the Jews declined. Some even made fun of him for his grandiose ideas. When one Jewish poet did so in satirical verse, his head was severed and laid at Mohammed's feet. After the Jews rejected converting to Islam, Mohammed viciously turned against them. At one point in Mohammed's sojourn in Medina, the Quraish tribe of Mecca (his original tribe) marched against him and laid siege to Medina. When eventually Quraish gave up the siege and left, Mohammed turned against the Medina Jews, accusing them of giving material aid to Quraish. When they surrendered to his army, Mohammed gave the Jews of Medina the choice of death or conversion to Islam. They chose death. And eight hundred men were beheaded and their women and children sold into slavery. Mohammed himself took a captured Jewish woman, who had just lost her husband and all her male relatives, as a sexual slave.

Mohammed's obsession with the Jews did not end until his death. Muslim intolerance and violence against Jews is firmly rooted in Mohammed's actions against them in Medina. The fate of the Jews of Medina is a dark chapter of history that Muslims have found it necessary to camouflage in order to find an ethical justification for Mohammed's violence against the Jews. Thus, they had to be portrayed as evil, sons of pigs, apes, and enemies of Allah. Instead of simply wanting to remain true to their own religion, Jews were accused of betraying Mohammed and Islam itself. Rejection was considered defiance to the supremacist culture of Arabia—and Allah and his prophet Mohammed. Allah made it clear in the Qur'an that Arabs are the best people ever created.[5] That dark part of Muslim history against the Jews in the later days of Mohammed is very hard to explain away without vilifying the Jews. If the Jews were not villains, then Mohammed's actions against them were unholy, and he would have been wrong in killing them, an unacceptable sin by a prophet of God. Thus their role as evil and deserving of their destruction must be preserved and hammered into the mind of every Muslim, and it was indeed preserved until judgment day in the Qur'an and Hadith. Islam could not have done otherwise. Either Mohammed was evil, or the Jews were evil. The first option would have ended Islam and the supremacy of Arabia.

For this reason, the later sayings of Mohammed differ greatly from the earlier ones. For example, Abu Huraira reported

Mohammed as saying: "The Hour Resurrection will not take place until the Muslims fight the Jews, and kill them. And the Jews will hide behind the rock and tree, and the rock and tree will say: oh Muslim, oh servant of Allah, this is a Jew behind me, come and kill him!"[6]

With the above hadith, the destiny of the Muslim relationship with Jews was sealed. Mohammed's deep feeling of rejection by the Jews was not quieted by his beheading eight hundred males of a Jewish tribe and enslaving their women and children. His rage against Jews continued until his death. He left his Muslim followers a commandment they were to follow until the end of time, an order made very clear in the above hadith: kill them everywhere and look for them even if they hide behind a rock or tree. For anyone who doubts the impact of the above hadith on Sharia laws regarding non-Muslims and on the behavior of Muslims, just look at the history of Muslim attitudes toward the Jews, which persists to this day.

After the rejection of the Jews, Mohammed went back to his roots in Mecca, the holy pilgrimage center of paganism in Arabia. Instead of facing Jerusalem during prayers, he now instructed his followers to face the *Ka'aba*. In Qur'an, verse 2:142–143, Allah says he changed Qiblah (the direction to which Muslims pray) to distinguish between Muslims and non-Muslims. However, Maulana Maududi, the ideological guru of the current Islamists, elaborated on this verse in his book *Tafhim-ul-Qur'an* by saying:

This constitutes the proclamation appointing the religious community (*ummah*) consisting of the followers of Muhammed to religious guidance and leadership of the world. In the second place there is an allusion to the change in the direction of prayer from Jerusalem to the Ka'bah. People of limited intelligence could see no significance in this change of direction although the substitution of Jerusalem by the Ka'bah amounted to the removal of the Children of Israel from their position of world leadership and their replacement by the ummah of Mohammed.[7]

Mohammed was sending the message that Muslims had thus replaced the Jews as the chosen people. But in Islam, the word *chosen* does not carry the same meaning of the Bible. The Jews regard being chosen as a heavy responsibility to follow God's commandments and to repair the world. In Islam it simply means superiority.

With Ka'aba now being the center of Islam, superiority was given to the culture and language of Arabia. Inside the Ka'aba is a black stone that had already been worshiped for generations before Mohammed and Islam. Now all Muslims, wherever they may be, must bow five times a day to the original tribal home of Islam, Mecca, where Muslims worship, kiss, and pray to the Black Stone—ironically the very symbol of the pagans Mohammed initially revolted against and fiercely fought. Mohammed and Islam had come full circle, first by rejecting the idols in the Ka'aba, then borrowing aspects of Christianity and Judaism and merging them with Arabian culture and pagan rituals. The culmination was a unique religion that Mohammed and his followers believed would fit Arabia better, finally going back to the center of his ancestors' place of worship, the Ka'aba in Medina, after the Jerusalem people had failed him.

Mohammed eventually succeeded in converting all of the tribes of Arabia to Islam, except for the Jewish tribes who continued to refuse to accept Mohammed as their prophet. The fate of the two other religions in Arabia was sealed when Mohammed declared he was the last and final prophet, making Jews and Christians the enemy. Islam thus forbade the existence of any other religion in the Arabian Peninsula. As a result, both Jews and Christians in Arabia were severely punished, expelled, and killed. To this day, Jews and Christians are not allowed in Mecca and Medina, the sacred holy land of Muslims.

When it comes to Muslim countries, other religions continue to be taboo. Christianity and especially Judaism are considered enemies and will be until "judgment day." This fight, which started in the seventh century, still continues today. Jews have been chased out of most of the Middle East and are even threatened within their own holy land.

One of Mohammed's aims for the new religion was to unify all the warring tribes of the Arabian Peninsula—yet preserve their unique warring culture. The genius of Islam was that it found a way to reconcile these two competing goals. Islam retained the superiority of the male, the submission of the female, slavery, and the culture of raiding and male violence by channeling it toward the outside world in an institution called *jihad*. Arabia was now to consider itself as one big tribe under Islam called *Dar al-Islam* (house of Islam), against a common enemy, the outside non-Muslim world called *Dar al-Harb* (house of war). Thus, under the concept of jihad, Islam retained and institutionalized the same mechanisms that made the tribe proud, but on a much larger scale. The only difference was that now the raiding was against the outside non-Muslim world instead of the nearby tribe.

As children growing up in a Muslim society, we were taught the stories of Mohammed's conquests and great battle as heroics. Muslim boys and girls, like me as a child in Egypt and Gaza, were fascinated by the tribal wars of Mohammed and his divine conquests, booty, and subjugation of the pagans. In the Islam classes I attended as a young girl in school, the raids of Mohammed were taught as a source of Muslim pride as victory for Allah and his prophet. I remember hearing songs on the radio, over and over, about jihad and martyrdom to destroy the infidels, the ones who rejected Mohammed. We were taught from childhood that jihad was not only honorable but also a mandate for every Muslim. Rejecting Islam was regarded as betrayal and was not a choice for anyone. It was thus our duty to wish for battle for the sake of Allah.

The ambition of bringing unity to Arabia was accomplished without major modification to the culture when conquest and raiding was shifted from neighboring Arab tribes to the outside world. Mohammed's concept of heaven also enhanced and shifted the rewards of battle. A hero's death in the battle to expand and glorify Islam is the only guarantee for any Muslim to go to heaven. The tribal hero would earn infinite rewards for protecting the "tribe" of Islam and dying for its survival and expansion. First of all, if he died in battle, his name would never be forgotten. He would be honored as a *shahid* (a martyr and hero) forever to remain immortal in the minds of Muslims on earth. The Dar al-Islam tribe would give him the same appreciation, pride, and respect a victorious warrior received as he returned from raiding a caravan. He became the pride of not only the tribe but Islam itself.

Furthermore, men could now reap their prize of female sexual ownership both in this life and in the afterlife. Just as in the glory days of old Arabia when he returned from battle with booty and sexual slaves, he would also get virgins in heaven. In fact, his reward would be even greater than had he survived a battle on earth—he will get perpetual virgins—described as alluring, beautiful, "high-bosomed," and "bashful dark-eyed houris."[8] The Muslim heaven, as described in the Qur'an, will reward him, the savior of the tribe of Islam, with all that was scarce or forbidden in Arabia—trees; fruits; shade; rivers of wine, milk, and honey; and even beautiful little boys like pearls to serve him.[9]

Sharia Became the Answer
after Mohammed's Death

Mohammed died in 632 CE following a brief illness. After an initial period of confusion, a council of his followers chose Abu Bakr, Mohammed's father-in-law, to be his successor. Disagreements over how this transition came about and whether or not it was legitimate persist to this day and account for the bitter division between Shi'ites and Sunnis. The Sunnis hold that Abu Bakr was chosen by Mohammed, and that all future caliphs (Islamic heads of state) should be chosen by consensus or election of the community (council), while the Shi'ites believe that Mohammed divinely ordained his cousin and son-in-law, Ali ibn Abi Talib, to succeed him, and thereafter the position was to be handed down according to bloodline.

After Mohammed's death, the struggle over his legacy and the fear of loosing Arabian culture and Islam, which preserved it, reappeared when many Muslims abandoned Islam. Muslims were heading for a catastrophe. Muslim leaders used violent and bloody *reddah* (meaning "bringing back to Islam") warfare to reclaim the large number who had left the faith. Islamic warriors fought fiercely and brutally. Within two years, the rebellious Arabian desert tribes had all been won back for Allah.

The hundred-year period after Mohammed's death was a time of bloody civil wars, assassinations, revolutions, counter-revolutions, and mass killings. Caliphs competed in linking their lineage to the prophet Mohammed to claim legitimacy and were killing each other and calling each other apostates. Yet simultaneous with the in-fighting, the mighty armies of Islam were continuing Mohammed's mission to march across the known world conquering and converting by the sword.

After a hundred years of fighting, the immense empire of the *Caliphate* (the divine Islamic State or Empire) was falling apart, and they needed to legitimize their rule by holy divine laws. This was especially true in the newly conquered territories outside of Arabia with their diverse culture, religions, languages, and needs. Muslim leaders needed more than just the Qur'an and bloody wars to get them to surrender to Islam. Mohammed left his followers with an ambiguous, inconsistent, and incomplete book, which by itself could not provide the foundation for an Islamic constitution. They needed a brutal but divine law to guarantee total submission—penalties of death, amputation of limbs, flogging, and stoning. Just another holy book was not going to be sufficient to give divine power to the caliph, who needed to legitimize his totalitarian power. Muslims went on a mission to collect the hadiths of Mohammed in order to form their Sharia laws. The combination of both Qur'an and Hadith gave them more material, but at the same time, the inconsistencies still remained.

Thus Sharia was written down, codifying seventh-century Arabian Peninsula culture as law for all Muslims to follow for any time and in any place. Over the next fourteen centuries, through Sharia, Arabs would spread not only their religion but also their language, culture, and way of life.

Under the Caliphate, particularly the *Umayad* rulers, Sharia was formulated by seven *imams* (religious leaders and authorities on Muslim principles of jurisprudence).

Interestingly enough, the caliphs were exempted from being punished under Sharia for cases of theft, adultery, killing, and drinking. One specific codified Islamic law attributed to Imam Abu Hanifa states: "An Islamic State Head cannot be charged for adultery, robbery, theft, or drinking."[10] In a supreme irony, Imam Abu Hanifa, who supposedly wrote the law making Muslim political leaders above the law, was himself killed by the reigning caliph.

The writers of Sharia had the precedent of Mohammed himself when they came up with exemptions for the Muslim caliph. Islam gave Muslim men up to four wives, but Mohammed had up to eleven wives at a time in addition to concubines. Many caliphs later pushed the numbers way beyond Mohammed's, with harems of thousands. The effects of this divine exemption are still felt today in the Muslim world where rulers are above the law and the Muslim public accepts and expects it. It is taken for granted that leaders will be corrupt, a phenomenon we will examine in greater depth in chapter 6.

Islamic Sharia, which was written by learned and respected

imams under the authority of reigning caliphs, had a sad ending for the imams who wrote it. The following was the destiny of eight prominent imams after some of them fulfilled their duty of writing the laws of Sharia:

- Imam Abu Hanifa (699–767 CE): Poisoned in prison by Caliph Al Mansur

- Imam Shafi'i (767–820 CE): Imprisoned by Caliph Harunar Rashid

- Imam Malik (712–795 CE): Punished, hand severed by Caliph Al Mansur

- Imam Hanbal (778–855 CE): Imprisoned for fifteen years by Caliphs Mamunur Rashid, Al Mutasim, and Al Wasiq

- Imam Jafaar Sadiq, a Shi'ite imam: Poisoned in prison by Caliph Al Mansur

- Imam Musa Kazim, a Shi'ite imam: Poisoned in prison by Caliph Harunar Rashid

- Imam Bukhari (810–870 CE): Exiled to Samarkhand by governor of Bukhara

- Imam Taymiyah (1263–1360 CE): Poisoned in prison by Caliph Al Hisham

As a thank-you for writing Sharia, those imams all met their demise. (Perhaps it was feared that if they were set free, they might change what they wrote.) Writing exemptions for the caliphs brought not only the demise of the imams but also the demise of freedom in all the countries conquered by Arabia. The most important aspect of Sharia law is total control of the large and diverse Muslim empire—everyone's behavior, loyalty, mind, and even soul. The conquered were required to become as Arab as the Arabian tribe itself.

❖ ❖ ❖

To the Western mind, it is difficult to understand how a religion can control its followers to the degree that Islam does. The Qur'an, a book—no matter how much it is regarded as divine— alone could not have done it, especially in the newly conquered territories of settled civilizations such as Egypt and Persia. Through Sharia, the Muslim Caliphate succeeded in bringing conquered populations into total dependence and submission, the way desert tribes had always subdued vanquished tribal foes. Now they had a "divine" tool to accomplish this, one that regulated every detail of life.

Some fourteen hundred years later, the laws that codified the brutal seventh-century desert tribal way of life still rule over 1.2 billion people around the globe. They all must bend over five times a day, worshiping Allah in the direction of Mecca, Saudi Arabia. Arabia is perhaps one of the most supremacist and ethnocentric cultures on earth, one that succeeded in exporting and preserving their language and culture values, customs, and desert laws to fifty-four nations through forced religion. Muslims have no choice but to live as captives within the confines of a psychological "iron curtain" of Sharia from which they cannot escape. They are living under the most brutal, degrading, and humiliating laws in human history; laws that are obsessed with the sexuality of women, that subjugate and humiliate non-Muslims, and that ultimately produce a dysfunctional angry society.

Without Sharia, Islam could not have survived, especially in the conquered lands. Islam now has become Sharia, and Sharia has become Islam. They are inseparable for survival. If Islam is a policeman, Sharia is his gun. Now let's take a closer look at Sharia and how it specifically impacts women, men, relationships, the family, and society.

Two

The Marriage Contract: The Lock on the Gender Cage

Growing up female in the Middle East, my life was impacted by the legacy of Sharia from the moment of birth. As a young girl in Egypt, I dreamed of love and marriage, but for a girl to pick a mate in a gender-segregated, Sharia-ruled society was nearly impossible. In Muslim society, a girl is picked, and she can say either yes or no, but she can never pick a marriage partner. She cannot even date. She must always be concerned with her reputation and honor—and above all her virginity. Her virginity is the very focus of the Muslim societal institution of "honor." It is one thing that Muslim men must protect in their female relatives in order to preserve the family's honor.

When I was a young teenager in Egypt, I was always warned against trusting young men. Even a simple smile or greeting directed at a boy—let alone going on a date—could be detrimental to a girl's good name and reputation. Aside from the gossip spread by anyone who might see them together, the boy himself was likely to be the first one to spread rumors against the girl who entrusted him with as little as a smile. I heard claims by Muslim boys against girls who had crushes on them from afar, saying they were "easy" or "asking for it." Thus, the best choice for a Muslim girl is to protect her reputation and wait for a marriage proposal through her family.

I was lucky to have a Western-style education, but that made my marriage prospects harder. The pool of eligible men was very limited in Egypt and many other Muslim countries where the population is about 65 percent illiterate. The percentage of Egyptian young men and women of my generation who had Western schooling and college education was extremely low in comparison to the population—probably less than 3 percent. That placed Muslim girls like me at a major disadvantage. Islamic law prevented us from marrying anyone but Muslim men. However, that limitation did not apply to men. Sharia law gave them the freedom to marry non-Muslim women. Thus, the already small pool of marriageable educated young men was getting smaller and smaller. Naturally, a good number of the eligible Western-educated young Muslim men were very likely to marry Western or Christian girls. Many of these young men emigrated alone to the West, but we could not do that since a Muslim girl could not travel and live on her own. There was no choice for us but to graciously wait for a marriage proposal from the ones who stayed unmarried in the Middle East.

Because of the Sharia law prohibiting Muslim girls from marrying none other than Muslim men, many beautiful, Western-educated Egyptian women of my generation ended up unmarried. When I visited Egypt a few years ago, I met at least two women graduates of the American University in Cairo who had never been married, and it was not because they did not try. This phenomenon was becoming so prevalent among all classes and educational levels in Egypt, that TV programs in Egypt began discussing the topic of unmarried, middle-aged Muslim women who managed to stay virgins all their lives the way Islam demanded from them.

The cruelty of these unequal laws concerning marriage choices has destroyed many lives. By giving men the freedom to marry Christian and Jewish women, it was thought that the number of Muslims would increase, since under Islam the children automatically become Muslim. But the law disregarded its effect on Muslim women.

Like everyone else in the Middle East, I never dared to challenge such laws, nor did I fully comprehend them from my religious education or society. As a young Muslim girl, I was told never to question and simply to wait for a Muslim man to propose marriage. This is Allah's law, they told me, and we must obey it. Those who didn't obey were considered apostates who should be killed. Challenging Sharia was the last thing we women wanted to do, since challenging Allah's law was like challenging Allah himself. The majority of us just accepted our destiny and worked around it.

When I was about sixteen, a Saudi man saw me in public and asked friends if he could propose to me. My family's reaction was that Saudis follow strict Islamic Sharia and that I might have a horrible life sharing a man with other wives in Saudi Arabia, so such a marriage proposal was out of the question. Thank goodness. Conservative Islamic Egypt, which followed a milder form of Sharia than Saudi Arabia, felt like heaven in comparison.

At age twenty-one, I accepted an engagement with a perfect stranger, arranged by our families in the usual fashion. He was from a wealthy family, and I was assured he was a good catch. After the engagement party, his parents invited me to their home prior to going out to a restaurant. My fiancé's mother handed me her son's shirt to iron. Having grown up with maids to do such work, I didn't know how to iron. I burned the shirt. If that was the test for suitability as a wife, I had failed miserably. To make a long story short, I handed back the ring the next day, making it one of the shortest engagements in Egyptian history!

Eventually I chose to move to freedom. At age thirty, I immigrated to the United States in late 1978 with my Christian Egyptian husband who nevertheless had to convert to Islam for my own protection.

Only when I arrived in the United States did I begin freely and objectively reading about my religion and its Sharia away from Muslim denials, objections, threats, and claims of conspiracy theories, misinterpretation, and misunderstanding by the West. I lived for thirty years under Islamic laws, taboos, restrictions, and controls of women, but I never understood how or why. I did not understand why women were always blamed for an unhappy marriage, why every time a marital problem arose the woman was the one responsible and the one who must compromise. Relatives would always whisper in women's ears, "Listen to his wishes; be submissive and respectful; obey your husband; get up and look after him he is the man of the house, so don't answer back or object to what he says." We always listened to sayings such as "The back of a man is better than the back of a wall" or "A wise woman should kiss the ground that her husband walks on." I discovered that it was the women who were in denial, and, for the first time, I was able to connect the dots and discover that for every ill and tragedy in the Muslim world, there was a theological basis underlying it. Things that had never made sense in Muslim society started making sense to me. I learned that the misinterpretation and misrepresentation and even the conspiracies were created by my culture of origin in order to camouflage horrific laws with pretty explanations. And when things could not be explained away, we were told it was "Allah's will." The oppression of women, sexual enslavement, and even violence and murder were given honorable names.

Now I look back on my Muslim society with sadness and ask how this could have happened to once great nations like Egypt, Persia, Iraq, Syria, and Turkey. How could they have strangled themselves with the most barbaric, oppressive, and demeaning laws on earth for fourteen hundred years?

A Different Way of Marriage

As a young teenager in the mid-1960s, I saw a church wedding for the first time. I was visiting my aunt in Suez, Egypt, and we had gathered around the state-run TV channel to watch an old Hollywood movie. I was very touched by the traditional Christian wedding portrayed in the movie, with church bells and music accompanying the bride as she walked with her father toward the priest where the groom stood waiting. I listened carefully to the sacred marriage vows first recited by the priest and then repeated by the groom and the bride. It was especially moving for me to watch the groom vow to be loyal, love, honor, and cherish his one and only wife as a sacred covenant between the two before God. They were obviously in love, and the love was reinforced by the words that their religious leader told them to repeat to each other.

I wept over the holiness of the event and the beauty of the words, but most importantly the equality of the vows. I listened to the solemn words of the priest explaining that the man and woman would leave their father and mother and start a new beginning. In marriage one man and one woman are held together as one flesh; from then on they function together as one. That was when I realized there was a huge difference between marriage under my religion and the Christian marriage, but I could not pinpoint what it was exactly. Was it the ceremony?

I asked my aunt, "How come we do not have weddings like that?" My aunt could not help but notice my ambivalence and said, somewhat defensively, "We have glamorous weddings too." Her answer missed the point that I was addressing and eager to understand.

Even though I was too young to understand all the dynamics, I noticed that the Christian marriage brought the husband and wife to stand together as equals and apart from their families. The wife was not represented by her father, and no one else recited the vows for her. There was no virginity check, and the father did not negotiate any dowry for the bride. The bride's dignity was kept intact. More importantly the husband had to vow loyalty to his one and only wife.

The Sharia Wedding

What I was seeing in the movie was a completely different meaning of marriage than what I was brought up to expect. Under Sharia, marriage is a legal and financial contract between families, and not a covenant with God between one man and one woman. The contract is usually signed at the home of the bride (not in a mosque), with the bride waiting in a separate room while her father and groom and their male relatives sit together in the presence of a government official called a *maathun*, who is licensed to perform marriages. After the contract is signed by the groom, it is then taken to the bride for her signature. Not much attention is paid to what is written in the contract—everyone already knows what's in it, and it is carved in stone in the Muslim culture.

After the signatures, the celebration begins, usually in a hotel or a hall for those who can afford it. Among the poorer classes, it could be right in the unpaved main street of the village in the open air or under a colorful rental tent. Belly dancing and wedding songs are heard among loud *zaghrouta*, the traditional ululation. It's a long, wavering, high-pitched sound reserved for special celebrations, a sound that in our culture can really bring shivers of joy to the ceremony. When I was thirteen years old, I witnessed one of these Bedouin-style weddings while vacationing on the beach in Suez. Held in the open air, it was very different from what we city dwellers had. The men and women were separate, and the dancer had full black dress on. We were fascinated. I felt like a foreigner as I watched the rituals. But what shocked me the most was when the bride left toward the end of the wedding and someone came later waving a white cloth with a blood stain on it announcing her virginity.

All traditional Egyptian marriages have a virginity check, but educated and middle-class marriages no longer do it publicly. I remember my aunt had something wrapped in a box hidden in her closet and when I asked her what it was she blushed and said to me, "You will know what it is when you get married." Later, I learned that it was a white handkerchief stained with the blood that proved her virginity on the night of her wedding. But in the villages, the virginity check is no secret. As I had witnessed in Suez that day, the bride's virginity proof is displayed for all the public to see.

Whether public or private, the virginity check creates an atmosphere of anxiety and distrust between bride and groom. This is the night when a girl who has never had sex before needs a tender and loving beginning. Instead she must worry about an unromantic and potentially painful act to prove she is honorable. Girls who have lost their virginity prior to marriage are condemned to a life of unmarried disgrace—or worse. They can be killed by male family members, or—if they are lucky and rich enough—with today's medical miracles they can become virgins again. Surgeries to reconstruct the hymen before the wedding are increasing in number in the Muslim world. Virginity is that important to the Muslim woman; it is literally a matter of life or death.

Akd Nikkah

Perhaps the best way to explain the meaning of marriage in Muslim society is to look at a marriage contract. The Muslim marriage contract is traditionally called *Akd Nikkah*, and the literal meaning of the word *nikkah* in Arabic is "sexual intercourse." Until recently Egypt used Akd Nikkah to describe the marriage contract, but it has now changed it to *Akd Zawag* (marriage contract). In Pakistan, however, the name is still *Nikkah*. (They probably have not changed it because Pakistanis do not speak Arabic, and the word is not as offensive.) The use of the word *nikkah* to describe marriage was not a mistake or mistranslation; it is the word often used in the Qur'an and Hadith to describe marriage.

The following is a translation of a Muslim marriage contract from Egypt.

In the name of Allah the most merciful most gracious

Marriage Contract

Translated From Arabic Into English
By Dr. Mark A. Gabriel

Recorded in the Civil court under number _____ Date _____.
Signed by the Religious civil servant and using the husband and wife finger prints.

The two parties, or those who represent them, agree to record the marriage. After informing both of them about the civil and religious regulations, they declare that they comply with those regulations and that they have no diseases that can cause a legal separation between the wife and husband.

On the day of ____, month of_____, year_____A.H. (after hijrah)_____A.D.

By my presence as the Religious civil servant, civil court_____, city _____, house number _____.

The marriage has been confirmed between:

A- Husband or his representative declaring the marriage.

His name _____

Nationality _____ Religion_____Birth Date _____

Occupation _____ Address _____

Work Address _____ ID No. _____

Issue Date _____ Expiration Date _____ City _____

Name of the husband's mother _____

The Couple's Address _____ / _____ / _____

Either the husband declares that he has no other wife or he has other wives as follows:

Wife No. 1- Name _____
Address _____ / _____ / _____

Wife No. 2- Name _____
Address _____ / _____ / _____

Wife No. 3 Name _____
Address _____ / _____ / _____

B- Wife's Name or her representative and her condition of virginity:

_____

_____

Nationality _____ Religion _____ Birth Date _____ / _____ / _____

Occupation _____ Address _____

ID No. _____ Issue _____ City _____

Name of wife's mother _____

Address of Couple No._____ City _____ Province _____

Sadaq: Amount of _____ Deposit to Be Paid _____ Late _____

The declaration of the marriage has been confirmed according to the laws of Allah and his messenger. The married couple agreed upon this contact.

Witnessed by:

1. Name _____ Nationality _____ Religion _____ Birth Date __/__/__

Place of Birth _____ Occupation _____ Address _____

ID_____ Issued by _____ Date __/__/__

2. Name _____ Nationality _____ Religion _____ Birth Date ___/___/___

Place of Birth _____ Occupation _____ Address _____

ID_____ Issued by _____ Date ___/____/____

This contract was written and copied three times, once for the husband, once for the wife, and once to go to the civil court.

Fee amount _____ has been paid. Date ___/____/____

Husband (or representative) Wife (or her representative) Witnesses

_____   1_____   _____

                            2_____   _____

Religious legal servant   Civil court stamp

The Sharia marriage contract is essentially a document grant-ing sexual intercourse rights to the male and giving him total control over his wife or wives. The contract asks the bride about her virginity status, and it states the amount of the dowry. But what is most glaringly noticeable are the three spaces for the groom to fill out: the name and address of wife number one, wife number two, and wife number three. The bride signing the contract sees those three spaces and knows that they could one day be filled out by the groom or left empty. It is totally up to him as his Sharia-granted right. Even if those lines remain empty, the damage has already been done. The simple fact that the choice exists damages any expectation of loyalty or commitment from the husband to the wife. A commitment or vows of loyalty from the husband to the wife is neither required nor expected. And if her husband does stay loyal, there is no way for her to ever know whether it is out of economic considerations or from devotion to her.

The religious sanction of polygamy utterly destroys the idea that a man and a woman are one in marriage. The message to the Muslim woman even on her wedding night is: "You can be replaced." In the back of every Muslim woman's mind is the threat right before her as she signs the marriage contract and as her father accepts the dowry. Even the Qur'an itself tells the wife that she can be replaced: "Maybe, his Lord, if he divorce you, will give him in your place wives better than you, submissive, faithful, obedient, penitent, adorers, fasters, widows, and virgins."[1] Fear and distrust is everpresent in the mind of the Muslim wife, who even if her husband never marries another, must thank her lucky stars for her husband's faithfulness. His faithfulness to her was never a divine order from Allah. He has a divine right to four wives, plus a man is entitled to any number of temporary "pleasure" marriages as long as he pays for them.

How can this contract tie the bride and groom in a love relationship? How can a marriage relationship be sacred? Where is the love? These are questions that stand in the way of a happy Muslim marriage. It does not mean that there are no happy Muslim marriages, but if there are any, it is not because of the marriage contract, but in spite of it.

Some marriages are permanent, and some are temporary. It is all in the hands of the man—since divorce is an option only available to men—and is as easy as saying, "I divorce you" three times. In addition to being allowed up to four wives and an unlimited number of captive women, men are also given the choice of three kinds of marriage: the typical first marriage acknowledged in public and recorded in the courts; *urfi*, which is not registered in the courts but is just as legitimate and usually done in secret with witnesses; and *mutaa* (pleasure marriage), a temporary marriage contract to sanction a night of pleasure. Justification for these marriages comes straight from Qur'an 4:24, a verse we'll look at in detail in the next few pages.

Temporary marriages for the purpose of sexual pleasure, whether urfi or mutaa, are practiced by both Sunni and Shi'ite Muslims. As Egypt has become more radicalized after the 1970s, there has been an increase in the phenomenon of urfi marriage among Islamists. In the Muslim world today, mutaa marriage matchmakers can arrange these temporary marriages for Muslim men. Women who are otherwise covered from head to toe on the street are treated and act like prostitutes in these religiously sanctioned paid-for mutaa deals—all in the name of a religiously sanctioned temporary "marriage" that could last for an hour. Nevertheless, in Iran, government officials have actually encouraged temporary marriages as a way to fight "illicit" sex.

There is also an additional lesser-known temporary marriage called *misyar*, or "traveler's marriage." It is gaining popularity in Saudi Arabia. This form of marriage is designed to accommodate the male sexual appetite while traveling. The fact that it is allowed under Sharia is an obvious example of the sexual nature of the Muslim marriage contract—where pretty much any sex is allowed as long as the dowry is paid in exchange for nikkah.

Some Muslims are appalled at today's Muslim leadership for allowing temporary marriages in this day and age. Those Muslims do not understand that such marriages are part and parcel of Allah's law and no Muslim leader can abolish them. Such marriages are clearly supported by the Qur'an, Hadith, and Sunnah.

Since quite a lot of the justification comes from a rather curious passage in Qur'an 4:24, let's examine that verse and the centuries of interpretation that surround it. That verse came about when Mohammed's men were having their customary, privileged sex with married women captured in battle. They felt awkward about having sex with women who had husbands and so asked the prophet whether it was allowed. Qur'an 4:24 gave an answer that has caused untold suffering over the last fourteen hundred years. The English translation of verse 4:24 says:

> And all married women (are forbidden unto you) save those (captives) whom your right hands possess. It is a decree of Allah for you. Lawful unto you are all beyond those mentioned, so that ye seek them with your wealth in honest wedlock, not debauchery.

And those of whom ye seek content (by marrying them), give unto them their portions as a duty. And there is no sin for you in what ye do by mutual agreement after the duty (hath been done). Lo! Allah is ever Knower, Wise.

Muslim interpreters of this verse say that it is about marriage and not sexual intercourse. The first section tells the Muslim man that married women are forbidden. But Muslim women cannot have two husbands anyway, so why would it specify that a Muslim man cannot marry them? The question is, did the Qur'an order men not to *marry* married women or not to *have sex* with married women? The obvious meaning is that a man can't have sex with married women unless they are slaves obtained in war (whom you may rape or do with whatever you like). Does that mean the Qur'an allows polygamy for married slave women? Obviously not. This verse is not about marriage, but about sex with owned captives.

Verse 4:24 also states that there can be no blame about what is mutually agreed upon. When I read the original Arabic, I do not see any word that means mutual. I see the word *taradaytum*, which means a kind of agreement, but it is not clear on what the agreement is about—is it the sex or the amount of the wage? And is there anything in Islam that indicates the permanency of marriage until death? I do not see it.

The Qur'an, without all the dressed-up interpretations, has given a man immense sexual rights over women, even with those whom he captures in war or who are in his home as slaves right in the presence of his wife or wives.

Today, Muslims who believe that the Qur'an is the permanent, holy words of Allah solve the embarrassment about "married slave women whom your right hand possess" without thinking twice; they say there are no more slaves today, thus the slave problem no longer applies. However, the Qur'an itself never forbade sexual slavery to men, and in fact, under some circumstances, encourages it.

As to the argument that slavery, including sexual slavery, no longer exists in the Arab world—tell that to the persecuted non-Muslim slave women in the Sudan today, tell that to the Philippino maids working in rich Saudi Arabian homes, and tell that to maids and needy poor who work in the homes of Muslims across the world who are still treated as slaves.

One can't help but ask how a holy book can support sex with owned slaves and captive women, even if they are married. How can the male master of slaves feel that Allah is blessing his sex with a captured woman even if she agrees when she is under his mercy? How can Allah care more about the sexual appetite of Muslim men and forget the rights of such slaves and women captured in war? Didn't Allah create them too? Sexual slavery is appalling to all human beings, even atheists. Is it any wonder that the abolishment of slavery in the world did not come from the Muslim world or its Sharia? It actually came from the land most hated by Muslims—*Dar al-Harb*. It was the Judeo-Christian West that abolished slavery and embarrassed Muslims into it. But Sharia stands until today—supporting slavery in its many forms as long as Muslims insist on literally applying that verse from the Qur'an.

When I and many other ordinary Muslims read the Qur'an in Arabic, we often cannot differentiate between the terms "sexual intercourse" and "marriage," which are often interpreted with the same meaning. One has to depend on the pretty interpretations of embarrassed imams, who want the Qur'an to be more appealing to the general public. They tell us when the Qur'an is talking about marriage and when it is talking about sexual intercourse. And they say when the Qur'an is talking about a wage to a captive woman in return for sex and when it is talking about a "dowry" in a respectable, permanent marriage.

In the Qur'an, the dowry is often called *ujur*—the word *ujur* in Arabic literally means "wage." So to make the meaning less repulsive, *dowry* was given a different word from that of the

Qur'an. It is now called *mahr* in Egypt. *Mahr* (dowry) is a techni-
cal term denoting the money that must be given to the woman in
the marriage contract in exchange for enjoying her—it is simply
payment for sex. And giving them their "wage" is a *faridah*, meaning an obligation. Ibn al-'Arabi, a Muslim spiritual leader who
lived from 1165 to 1240, confirms that the man's sexual rights by
virtue of paying the dowry is grounded in the Qur'an. He went as
far as saying that the payment of the dowry creates a master-ser-
vant relationship between the husband and the wife.

This significance of the dowry as a woman's wage for man's
sexual enjoyment is rooted in Islam even in a non-marital sexual relationship. In a contemporary work on Islamic law by the
modern scholar Gaziri, he writes, "If a man has sex with a married woman, by mistake, thinking her to be his wife, he must
give her a dowry equal to the dowry given to a woman of her
social worth. This dowry becomes the property of the wife and
not her husband."[2]

How can a Muslim man have sex with a married woman *by
mistake*? Does the word *sex* here mean "marriage," as the Qur'an
sometimes confuses the two? What kind of sex is that? Isn't that
adultery—for which both he and she should be killed according
to Sharia? If this is adultery, then why is the man asked to give
her a dowry if she obviously must be killed for having sex outside of marriage? This suggests the possibility that the sex
outside her marriage was not her idea in the first place. What
kind of dowry is that given to a woman married to another man?
And how can the Muslim male, who just had sex with her,
order her to keep the money to herself and not to her husband?
Is this perhaps simply the price a man must pay for raping a
married woman?

Muslims in general disagree with many of these straightforward interpretations of Sharia, but how can they deny the Shafi'I
that says: "A man is obliged to pay a woman who was forced to
fornicate with him the bride-money without marrying her"?[3]

And in this case, is the payment to the victim the only consequence for rape?

This gets even more interesting in the following statements made by some of Islam's most eminent scholars: "The dowry is given in exchange for the woman's sexual organs."[4] "He who so gives two handfuls of flour or dates as dowry of his wife has rendered her (private parts) lawful."[5] The dowry, which is called "marriage payment" in Sharia books, clearly links the act of sexual intercourse to the dowry: "The bride may refuse to have sexual intercourse until her husband gives her the marriage payment."[6]

Marriage implies a permanent relationship, but as verse 4:24 mentioned earlier, along with the many other hadiths above, it does not convey a permanent relationship between a man and a woman. To every honest Arabic-speaking person, this verse does not speak of marriage as we all know it. My interpretation: if you have pleasure from a woman, give her a wage. No husband who has the pleasure of marital sex needs to be reminded by Allah's law to pay his wife a wage. She is already under his financial support. That verse of the Qur'an (4:24) is simply sanctioning via religion a form of prostitution—nothing holy and no permanent commitment. Yet under Islamic Sharia, this "prostitution" is deemed a form of marriage—all done for the sake of meeting the sexual pleasure of men at the expense of women. Nothing more and nothing less.

The majority of Muslims deny this kind of interpretation, but it's much more difficult to deny the interpretation of one of the greatest and most revered Muslim theologians, Imam Ghazali (1058–1111). He defined marriage for generations of Muslims when he said: "Marriage is a form of slavery. The woman is man's slave, and her duty therefore is absolute obedience to the husband in all that he asks of her person. A woman, who at the moment of death enjoys the full approval of her husband, will find her place in paradise."[7]

Another of Ghazali's interpretations of marriage states, "A

woman given in marriage is either one who is taken as a lawful wife, or one who is taken for enjoyment and the attainment of certain purposes."[8] Ghazali was among the harshest imams on women. He said, "Women are prisoners in a man's hand. Men have taken them as trusts from God and God has made their sexual parts lawful for men."[9]

In the Muslim marriage, the rights of the husband are many, and the rights of the wife are few. Indeed, let's look at these rights in detail, focusing first on the rights given to men and later on those given to women.

Gender Rights under Sharia

Divorce

The Arabic word for divorce is *talak*, which literally means "set free" or "let go." Under Sharia laws, instant, final divorce is the right of the husband only. And all it requires is to repeat the words "I divorce you" three times. Actually, verbally saying it is not even required. He can hold up a thumb and two fingers as he says it. He can also do it by sticky note, by leaving a message on an answering machine, and now, say the scholars, by e-mail or text messaging, thus bringing the seventh-century desert code of instantly getting rid of a wife into the twenty-first century. Sharia places no restraints on a man's divorcing his wife or wives, and no reason is required. Bukhari reported a hadith on divorce that treats the woman as mere property: "A man may say to his brother (in Islam), 'Have a look at either of my wives (and if you wish), I will divorce her for you.'"[10]

The ease with which a man can get rid of his wives is no joking matter. Theoretically, he can get rid of his four wives and start a new cycle with four new wives plus "slave wives." There is even a law that states that final divorce takes place even if the husband divorces while intoxicated, under the influence of narcotics, or in pain of disease—or even in a joke.[11]

There are, however, conflicting attitudes concerning divorce. While divorce can be as easy as three words uttered by a man, a well-known hadith states, "Of all the lawful acts the most detestable to Allah is divorce."[12] If divorce is so detestable in the eyes of Sharia, why does Sharia make it so easy for the man to divorce, even by simply uttering "you are divorced" while intoxicated? This is just one of the many contradictions in Islam.

The contradictions become extremely obvious when a divorce occurs even against the will of both husband and wife: "Narrated Abdullah ibn Umar: A woman was my wife and I loved her, but Umar hated her. He said to me: Divorce her, but I refused. Umar then went to the Prophet (peace be upon him) and mentioned that to him. The Prophet (peace be upon him) said: Divorce her."[13]

Third-party divorce cases have happened in many Muslim countries and continue to occur. In case anyone doubts that a couple can be unwillingly divorced by outside parties, Hanifa Law states: "If one person compel another to divorce his wife, and this person accordingly divorce his wife, such divorce takes effect."[14] Also a marriage is immediately annulled if one of a couple who is non-Muslim becomes a Muslim or if a couple leaves Islam.[15]

In February 2006, Saudi police knocked on the door of Fatima and Mansour al-Timani to serve divorce papers on Mansour. Fatima's relatives sought the divorce on the grounds that she had married "beneath her." It was all very legal, and the couple, who are deeply in love, were forcibly separated. They have appealed this Sharia ruling to the king, and as of January 2008 it remained unresolved. Fatima has publicly stated that if the divorce cannot be reversed, she will commit suicide.

In Egypt, the state Sharia courts threatened to divorce a famous couple, the liberal Islamic scholar Nasr Abu Zayd and his wife, Dr. Ibthal Younis, because their views were too secular. The courts declared their marriage null and void in 1995, and the couple had to flee the country in order to continue living together.

A husband can take his wife back after a first or second divorce "whether she wishes to return or not."[16] It gets even stranger.

According to accepted Sharia law, if a man divorces his wife and wants her back, in order to get reunited with the previous husband, a divorced wife must marry another person, have complete sex with him, and be divorced by him voluntarily.

What is a woman's right in divorce? First of all, she cannot initiate a divorce. She can ask for a divorce, but only a man can grant that request. And he can refuse, effectively preventing her from ever marrying again, even though he has abandoned her.

In some countries, the only way for a wife to get a divorce is to convince the Sharia court and also to pay money to her husband. She could achieve through *khul*, which means "a release for payment," whereby a wife pays the husband in return for divorce.[17] In this case a woman must pay her dowry back to her husband, who often asks for a lot more to grant her a divorce. So after a life of slavery with a man, if a woman initiates the divorce, she does not deserve to keep the "wage" or dowry she was given in return for marriage.

What rights does a woman have after being divorced? She only receives financial support after a divorce for a maximum of three months. Plus she may very well lose her children.

Custody of children

In cases of divorce, custody goes to the mother, provided she prays and does not marry a stranger. But after the age of seven or nine—there is some variation in interpretation on the age—boys and girls belong to the father.

The husband is the privileged party in cases of custody of the children because he takes them from the wife as soon as the difficult years of early childhood are over. Gaziri, a modern scholar in Islamic law, wrote:

> The conditions of the custody of the children is as follows. First the wife should not reject Islam. If she rejects Islam, she has no right to the custody of the children. Second, she must be of good character for if it was proven that she is corrupted by illicit sex,

or theft, or has a low trade such as a professional mourner or a dancer, she loses her right to custody. Third, she is not allowed to marry anyone except the father of the child. If she remarries, she has no right to custody, unless her new husband is related to the child as a paternal uncle. But if she marries a foreigner she has no right to custody. Fourthly, she must not leave the child without supervision. Especially if the child is a female, because females need protection. So if the mother had to go outside for a long period and so neglect her child, she has no right to the custody of the child. Fifthly, if the father is poor, and the mother refused the custody of the child except for payment, and his aunty said "I will look after him for free," then the aunt will have the right to the custody of the child.

To follow the religion of Islam is not a condition to the right to custody, for if the husband is married to one of the people of the Book, she has the right to custody as long as he is safe from apostasy or corruption. But if that is not so, if, for example, he saw her taking the child to a church, or feeding him pig's meat, or giving him wine, then the father has the right to take the child from her, and sanity is a pre-requisite that is agreed upon by all.[18]

As to the period of custody, Gaziri added,

The Hanafites said, "The mother has the rights to the custody of the boy until he is seven years old." Others said, "Until he is nine." But the first opinion is the one that is legally accepted. For the girl there are two opinions. The first is until she menstruates. The second until she reaches the age of puberty, which was set in Sharia to be nine years old. This is what is accepted legally.[19]

The endless list of the marriage rights of men includes the man's right to prevent his wife from caring for her child from a previous marriage. "The husband has the right to prevent his wife from looking after and breast-feeding her baby, from her previous husband (if she was living in the husband's house), because that will make her too busy to attend to the husband, and it will affect her beauty and cleanliness, all these are the rights of the husband alone."[20]

The issue of custody of children can become an international issue even in cases where there is no divorce. Many a Western woman married to a Muslim man has awakened one morning to find that her husband has disappeared with the children, taking them back to Iran, Saudi Arabia, or whatever his country of origin. He is perfectly within his rights to do so under Islamic law, and getting the children back is often impossible for these distraught mothers. We are hearing of such cases with alarming regularity.

Wife support

There is no community property in Islam between husband and wife. The concept of community property doesn't make sense with the possibility of four wives in addition to slave sexual partners. Also, women under Sharia can keep their own wealth without merging it with the husband's. That's because with divorce solely in the man's hands, it raises the complication that her property might go to other wives and other sets of children under a divorce.

The tenuous and temporary nature of Islamic marriage is evident in how Sharia spells out the financial obligations of a husband to his wife/wives. Husbands are bound to provide only food, clothing, and accommodation, not doctors' fees, medicines, and cosmetics; a rebellious wife doesn't get anything.

The followers of the Hanafi school said: "The support of the woman is obligatory on the man in return for the woman being locked up in the man's house, and for being exclusively his." However there are exceptions. For instance:

There is no support for the woman if she is (1) rebellious (*nashiz*), that is the woman who goes outside the house of the husband without his permission and without a justifiable reason, or refuses surrendering herself to him so she does not enter his house. But if she refuses to have sex with him (even though that is unlawful) that refusal is not a reason for stopping her support because the qualifying reason for the support does exist and that is her being locked up in his house. (2) The renegade woman. (3) The woman who obeys the husband's son or his father or kisses either with lust or anything that might put her relation with her husband on a prohibited degree. (4) The woman whose marriage contract is imperfect, and the woman who had sex with someone by mistake, the man thinking she was his wife. (5) The wife who is too young to have sex. The Islamic law knows no minimum age for a legal marriage. (6) The wife who is imprisoned, even if she is innocent, if he cannot have access to her (as a wife). (7) The sick wife who, due to severe illness, did not move after the ceremony to the husband's house, because she did not surrender herself to the husband. (8) The wife who was raped by another man. (9) The wife who goes to perform pilgrimage . . . there is no support for her because she is not "locked up."[21]

The followers of Imam Shafi'i said:

The conditions of the man's maintenance for the woman are as follows: First, she must avail herself to him by offering herself to him, such as saying to him, I am surrendering myself to you." The important thing is that she must notify him in advance that she is ready for his meeting with her, and of his entrance upon her as he wishes. If she does not notify him that she is ready, she has no right of maintenance, even if she does not refuse his request to meet with her. So maintenance is conditional upon the woman's notification to her husband that she is ready for his meeting any time he wishes, and that she must avail him of herself anytime he wishes. So if she works during the daytime, and he cannot meet with her, her maintenance would be denied. Secondly, she must be capable of having sexual intercourse. If she is a small girl who cannot cope with intercourse, she is not entitled to the maintenance. Thirdly, she must not be rebellious, that is, disobeying her husband, which can take the form of preventing him from enjoying her by refusing his touch and his kisses and refusing to have sex. If she denies him any of the above, her maintenance will be cancelled for that day, because maintenance is due day by day. . . . And the rebelliousness of one day cancels his provision for clothing her for a whole season.[22]

The followers of Imam Malik said: "The condition for the man's maintenance to the woman is that she should avail herself to the man for sexual intercourse, so that if he requested it from her she would not refuse. Otherwise she would have no right to the maintenance."[23]

The followers of Imam Ibn Hanbal said:

The wife's daily maintenance is due upon the husband if the wife surrenders herself to her husband completely . . . for the daily maintenance is given to the woman in return for the husband's sexual enjoyment, so when the wife surrenders herself her daily maintenance is obligatory as long as she had reached nine years old . . . so if she was well physically and surrendered herself for the enjoyment of the husband but without sexual intercourse, she has no right for the daily maintenance. So if the wife refuses to surrender herself so that the husband might have sex with her, her daily maintenance is denied, so if she then has a problem that prevents her from having sex with her husband, but surrenders herself to her husband after that, her daily maintenance is not given to her as long as she is sick, as a punishment for her because she refused to surrender to her husband when she was well.[24]

Consider for a moment the incredible stress of having one's maintenance on the line every day—on a day-to-day basis, under the threat of losing it for being sick or other circumstances

which may be beyond your control. Furthermore, what is striking in all of the above conditions of maintenance is the view of
women not as persons but as receptacles for a man's pleasure, as
well as the assumption that payment for sex is the whole basis for
the institution of marriage.

A husband may beat and sexually abandon his wife

According to the Qur'an, the man has the responsibility to
admonish his wife, and the right to desert her sexually, and finally
if that does not work, to beat her to correct any rebelliousness in
her behavior.

The Qur'an 4:34: says, "Men are the maintainers of women
because Allah has made some of them to excel others and because
they spend out of their property; the good women are therefore
obedient, guarding the unseen as Allah has guarded; and (as to)
those on whose part you fear desertion, admonish them, and leave
them alone in the sleeping-places and beat them; then if they
obey you, do not seek a way against them; surely Allah is High,
Great."

Sayyed Qutb, whose teachings are respected by many Muslims,
was an Egyptian Muslim brotherhood Leader executed by
Nasser in 1966. He explains the dynamics of deserting the wife
sexually if admonishing her does not work:

"Here comes the second phase . . . the man has to make a superior psychological move against all her attraction and beauty, by
banishing her to her couch, for the couch (the bed) is the place of
temptation and enticement, where the rebellious woman reaches
the summit of her power. If the man can conquer his disposition
against her temptation, then he has disarmed her from her sharpest
and most treasured weapon."[25]

Other modern scholars support the above views by saying:
"This sexual desertion is a remedy that curbs the rebelliousness
of the woman, and humiliates her pride, in that which she treasures most, her femininity . . . thus inflicting the most humiliating

defeat on the woman." If sexual desertion doesn't work, then the man has the right to "beat them."[26]

Some English translations of the order to beat tell the Western reader "to beat lightly" but the word *lightly* does not appear in the original Arabic text. Beating the rebellious wife is the last resort before divorcing her.

But just what, in the first place, is defined as rebelliousness? What must a wife do to deserve a beating?

According to a fatwa by Qazi Khan in Mishkat Al-Masabih, "beating the wife mildly is allowed in four cases (1) When she does not wear fineries though wanted by the husband, (2) When she is called for sexual intercourse and she refuses without any lawful excuse, (3) When she is ordered to take a bath to clean herself from impurities for prayer and she refuses and (4) When she goes abroad without permission of her husband."[27]

This beating is the husband's unquestionable right. He does not have to justify it to anyone. The Hadith says: "A man will not be asked as to why he beat his wife."[28]

This right for man to beat his wife isn't just a practice belonging to the distant past. The *Guardian Weekly* reported, "In 1987 an Egyptian court, following an interpretation of the Koran proposed by the Syndicate of Arab Lawyers, ruled that a husband had the duty to educate his wife and therefore the right to punish her as he wished."[29]

Sayyed Qutb tries to justify the provision for a man to beat his wife, dressing it up in contradictory psycho-babble:

The facts of life, and the psychological observations of certain forms of deviations indicate that this approach (beating the wife) is the most appropriate one to satisfy a particular form of deviation, reforming the behavior of the person . . . and gratifying her . . . at the same time! Even without the existence of this form of psychological deviation, perhaps some women will not recognize the power of the man whom they love to have as their guardian and husband, except when the man conquers them physically! This is not the nature of every woman. But this kind does exist. And it is this kind that needs this last treatment to be set straight, and remain within the serious organization marriage in peace and tranquility.[30]

Even if this treatment is of benefit to the minority of women who are perverted, does this justify the command to beat the wife who rebels for any and every reason?

Now let's turn the tables. What are the woman's rights concerning a rebellious husband? She cannot resort to the same measures her husband uses, as is clear from the following verse: "If a woman fears rebelliousness or aversion in her husband, there is no fault in them if the couple set things right between them; right settlement is better."[31]

It is clear from verses 4:128 and 4:34 that the Qur'an commands diplomacy when a woman fears rebelliousness in her husband. But when the man fears rebelliousness in his wife, the Qur'an commands the use of force and sexual desertion.

Unlimited rights to a woman's body

Men's rights in the area of marital sex—and the attitude toward women that such rights suggest—are shocking to the average sensibilities and seem to fly in the face of all human decency. The Qur'anic verses and supporting hadiths speak for themselves: Marriage gives the man the right to enjoy a woman's private parts.[32] A wife must shave her pubic hair if her husband returns home at night after a long journey.[33] A woman must keep her sexual organs ready for service at all times.[34] If a woman claims to be having her period but her husband does not believe her, it is lawful for him to have sexual intercourse with her.[35] A husband deserves total submission and gratitude.

According to 'A'ishah: "A young girl came to the Prophet and said, 'O Messenger of God, I am a betrothed girl but I detest marriage. What are the husband's rights from the woman?' He replied, 'Were he covered with pus from the tip of his head to the soles of his feet, and were she to lick him, she would not compensate him enough.'"[36]

Furthermore, a fatwa by Qazi Khan reads, "No wife shall refuse her husband what he wants from her except on religious grounds, i.e., at the time of menstrual flow or fasting. Some theologians regard this refusal as unlawful as the husband may get enjoyment from his wife in other ways, by embracing, kissing, etc. The duty of the wife is to give him comforts in his bed whenever he wants her." According to Khan, beating the wife mildly is permitted when she is called for sexual intercourse and she refuses without any lawful excuse.[37]

The husband's rights and desires are always urgent and must be met immediately. The Messenger of Allah said: "By Him in Whose hand is my life, when a man calls his wife to his bed, and she does not respond, the One Who is in the heaven is displeased with her until he (her husband) is pleased with her."[38] He also said: "If a husband calls his wife to his bed (i.e. to have sexual relations) and she refuses and causes him to sleep in anger, the angels will curse her till morning."[39]

This is all because the husband's rights are divine. The woman is not even left alone after death. Her obedience to the husband is her key to paradise. Thus women are being led to believe that Allah's approval and her guarantees to heaven are earned through her obedience to her husband. "The prophet once said to a woman: 'Watch how you treat your husband for he is your Paradise and your Hell.'"[40]

Imam Al-Suyuti (1445–1505), commenting on Qur'an 4:34, said: "There are three (persons) whose prayer will not be accepted, nor their virtues be taken above: The runaway slave until he returns back to his master, the woman with whom her husband is dissatisfied, and the drunk until he becomes sober."[41] In another place, "Whosoever female dies while her husband is pleased with her, will enter Paradise."[42] Very few rights for women and slave women are mentioned. While the Hadith enumerates the husband's rights, the woman's rights are simple, as the following hadith shows: "'O Messenger of Allah! What right has the wife of one among us got over him?' He said: 'It is that you shall give her food when you have taken your food, that you shall clothe her when you have clothed yourself, that you shall not slap her on the face, nor revile her, nor desert her except within the house.'"[43]

The revered Islamic scholar Ghazali, who has been called "the greatest Muslim after Mohammed," writes that the role of a Muslim woman is to "stay at home and get on with her sewing. She should not go out often, she must not be well-informed, nor must she be communicative with her neighbors and only visit them when absolutely necessary; she should take care of her husband . . . and seek to satisfy him in everything. . . . Her sole worry should be her virtue. . . . She should be clean and ready to satisfy her husband's sexual needs at any moment."[44]

Polygamy–A man's right to multiple wives

The verse Qur'an 4:3 is translated as follows: "If you deem it best for the orphans, you may marry their mothers—you may marry two, three, or four. If you fear lest you become unfair, then you shall be content with only one, or with what you already have. Additionally, you are thus more likely to avoid financial hardship." This is another translation of the same verse: "If you fear you can not treat orphans (girls) with fairness, then you may marry other women who seem good to you: two, three, or four of them. But if you fear that you cannot maintain equality among them, marry only one or any slave girls you may own. This will make it easier for you to avoid injustice." Thus, a provision is made for a man to marry more than one woman.

I was puzzled by the reference to orphans. But one has to think of the desert world of Mohammed. It was a time of constant bloody tribal warfare. Many men died in battles, and this must have left many young girls without fathers and other male relatives to protect them, both within Mohammed's followers and conquered tribes. Thus in a culture that offers sexual rewards to warriors, and a culture where sex with children was condoned, the orphans must have presented a temptation, especially with no male relatives to protect their honor.

Commentators have sidestepped the orphan references and chosen to focus on wives in general, with special attention to "fairness" and "equity among wives." Some Muslims, however, have argued that since maintaining equality among wives is impossible, then marrying one wife is best. But the fairness and equality argument does not make sense since Mohammed himself had several wives and concubines and was proud to say that Aisha was his favorite wife! He himself had preferences. The Prophet, like the Muslim caliphs after him, was given privileges forbidden to the ordinary Muslim. Four wives were not enough. Mohammed had up to eleven wives in addition to women slaves. This is confirmed in Qur'an 33:50:

> O prophet! We have made lawful to thee thy wives to whom thou hast paid their dowers; and those whom thy right hand possesses out of the prisoners of war whom Allah has assigned to thee; and daughters of thy paternal uncles and aunts and daughters of thy maternal uncles and aunts, who migrated (from Mecca) with thee; and any believing woman who dedicates her soul to the Prophet if the Prophet wishes to wed her this only for thee, and not for the Believers (at large); We know what We have appointed for them as to their wives and the captives whom their right hands possess in order that there should be no difficulty for Thee. And Allah is Oft-Forgiving, Most Merciful.

When it came to marriage and sexual privileges, Mohammed was more privileged than the rest of the believers.

So how do Muslim commentators get themselves out of yet another quagmire? They say that the equality in Qur'an 4:3 is concerned with apportioning time and money, while the equality mentioned in Qur'an 3:129 is concerned with the affection and love of the man toward his wives.

This only further increases the contradictions, since we know that Mohammed himself was not impartial in his affections toward his wives, for he loved Aisha more than any of his wives. But as long as the husband can be fair in apportioning his time and money, he can marry up to four. That interpretation makes it easier for men to be polygamous and not have to worry about loving one wife more than another.

The reason for marrying more than one woman is given by Ghazali, the great Muslim scholar: "Some men have such a compelling sexual desire that one woman is not sufficient to protect them from adultery. Such men therefore preferably marry more than one woman and may have up to four wives."[45]

And the reason for having sex with the slave girls instead of one's wives is also given by Ghazali: "Since among Arabs passion is an overpowering aspect of their nature, the need of their pious men to have sex has been found to be the more intense. And for the purpose of emptying the heart to the worship of God they have been allowed to have sex with women slaves if at some time they should fear that this passion will lead them to commit adultery. Though it is true that such action could lead to the birth of a child that will be a slave, which is a form of destruction . . . yet enslaving a child is a lighter offense than the destruction of religious belief. For enslaving the new born is a temporary thing but by committing adultery eternity is lost."[46] Also according to Ghazali: "For if a man purchases a slave girl, the purchase contract includes his right to have sex with her. This contract is primarily to own her and secondarily to enjoy her sexually."[47]

The commentator Qortobi said, regarding Qur'an. 4:3 that

slave girls used as such by the free Muslim man "have neither sexual rights, nor financial rights. For God made the 'one free woman' and the 'slave girls you may own' of the same category. The man however owes the slave girls the appropriate rights of ownership, and the kindness that befits slaves."[48]

Muslim women will not be rewarded by a monogamous marriage in heaven. Even in heaven, women are kept on their toes, in constant competition with other women. Their men in Paradise will enjoy sex with perpetually exquisite virgin women. Women are thus not just threatened by other women on earth, but also by additional women of perfect beauty in heaven—they must compete with supermodels in Paradise. Read what these pure-eyed women are telling wives on earth in the following hadith by Mu'az reported from the Messenger of Allah who said:

"A woman does not give trouble to her husband in this world but his wife of the pure-eyed virgin ones (huris) does not say to her: 'Do not give him trouble. May Allah destroy you, He is only a passing guest with you and it is very near that he will soon leave you to come to us.'"[49]

The editor of Mishkat wrote in a footnote to that tradition: "No woman should give trouble and anxiety to her husband. She is to give him ease and comfort in the household. If she acts otherwise, she will not be able to be his mate in Paradise. There the pure-eyed virgin girls will be his consorts."[50]

The Paradise of the Qur'an promises devout men beautiful women in Paradise and unlimited sexual feasting:

> "Lo! those men who kept their duty will be in a place secure amid gardens and water springs, attired in silk and silk embroidery, facing one another. Even so (it will be). And We shall wed them unto huris fair ones with wide, lovely eyes."[51]

> "Therein maidens restraining their glances, untouched before them by any man or jinn . . . lovely as rubies, beautiful as coral."[52]

"The fair, the beautiful ones huris . . . with large dark eyeballs, kept close in their pavilions."[53]

"Surely for the godfearing awaits a place of security, gardens and vineyards, and maidens of swelling breasts, like of age, and a cup overflowing."[54]

The hadith even raises the number of Paradise wives to 72.[55] It also tells us: "In Paradise . . . every person would have two wives (so beautiful) that the marrow of their shanks would glimmer beneath the flesh and there would be none without a wife in Paradise."[56]

The one theme that runs through as a constant in many verses of the Qur'an and Hadith is this catering to men's sexual pleasures both on earth and in Paradise. That is in sharp contrast to the very few rights, sexual and otherwise, of the woman who must be perpetually used and abused for a man's purposes.

There is a misconception that Islam is sexually repressive to men. But the truth is the opposite, and Muslim religious leadership fully understands it and tries to play it down to protect their society. Sex for the male in Islam is a huge buffet of alternatives from which he can freely choose. And if he understands the game, the Muslim male can never be indicted for adultery or rape, no matter what he does.

But the most shocking sexual privilege Sharia grants to men is that they are allowed to seek sexual gratification with children. Urfi and mutaa marriages open the door to this kind of interpretation, as there is no legal age of marriage under Sharia and in Iran. For instance, a marriage may be lawfully consummated with a girl as young as nine. Furthermore, the revered Ayatollah Ruhollah Khomeini, The Supreme Leader of Iran, the Shia Grand Ayatollah between 1979 and 1989 (in large part responsible for the recent spread of radicalism across the Muslim world), said in an official statement:

A man can quench his sexual lusts with a child as young as a baby. However, he should not penetrate. Sodomizing the baby is *halal* (allowed by Sharia). If the man penetrates and damages the child, then he should be responsible for her subsistence all her life. This girl, however, does not count as one of his four permanent wives. . . . It is better for a girl to marry when her menstruation starts, and at her husband's house rather than her father's home. Any father marrying his daughter so young will have a permanent place in heaven."[57]

Khomeini is very specific about the allowed sex acts with infants: "It is not illegal for an adult male to 'thigh' or enjoy a young girl who is still in the age of weaning; meaning to place his penis between her thighs, and to kiss her."[58]

Ayatolla Khomeini didn't just make this stuff up. Mohammed was practicing thighing with Aisha at age six and consummated the marriage at age nine.[59] Mohammed's behavior was not unusual for the place and time in which he lived. But Islamic leaders promote the notion of *uswa hasana* (a model for all time), that whatever Mohammed did then is what Muslims must do throughout time and space.

In his famous book, *Tahrirolvasyleh*, Ayatollah Khomeini writes about his views of sex in excruciating detail—specifically sex with a nine-year-old child and how much to pay or not to pay for damaging the child's vagina, or whether to marry or not to marry her as a *Siqeh* (a temporary wedding).[60]

Marrying a child is not just a Shi'ite belief, but also a Sunni one. After an eight-year-old Yemeni girl filed for divorce from her thirty-year-old husband, the Yemeni Parliament rejected a request to legislate a minimum age for marriage. The rejection was based on its understanding of Islam. Commenting on minimum age in Muslim marriage, in June 2008, Saudi marriage official Dr. Ahmad Al Mubi said in an interview which aired on LBC TV: "There is no minimal age for entering marriage. . . . The Prophet Mohammed is the model we follow." In the same interview he said that the marriage contract can take place any time, even at age one, and then the marriage can be consummated at age nine.

By having no age limit for marriage in Islam, a girl can find herself born married, just like Aisha, wife of Mohammed. In that case, where is the consent of the girl that Muslims claim they must have from the bride? How can a one-, nine-, or twelve-year-old give her consent to marriage? The contradictions in Islam are staggering.

The above is not just an opinion of Muslim clerics, but pre-adolescent marriage is indeed codified in Qur'an 65:4 when it discusses divorcing a wife who has not had her period yet: "Such of your women as have passed the age of monthly courses, for them the prescribed period, if ye have any doubts, is three months, and for those who have no courses (it is the same): for those who carry (life within their wombs), their period is until they deliver their burdens: and for those who fear Allah, He will make their path easy."

Apologists for Islam today try to explain away what Mohammed did as "of the period" and then in the next breath, the same soothing spokesmen will insist that his "thighing" with Aisha, or the way he treated prisoners, or had others treat them, is valid and worth emulating for all time. The clerics wish to hide as much of this from us as they can. Yet in the age of the World Wide Web, that concealment is an increasingly tough act, considering that information is all merely a click away.

I recently heard on Arab television the brave Bahreini feminist Ghada Jamsheer refer to the Khomeini writings and the sanctioned sex with children. Her stunned interviewer didn't know what to do. He tried to interrupt her and argued that she was saying such things because she was a Sunni, but he did not once deny that what she was saying was true. Ghada Jamsheer is no longer allowed to speak out. She has been silenced, but the TV interview rapidly spread over the Internet. Now all of the dirty laundry is out in public, and

Muslims themselves are beginning to hear about the allowed sexual uses of children right on their TV sets.

Legalized pedophilia—whether thighing of infants or raping nine-year-old girls—will continue in the Muslim world as long as "Allah" encourages men to be owners instead of husbands and fathers.

Many Muslims themselves are embarrassed by this and are trying to hide these facts about male sexual rights—even from their sons. Sharia's sexual generosity to the male is a hush-hush truth that no Muslim leader has the courage to speak out against. To the world they deny and excuse it away, but in private they cherish and want to maintain such horrendous rights. After all, it is their gift from Allah. For the well-informed Muslim man, the sky is the limit in satisfying himself sexually beyond marriage. It is perfectly within Sharia's limits, beyond society's condemnation, and all with Allah's approval.[61]

Not all Muslim men take advantage of the rights granted to them in Islamic teachings, nor do they reflect the demeaning views of women expressed in those teachings and laws. But in times of trouble, because the laws are there, even a good man may fall back on his "rights." Being a committed believer can get him out of a lot of obligations to his wife. Under the Sharia marriage contract and all that it means and implies, no Muslim wife can truly feel secure in a society that treats her no better than a paid prostitute, even if her husband is a loving and faithful husband and father.

I ask myself—how could all these laws have survived fourteen hundred years in Muslim countries without proper reform? The only reason I found after having lived as a Muslim for thirty years under Sharia, is that because clerics figure such embarrassing laws would repulse any average Muslim, they are kept as deep secrets and only mentioned to a few select Muslims getting degrees in Islamic theology. Such horrific laws survived by hiding and suppressing the truth and misrepresenting Sharia, especially to the victims of Sharia—women.

The fourteen-hundred-year-old Muslim marriage contract is defective and must be not just reformed, but replaced. It is time for Muslim society to end the unholy alliance between men and women under a dysfunctional marriage contract that can never produce a happy and functional union, but only a mean-spirited relationship based on cruelty and misery, which poisons the whole family. The Muslim women and men of today deserve much better.

Three

Women:
The Center of
Oppression

WHEN KAREN HUGHES, A SENIOR BUSH ADMINISTRA-
tion official, spoke before five hundred women covered in black
at a Saudi university, she expressed the hope that Saudi women
would be able to drive and fully participate in society. She was
quickly challenged by her audience. "The general image of the
Arab woman is that she isn't happy," one Saudi woman said.
"Well, we're all pretty happy." The room, full of students, faculty
members, and some professionals resounded with applause. Other
Saudi women said that they do not need to drive because they
have chauffeurs.

Western media quickly judged Hughes's mission to be a failure.
That would be the case if you take Saudi women's words at face
value. Arab culture cannot be taken at face value; it is complicated,
proud, deceptive, and driven by a deep urge to put down Western
culture and values. I believe that Mrs. Hughes's visit did make a
difference. The women who attended that event, even the ones on
the defensive, all went home with something to think about.

Like all societies, there are educated, wealthy, and sophisticated Muslim women who are quite impressive. But that does
not represent the great majority of Muslim women, who are

among the poorest and most oppressed in the world. But rich or poor, educated or not, wearing Western clothes or covered up, they all live, to one degree or another, under the sword of Sharia. Their lives resemble a maze where the direction of their daily activities is largely limited to the home, and their interactions are limited mostly to other women. On the street, the Muslim woman must not be identified and must never be with a man other than her husband or a close blood relative. Rich or poor, they all must live in the same cage of Sharia. It may be a gilded cage, but it is still a cage.

Being associated with the wealth of petrodollars does not protect Saudi women from being humiliated or arrested by the "virtue police," or from being flogged or jailed for things that many women around the world take for granted. She cannot be rescued by the police when beaten by her husband, and she has no recourse but to share her husband with other wives if he so desires.

In 2007, a prominent Saudi television presenter made international headlines when she permitted newspapers to print horrific images of her bruised and swollen face, which she claimed were from a beating by her husband. She explained that the reason for the brutal beating was because when he came home he could not immediately find her, as she was in the upstairs apartment visiting his sister. The Saudi woman was hospitalized and required multiple plastic surgeries on her face. When the husband was interviewed on Arab TV, he was not ashamed nor did he express any regrets. Nevertheless, her punishment for going public with her story and embarrassing her husband was that she was forbidden to work anymore by her husband who also said he would take a second wife. That is what can happen to even a prominent, wealthy, and educated Saudi woman under Sharia.

How could a husband not be ashamed for beating his wife? As explained in the previous chapter, wife beating is allowed, even prescribed for a "rebellious" woman. And technically, a wife not being there to cater to a husband's needs when he arrives home is in the list of serious offenses. However, since domestic violence is not an acceptable thing in polite, civilized society, Muslim leaders try to downplay it by claiming that Muslim men are allowed to beat their wives only under extreme cases when nothing else works. Yet this is contradicted by the following hadith: Umar reported the Prophet as saying, "A man will not be asked about why he beat his wife."[1] Thus, the Sharia law allowing beating for the disobedient wife is actually strengthened by the husband's right to not give an explanation to anyone, including the police, for why he beats his wife.

Given all that Muslim women suffer, Westerners find it difficult to understand why the majority of them deny their oppression especially to the West, yet it makes perfect sense to those who have lived under Sharia. Muslim women are held hostage under the law, and that's no exaggeration. The Qur'an, various hadiths, and Sharia all prescribe severe punishment for the rebellious woman. Complaining outside the family about a husband's treatment is taboo in Muslim society and is considered rebellion. A complaining woman can be viewed as a rebellious woman (even if the complaint is about a beating). A rebellious woman can be beaten by her husband and ordered by the Sharia court to never leave the home without his permission in *beit al taa*, meaning "house of obedience," a practice that amounts to house arrest.

Also, a woman's financial support is tied to her total obedience. A Muslim wife complaining to strangers or the media is considered an insult to her husband, family honor, and above all to Sharia itself. Thus complaining about Sharia's harsh laws in public, especially to an infidel American official, would be an act of rebellion against Islam itself. It can also be considered an act of treason against the state. So why would any Saudi woman acknowledge dissatisfaction with her life to Karen Hughes or any other Western stranger? It would be unthinkable, and she would suffer untold consequences.

In a case that made international headlines, a Saudi girl who had been gang raped was sentenced to jail and flogged for placing herself in a car with a male. Predictably, the sentence was made harsher after she spoke to the media. Muslims are very sensitive to criticism, and because this story became internationally known, the Saudi king was forced out of embarrassment to show his compassion by overturning her sentence.

A more realistic view of the life of Saudi women was expressed by Saudi women's rights activist Wajiha Al-Huweidar, which aired on Al-Hurra TV on January 13, 2008: "Saudi society is based on enslavement—the enslavement of women to men and of society to the state. People still do not make their own decisions, but it is the women of Saudi Arabia who have been denied everything. The Saudi woman still lives the life of a slave girl. So in what way are we different from Guantanamo? At least in the case of Guantanamo, many prisoners have been released, while we remain in this prison, and nobody ever hears of us. When will we be freed? I don't know."

Another Saudi woman, Dania Al-Ghalib, wrote in the Saudi English-language daily *Arab News* an op-ed titled "The Saudi Woman Is Always Guilty" in which she said,

The Saudi woman is born unwanted . . . the Saudi woman is guilty of being haunted by spinsterhood and not accepting *misyar* (pleasure marriage) and all other types of male-invented marriages. She is also guilty if she accepts being abandoned by her husband when he feels tired and bored with her and wants a new wife. She is guilty if she objects to anything and her legal guardian beats her until he breaks her ribs or permanently disfigures her. His right is to beat her and make her obey and listen, even if that means deforming her physical features as a woman and taking away her beauty. She is guilty when others confiscate her property or real estate by impersonating her, and her greatest sin is that her identity stems from her guardian. The Saudi woman is always guilty, and anyone who thinks of dealing with her humanely is a criminal.

The above two Saudi women's views paints a far different picture from that of Karen Hughes's audience. The ultimate abuse is when the slave is not allowed to rebel or speak out. The last thing a Muslim woman wants is to be in a Sharia court where all the laws are stacked against her; *nashiz*, which is Arabic for "rebelliousness of a woman," is a crime under Sharia. Muslim women are in an impossible situation, and denial has become the only comfort to many of them. Who can blame them?

But people on the outside living in Western democracies should not be fooled by the double-talk that the Arab culture is famous for. The West's dilemma is understandable, but they must understand how grave the situation is under Sharia, and how it often produces a deeply unhealthy reaction to victimization by the victim herself. Sharia has produced people who guard their own prison, making it very hard to rescue a victim who is defending the victimizer.

If I were to mention all the misogynist Sharia laws, I would need far more than just one chapter. However, I would like to summarize a few: a Muslim woman who commits adultery is to be stoned to death; unmarried girls who have sex must be flogged; women's testimony in court is half the value of a man; women get half the inheritance of a man; there is no community property between husband and wife; if a woman is killed, her indemnity money is half the indemnity money of a man; if her family follows Shafi'i law, then her clitoris must be removed at a young age—that is female castration in order for the man to make sure her sexual appetite is suppressed; she needs her guardian's permission for marriage or else it is void; she needs her husband's or male relative's permission for travel; she must cover all her body except her face and hands. (Other, more radical Hanbali-Wahabi views require that every inch of a woman be covered including her face and hands, and she can only have a hole in front of her eyes through which she can see.)

The above laws become more brutal when combined with

other laws, simply adding a greater stranglehold on women. For example, to prove rape either the rapist would have to confess or there must be four male witnesses to the rape (and how likely would that be?). No other evidence is allowed. That makes it very difficult for any woman to prove rape. Thus when she loses her virginity as a result of rape, she may become a victim of honor killing or be flogged by the Islamic court for having pre-marital sex. That does not apply to the male rapist who could theoretically be punished by flogging or jail, but without four witnesses he is a free man. And as we have seen in the previous chapter, a rapist can get away with it by paying the bride-money to the rape victim without marrying her.

While Islam claims respect for the woman's body, the laws do not support that claim. Sharia stones women for adultery, but men are not stoned for rape—such inequity contradicts any claims of Islam's honor of women.

Qur'an 24:33 absolves a man from using a slave girl for prostitution: "And do not compel your slave girls to prostitution, when they desire to keep chaste, in order to seek the frail good of this world's life; and whoever compels them, then surely after their compulsion Allah is Forgiving, Merciful." Under Sharia, the owner of a slave girl owns her body and can have sex with her whenever he wishes with the knowledge of his wives, but that is not what the above verse is talking about. It is about profiting financially by selling the body of the slave girl to other men. However, while the above verse tells men to not force their slaves into prostitution, it assures them that if they do, then Allah is forgiving and merciful.[2]

Exceptions to the rules of human decency have been made throughout the ages to protect men of power, and the laws of Islam have served power in that regard. Saddam Hussein's son systematically raped many girls during the brutal reign of his father. In fact, rape was used as a political tactic by Saddam Hussein's regime to frighten and humiliate Kurds and Shi'ites.

Saddam's army shamelessly raped many Kuwaiti women. As repugnant as this practice is, raping the women of your "enemies" can be justified by pointing to the example of Mohammed's conquering exploits.

In the famous story cited in the previous chapter, which resulted in the Qur'anic verse upon which laws on slave wives would be based, after one battle, "some of the winning Muslim soldiers did not like to rape the captive women in front of their husbands."[3] The story clearly shows that raping captive women in front of their husbands was a condoned military tactic and there was no punishment for it. Tragically, we have seen the tactic in the Sudan and other contemporary tribal conflicts in Muslim lands. This contradicts Islam's claim of respect for women.

It is obvious that men are the beneficiaries and women are the victims of Sharia's sexual laws, whether in times of war or peace. Seventy-five percent of women in jail in Pakistan are there for sexual crimes, many of whom were raped but were unable to prove it with four male witnesses. But still Muslims insist that Islam honors women.

Consider the quite typical view expressed by Mohammed Qutb, the brother of Sayyed Qutb, leader of the Muslim Brotherhood. He compared sexual relations between Muslim slave owners and their female slaves with what, in his view, is the depraved practice of casual consensual sex in contemporary Europe. He believes that sex with owned slave girls is less offensive than Western dating and consensual sex, a view that unfortunately many Muslims agree with.

What's important to notice here is that when criticizing the sexual attitudes and practices in the West, it is not the sex act per se that Muslims are upset about, but the notion of giving freedom to women to have or not have sex. What bothers them is freedom of choice in the West for women. But having sex with a slave who is unable to refuse her master or oppressing and beating noncompliant women, somehow that is okay.

Let us compare two cases in Islam: (1) a man who has forced sex with his owned slaves, and (2) a single Muslim girl who is caught sleeping with her lover. In both cases sex outside of marriage has occurred; however, one is blessed by Allah's law and the other is severely punished by flogging with the female often dying in the process. (For a woman, the difference here is *choice* and not the sex act itself. Only the male master in Islam can have the privilege of choice, and the woman should only be the passive recipient of sex.) If she survives the flogging and goes home, she will probably be subjected to vigilante justice by her father who will honor kill her and get away with it.

Killing for Honor

Contradictions in Sharia are glaring when it comes to honor killing. It is true that there are no Sharia laws that openly give men the right to kill their women to protect their family honor. Yet some laws exist that actually protect men who kill under such conditions. The following Shafi'i law puts punishment for the following crimes—adultery being one of them—in the hands of not only the judiciary but also the public: "There is no expiation (punishment) for killing someone who has left Islam, a highwayman, or a convicted married adulterer, even when someone besides the caliph kills him."[4] In other words, a killer—even though having no authority from the state—of an apostate, a robber, or an adulterer cannot be punished for murder under Sharia. Vigilante justice is thus allowed in Islam under certain conditions.

It is not a coincidence that murderers of certain Sharia violators go unpunished. Sharia's level of compliance is strengthened by appointing citizens as guardians and enforcers of Sharia. This gives ordinary Muslim citizens the right to be offended and angry with other Muslims and even non-Muslims for simple violations of Sharia. Thus, violators of Sharia must not only worry and fear the Muslim virtue police but worse, they must fear vigilante justice by the public—their friends, neighbors, relatives, and even a mother, father, brother, or sister. A convert out of Islam in Canada reported that his own mother had contracted someone to kill him by throwing him from a third floor of a mall because he has become an apostate.

The above Sharia law exempting certain murders can be abused by people who kill and then say, for example, "I caught her cheating," or "He was an apostate and insulted Islam." Exempting certain murders from punishment reduces the level of taboo against killing, resulting in relationships between Muslims that are based on fear, arrogance, and a holier-than-thou attitude. The ultimate result is a chaotic society. Increasingly we see death squads or street mobs taking "justice" into their own hands. On the Internet, we've witnessed scenes of a mob stoning girls and injuries to girls from acid thrown on them by boys who did not like what they were wearing.

The right to a degree of vigilante justice is not a coincidence in a draconian legal system that wants total control of society through oppressing and handicapping its women. I have never heard a Muslim leader firmly and unequivocally preach against vigilante justice or condemn such things as throwing acid on girls who do not cover up, or teach that honor killing is un-Islamic and should be harshly punished. But I often see imams from the pulpits of mosques inspire men to believe *they* are the victims and show them what kind of stick they can use to beat their wives.

Many Muslims insist that honor killing is a cultural thing and has nothing to do with Islamic Sharia. But how can we look at the above law that exempts certain types of murder and say that honor killing of a wife for adultery is not Islamic? Why does the phenomenon of honor killing exist only in Muslim culture? We cannot divorce Islamic Sharia from this tragedy so prevalent in Muslim society because there are indirect laws that promote this phenomenon. Another such law is *qesas* law, which exempts a killer from punishment of death if the family of the victim pardons him. In honor-killing cases, when both the murdered and murderer are within the same family, the family who had just lost a daughter or mother killed by a father or brother often does not want to lose more family members and opts to pardon the killer. Under qesas Sharia law, even the State cannot punish the killer by death if he is forgiven by his family, and that is known to men who often rely on that law for protection. Since the introduction of qesas law in Pakistan, honor killing has greatly increased.

Cases of honor killing in Egypt have always been ignored by the religious community and Sharia experts. It is only now that Muslims are showing some sensitivity about the topic because Western countries are becoming aware of and alarmed by incidences in their own backyard by Muslim immigrants. Sharia experts, who for centuries have seen honor killing of girls and looked the other way, are suddenly faced with the inconvenience of having to explain it to the international community. And now they feign surprise and concern and say it is un-Islamic. Some even go as far as accusing the West of ignorance about Islam and saying that this has nothing to do with Sharia.

Decades ago when I lived in Egypt, we were all aware of the hush-hush topic of honor killing. The religious community was silent about it, and we always presumed that it was supported by religion since no religious leaders ever condemned it. A petrified maid once told me about the body of a woman floating in a Nile River branch near her village. She said the body moved slowly down the river for days until it disappeared. Yet no one reported it. Even the village police looked the other way. The horrific scene she described to me was seen by the whole village, including the children, and nothing happened. Some people walked scared, while others murmured that women like that probably deserved their destiny.

One of the most moving Egyptian honor-killing movies was *Bidaya wa Nihaya*, meaning "beginning and ending." It made such an impression on me that I remember it vividly to this day.

In the 1960 film, Omar Sharif plays a young man in an extremely poor family. His older sister secretly works as a prostitute without her family's knowledge in order to provide for the family—and in order for her young brother, whom she loves dearly, to attend military academy to become an officer.

But one day, the newly graduated military officer, who is the pride of his family, is called by the police to identify a prostitute who claims she is his sister. In the jail, other imprisoned women, when they find out that the brother is an officer and would soon be coming to pick her up, begin picking on the sister about to be released, by singing, "Ya helwa Ya balaha Ya maamaa Sharafti Ikhawtik Larbaa," meaning, "Hey pretty pealed date, you have honored your four brothers."

Every Egyptian girl who watches the powerful and humiliating scene of that poor sister learns a good lesson about Sharia. This world-class movie shows Omar Sharif's agonized face as he recognizes his sister. She begs and follows him out of the jail in extreme shame to the whispers of the police officers behind them. The brother walks in the streets followed by his sister all the way to a bridge on the Nile and stands away looking at her. They do not talk. She stands up on the edge of the bridge, looking back at him from a distance. She knows what she must do . . . as he waits. A policeman comes from far off to try to stop the young woman from jumping to her death, but it is too late. She jumps. The camera focuses on the Nile, which has swallowed her without a trace. People walk by wondering what has happened, whispering about her reasons for suicide. The brother, who stood by forcing his beloved sister to jump, cannot take the guilt and devastation imposed on both of them by a merciless society. So after the crowd leaves, the brother also jumps to his death.

A few years ago, a real-life honor killing in Gaza occurred with a special twist. A young mother of two toddlers was rumored to have been forced into a suicide bombing after she was discovered cheating on her husband.

They say Islam has nothing to do with honor killing, but I have never heard a Friday sermon prohibiting it and quoting scriptures that condemn it. Men who commit that crime are rarely punished, and even then the punishment is very light. Preachers may not say in their mosques that honor killing is against Islam, but they surely tell that to the West when an embarrassing story of honor killing occurs in France, Germany, or London. Muslim sensitivity to shame before the West is behind the strong denial of any link of honor killing to Islam.

Why do Muslim leaders who tell the press that honor killings are un-Islamic never cry from the pulpits of mosques saying, "No, not in the name of Islam"? Isn't religion supposed to fix bad cultural habits? Why cannot the all-powerful authoritarian Islamic Sharia end this supposedly evil cultural habit in Muslim society? Why is it that draconian Sharia, which controls every aspect of a Muslim's life and more, has failed to notice that women and girls are being killed by their own male family members? Why is it that not one man has been stoned to death for killing his daughter to protect his honor, while women are stoned for having sex that was actually rape they are unable to prove?

The bottom line is that leaders of the "religion of peace" do not mind honor killing and have never harshly punished its perpetrators. Islamic Sharia becomes all the more powerful when yet another layer of fear is imposed on women, the main objects of victimization under Sharia. Relying on the justice system and the corrupt police cannot be totally effective in breaking the will of women and preventing them from rebelling. Thus, encouraging male family members to become the police, judge, and jury over women becomes the solution to achieve total female submission.

One honor killing touched particularly close to home. The unthinkable happened to our teenage maid who was my age when she was discovered to be pregnant out of wedlock. When my mother asked her what happened, she tearfully explained that she had been raped by her former boss in the home where she worked before coming to us. When the man's wife caught him, she blamed the maid and kicked the girl out in the middle of the night. My mother, who well understood the potential consequences, did not want to send the girl back to her family, so instead arranged for her to go to a government agency where she would be protected for the duration of her pregnancy.

We later learned her fate from the agent who had placed her in our home. He never used the word *killed*, but he whispered that her father and brother "took care of their honor." She ended up as one of those unreported deaths, very much like that body seen floating in the Nile until it disappeared. Nothing happened to the rapist, an upper-class married man with a bunch of children.

Looking back, the amazing part was how little discussion or questioning took place over such murders. Even my family was silent, and we hardly ever talked about it again. I wonder what would have happened if I had reported this to the police. Probably nothing. I was shocked and petrified but remained silent.

If honor killing was truly a crime unacceptable to Islam, Sharia Law could have certainly frightened men away from committing it. But honor killing falls into perfect harmony with the Muslim views of women and their sexual oppression. From the least to the most educated, from the least to the most religious, the reaction is the same: no one makes a public stand, and no one reports it, not even the religious leaders. Such murder victims are treated like a dead squirrel or a rabbit run over on the road. And now I cannot forget the face of that beautiful young girl who was just my age, always smiling and happy to bring me a cup of tea in the morning, during those few months she worked in our home.

Separate but Certainly Not Equal

The segregation of the sexes under Sharia law leads to some ridiculous situations in the twenty-first century. If a woman cannot be in the company of men who are not her relatives, then how can she have a job outside the home? An Egyptian fatwa recently tried to find a way around the dilemma. Dr. Izzat Atiyya, head of the Hadith Department in Al-Azhar University, issued a fatwa stating that a woman who is required to work in private with a man not of her immediate family—which is forbidden by Sharia—can resolve the problem by breast-feeding the man, which according to Sharia turns him into a member of her immediate family.

The issuance and publication of the fatwa raised a storm of protest both with the Egyptian public and the religious establishment. It also made international news, provoking ridicule worldwide. The embarrassed university suspended Dr. Atiyya. At their insistence, he retracted his fatwa as a "strictly personal interpretation of a certain hadith," but he continued to defend it. In an interview, he explained, "The religious ruling that appears in the Prophet's conduct (sunnah) confirms that breast-feeding allows a man and a woman to be together in private, even if they are not family and if the woman did not nurse the man in his infancy . . . providing that their being together serves some purpose, religious or secular." Atiyya further explained, "The adult must suckle directly from the woman's breast. . . . This according to a hadith attributed to Aisha, wife of the Prophet Mohammed, which tells of Salem, the adopted son of Abu Huzaifa, who was breastfed by Abu-Huzaifa's wife when he was already a grown man with a beard, by the Prophet's order." Dr. Atiyya also defended himself by saying: "The fact that the hadith regarding the breastfeeding of an adult is inconceivable to the mind does not make it invalid. This is a reliable hadith, and rejecting it is tantamount to rejecting Allah's Messenger and questioning the Prophet's tradition."[5]

The hadith in question is as follows: "Aisha is reported to have said that Salha, daughter of Suhail, came to the Prophet and said, 'Allah's Messenger, I see on the face of Abu Huzaifa (signs of disgust), on entering of Salem into (my house).' Upon this Allah's

Messenger said, 'Suckle him.' She said, 'How can I suckle him as he is a grown-up man?' Allah's Messenger smiled and said, 'I already know that he is a young man.' Then she suckled him, came back to the Holy Prophet and said, 'I did not see anything on Abu Huzaifa's face that I disliked afterwards.'"[6]

While the breast-feeding law was originally designed to allow an infant foster child to be considered a blood relative, the hadith cited by Dr. Atiyya clearly addressed the idea of suckling a grown man. Yes, of course it's ridiculous, but Atiyya indeed has a theological leg to stand on. The hadith on which he based his fatwa gives very definitive precedent, perhaps more so than the tenuous hadiths on which some of the marriage laws are based. Is it any more ridiculous than allowing one-night *mutaa* pleasure "marriages" based on the Prophet's answer to his soldiers' questions about raping slave women in front of their husbands? If one is to take the Qur'an and hadiths literally, breast-feeding an adult male is "sound." Why then did the Egyptian public get in an uproar over the breast-feeding fatwa? Embarrassment in front of the rest of the world was surely one factor. But other laws such as executing apostates or stoning a woman for unproved rape are equally if not more outrageous and embarrassing. Perhaps the ruling men of Islam want to preserve their control over women and their unlimited sexual privileges, so they support the Sharia laws that secure that. But they do not mind excluding an item on the menu of Sharia that gives other men freedom of privacy with their wives. Somehow that is going too far, so in this instance they find it easy to reject a seventh-century practice approved by the Prophet.

Female Circumcision

Another outrageous practice, supported by Sharia in many areas of the Muslim world, is female genital mutilation. When I was a young girl, I once heard my aunt talking about *tahara* (female circumcision). She was laughing about it and saying that for days, girls could not walk because of the "pain between their legs." I didn't understand what she was talking about, but I noticed my mother was nervous and quickly changed the subject. In my aunt and mother's generation, even the upper classes circumcised young girls. Fortunately, some in my generation escaped it. But today, genital mutilation still occurs in many small villages of Muslim and African countries.

Many moderate Muslim scholars insist that female circumcision is a societal practice unrelated to Islam. However, Dr. Muhammad al-Mussayar of Al-Azhar University, referring to reliable hadiths, stated,

> All jurisprudents, since the advent of Islam and for fourteen centuries or more, are in consensus that female circumcision is permitted in Islam. But they were divided as to its status in the Sharia. Some said that female circumcision is required by the Sharia, just like male circumcision. Some said this is a mainstream practice, while others said that it is a noble act.
>
> The Shafi'i school of Sharia considers circumcision of girls compulsory. *The Reliance of the Traveller*, a respected manual of Shafi'i jurisprudence, states: "Circumcision is obligatory (for every male and female) by cutting off the piece of skin on the glans of the penis of the male, but circumcision of the female is by cutting out the clitoris" (section e4.3). The English translation by Nuh Ha Mim Keller (certified by Al-Azhar University) disguises the true meaning of the Arabic by adding a bogus ending: "For men it consists of removing the prepuce from the penis, and for women, removing the prepuce (Ar. Bazr) of the clitoris (n: not the clitoris itself, as some mistakenly assert)."[7]

Female circumcision is commonly practiced among Indonesian Muslims, where Shafi'i Islam predominates. It is also relatively frequent in other regions where the Shafi'i school predominates, such as Egypt, southern Arabia, Bahrain, Kurdistan, Somalia, Brunei, and Malaysia, as well as Indonesia. In Indonesia, the practice had previously been unknown before Shafi'i Islam was introduced into Southeast Asia.The claim that female circumcision is not a religious practice doesn't hold up.

While many say that there is nothing in Islam requiring female circumcision, one of Sunni Islam's "Four Great Imams," Ahmad ibn Hanbal (from whom the Hanbali school of Islamic jurisprudence takes its name) quotes Mohammed as saying, "Circumcision is a law for men and a preservation of honor for women."[8]

The seventh-century desert culture routinely circumcised girls before the age of nine. Robbing a young woman of sexual pleasure by cutting out the clitoris was considered a way to protect the honor of young girls and to keep wives chaste when their husbands were off on jihad. And this, as so many other brutal desert tribal customs, was codified into law for all time. It continues to this day with dire consequences.

My Body, My Shame

Islam's view of a woman's body is the foundation of her virtual imprisonment. It represents a major contradiction between what outsiders are told and what the truth is. Muslims say that women must cover their bodies for their own protection as a way to honor women. But in reality a woman's body is considered a thing she should be ashamed of. According to many hadiths, a woman is an *awrah*, Arabic for "pudendum," the external genitalia. It is as if the main religiously sanctioned word for women in American culture was the detestable four-letter *c* word. A woman is an awrah, not "like an awrah," but she *is* an awrah, meaning a woman in her totality is an exposed genital area.

Ali reported the Prophet saying: "Women have ten *awrat* (plural of awrah). When she gets married, the husband covers one, and when she dies the grave covers the ten."[9]

Another hadith states, "The woman is awrah. When she goes outside (the house), the devil welcomes her."[10] So going outside the house for the woman is a form of exposure of her awrah. That is why women are discouraged from going outside the house, even to pray in the mosque, as the following hadith indicates: "A woman is closest to God's face, if she is found in the core of her house. And the prayer of the woman in the house is better than her prayer in the mosque."[11] This hadith explains why I and almost all Muslim women around me in the Middle East never had the privilege of praying together as a family in a house of worship. How can a woman be honored in Islam if the God who has created her considers her an awrah and prefers that she not worship him in the house of God?

Growing up as a Muslim never gave me the feeling that our bodies were holy, but rather something filthy that must be hidden. Most religions in the world preach that our bodies, both men and women, are holy and should be preserved holy for marriage. The treatment of a woman's body under Sharia is more like taming an animal than treating it as holy and respected of God's creation. Islamic law is more concerned with beating, flogging, and stoning than honoring women.

One of the most important responsibilities of a Muslim woman is to protect the honor of her male family members, and her body is the symbol of that honor. But protecting a man's honor goes beyond the symbol of her body to a life of secrecy about any abuse. In an article posted on the Internet, a Muslim female writer advises Muslim women "to guard your husband's honor as a Muslim wife." She says that "most Muslim women are careless about their primary obligation to protect their husband's honor." Her advice to fellow Muslim women includes the following: (1) Be careful of unintentional slips in conversations with other women. (2) Remember that mentioning your husband's weaknesses might initiate gossip about you. (3) Remember that protecting the husband's honor is one of *Allah's commands* for a Muslim wife. (4) Beware of the concern of even your biological mothers and sisters—it can sometimes be the *cause* of your marital troubles.[12]

The Dilemma of Hiding the Shame

Every part of a woman's body provokes sexual temptation to the Muslim male, who has been trained to regard them all as equally erotic as her private parts. His temptation and resulting sinful actions are therefore her problem and not his responsibility. This has become a great burden on the Muslim woman whose number one responsibility has become hiding and covering her shame, her body. She must shield and conceal it and live with no identity in public because the alternative could be humiliating corporal punishment by a male flogger.

Whether a Muslim woman wears only the traditional head cover allowing only her face and hands to show or whether she also covers her face and hands in what is called by some *nikab*, a woman's physical comfort, freedom of movement, and ability to drive or play sports is totally restricted. But according to Islam, that is secondary to her primary duty to protect her husband's, father's, and her own honor.

Sharia has solved the problem of male sexual temptation not by civilizing the male and teaching him self-restraint and respect for the female body, but by punishing the woman. The female thus must mold her life to hide her shame, her body, her awrah. Even in Muslim countries that don't enforce wearing the *hijab*, women who don't cover up are often harassed, ridiculed, or attacked. Even in the United States, I was told privately by some uncovered Muslim girls on U.S. college campuses, that Muslim Student Associations shame those who refuse to wear Islamic cover.

At the age when boys should have crushes on girls, they are given messages of hostility toward a girl's uncovered head, arms, and legs. The message given to boys is that it is their right to get offended, and those uncovered girls deserve to be disrespected. Thus we see incidences of Muslim boys attacking girls who are not covered. Women uncovered in the Islamic way are regarded as "asking for it." The normal boy sexuality has been twisted to feel hostility and extreme disrespect of an uncovered woman. And to cross the line further, boys are driven by an urge to do something about it even if the girl is a perfect stranger. In more liberal Turkey, boys threw acid on the legs of two schoolgirls whose skirts ended below the knee and not all the way to their feet. I wonder how many mosque sermons the following Friday condemned those boys or called their actions un-Islamic? The fear from such unexpected attacks have caused some Christian girls that I knew in Egypt to opt to cover up the Islamic way to avoid such attacks by perfect strangers.

By covering up women in such an extreme way, Muslim men have become unaccustomed to seeing a normal-looking woman. When they see Western women, some may completely lose control. A horrible incident happened during Ramadan in the Sinai to seven Israeli girls who were vacationing in Egypt after the peace treaty in early eighties. The girls were wearing shorts and T-shirts on the beach. An Egyptian soldier felt extremely offended because a man's fasting is cancelled during Ramadan if he looks lustfully at women. The soldier fired at and killed all seven girls. Furthermore, an Egyptian preacher who immigrated to Australia defended Muslim men who sexually assaulted several Australian girls on the beach, not by apologizing on their behalf, but by calling the girls "uncovered meat," a common phrase I often heard from Egyptian clerics. That has led many Muslim women to feel safe only when covered up from head to toe.

A Muslim friend of mine in Egypt told me that she was wearing her hijab not for religious reasons, but because of safety and social pressure. She insisted, "I am just comfortable this way." But how can anyone be comfortable in seeing the world through a hole? How can anyone be comfortable when every time there's a knock at the door, she must run and get the head cover lest the plumber see her hair? But that is the Muslim solution to the problem of male sexual temptation.

But even covering up doesn't necessarily absolve women of blame. In one hadith, "Those women who are naked even in their dresses and lead their husbands to astray will go to hell. . . . They incline to evil and make their husbands incline to it."[13] Whatever the woman does, she is condemned. When men imagine a woman naked, projecting their frustration onto them, the woman ends up blamed for the sexual violations even if she is totally covered! It seems to me that the above hadith is very telling: there is nothing that a Muslim woman can do to be respected.

Muslims use the words *nikab*, *burqa*, or *hijab* to basically mean the same thing. In Arabic *hijab* literally means "a barrier or veil" because it hides the face of a woman. But that is not all that it does; by covering the face and identity, the nikab also adds to the alienation and loneliness of Muslim women. What seventh-century Bedouin women needed to wear to have a small sense of privacy has become a shield of isolation and a symbol of subjugation in the twenty-first century. Besides the increased sense of alienation, the hijab is unfriendly. It sends the message, "I do not want to know you on a personal basis. I am just a shadow confined to the home." Hiding the face in particular can also be intimidating and frightening for others, because people do not know who is under the garb.

Westerners are sometimes baffled by the attitude some Muslim women in the West display regarding their covering up. Female Muslim medical students at several hospitals in Britain are objecting to a rigorous hand-washing campaign designed to stop the spread of dangerous bacteria in the hospital setting. Washing up to the elbow is crucial for safety, and the women medical students are complaining that being forced to bare their forearms above the wrist is immodest and prohibited by their religion. Believe it or not, some of the Muslim women at Birmingham University said they would change careers rather than comply.[14]

What baffles the West is why an intelligent, well-educated Muslim woman would by choice want to shroud herself in black from head to toe? In my opinion, a woman who wears the nikab by choice in the West is actually sending a hostile message. Instead of showing spirituality, humility, or modesty, she is in fact calling attention to herself. Wearing a morbid black cover-up makes her appear to love death more than life. It is a masochistic way of treating oneself in a society that does not require it and actually draws attention to the person who wears it. Cultures that love freedom, nature, and the outdoors see these shrouded women like ghosts or the walking dead rejecting the joys of life, not even allowing sunlight to touch their faces or a soft breeze to blow their hair.

I have no doubt that many women who wear the nikab by choice are militants who see themselves as holy warriors behind their male jihadists fighting the West to achieve their caliphate. Nor am I surprised when some of them celebrate the death of their husbands and sons who die in jihad. Make no mistake about it, these women are immune to ridicule and contempt and have one focus and one purpose: their absolute defense of Sharia. Such women must never be role models to young American Muslims, but must be regarded as poor souls who don't realize that they carry the seeds of their own destruction.

Confined to the Home

To add insult to injury, the great theologian Abu Hamid Al-Ghazali (1058–1111), referred to by the *Encyclopedia of Islam* as the second-most influential person in Islam, just after Mohammed, defined the role of women as follows:

> She should stay at home and get on with her spinning, she should not go out often, she must not be well-informed, nor must she be communicative with her neighbors and only visit them when absolutely necessary; she should take care of her husband and respect him in his presence and his absence and seek to

satisfy him in everything; she must not cheat on him nor extort money from him; she must not leave her house without his permission and if given his permission she must leave surreptitiously. She should put on old clothes and take deserted streets and alleys, avoid markets, and make sure that a stranger does not hear her voice or recognize her; she must not speak to a friend of her husband even in need. Her sole worry should be her virtue, her home as well as her prayers and her fast. If a friend of her husband calls when the latter is absent she must not open the door nor reply to him in order to safeguard her and her husband's honor. She should accept what her husband gives her as sufficient sexual needs at any moment. She should be clean and ready to satisfy her husband's sexual needs at any moment.[15]

Ghazali also outlined women's punishment under Sharia law with distinctive characteristics because of Eve's actions in the garden of Eden:

When Eve ate fruit which He had forbidden to her from the tree in Paradise, the Lord, be He praised, punished women with: (1) menstruation; (2) childbirth; (3) separation from mother and father and marriage to a stranger; (4) pregnancy; (5) not having control over her own person; (6) a lesser share in inheritance; (7) her liability to be divorced and inability to divorce; (8) its being lawful for men to have four wives, but for a woman to have only one husband; (9) the fact that she must stay secluded in the house; (10) the fact that she must keep her head covered inside the house; (11) the fact that two women's testimony has to be set against the testimony of one man; (12) the fact that she must not go out of the house unless accompanied by a near relative; (13) the fact that men take part in Friday and feast prayers and funerals, while women do not; (14) disqualification for rulership and judgeship; (15) the fact that merit has one thousand components, only one which is attributable to women, while 999 are attributable to men."[16]

Lest anyone think these attitudes are attributable to culture, but not to Islam and Sharia, let us examine more hadiths and verses of the Qur'an that deepen the feelings of guilt and humiliation of Muslim women:

Decked out fair to men is the love of lusts—Women, children, heaped up heaps of gold and silver, horses of mark, cattle and tillage. I once heard a Muslim writer address Muslim girls by saying, "Know that this temptation which afflicts the man is due to you." His opinion is not unusual and is a common belief in the Muslim world. That is why whenever a sexual scandal occurs in Muslim countries, the woman is blamed as the source of seduction. Muslim teachers often portray woman as the absolute and greatest affliction in a man's life. School girls are sometimes told that the reason the majority of women will end up in hell is because their failures causes men to stumble. The Prophet said: "I have not left any calamity *fitnah* after me more detrimental to men than women."[17]

Imam Ghazali in his two books, *The Revival of the Religious Sciences* and the *Book of the Counsel for Kings*, warns all men to be careful of women for their "guile is immense and their mischief is noxious; they are immoral and mean spirited." He then adds: "It is a fact that all the trials, misfortunes and woes which befall men come from women."[18]

The following hadith by Sahih Bukhari is considered by Muslim scholars to be the most authentic book after the Book of Allah (the Qur'an):

Once Allah's Apostle went out to the Musalla (to offer the prayer) on 'Id-al-Adha or Al-Fitr prayer. Then he passed by the women and said, "O women! Give alms, as I have seen that the majority of the dwellers of Hell-fire were you (women)." They asked, "Why is it so, O Allah's Apostle?" He replied, "You curse frequently and are ungrateful to your husbands. I have not seen anyone more deficient in intelligence and religion than you. A cautious sensible man could be led astray by some of you." The women asked, "O Allah's Apostle! What is deficient in our intelligence and religion?" He said, "Is not the evidence of two women equal to the witness of one man?" They replied in the affirmative. He said, "This is the deficiency in her intelligence. Isn't it true that a woman can neither pray nor fast during her menses?" The women replied in the affirmative. He said, "This is the deficiency in her religion."[19]

Many Muslims become very defensive when the above hadith is mentioned. Even some committed Muslim women have no choice but to live in denial, blaming this hadith not on their religion or those who gathered and documented such hadiths, but on the people who question it or even bring it up. An eloquent Muslim female on the Internet claims the above hadith is misinterpreted, and for that she does not blame the hadith itself for humiliating women, but she blames the people who repeat the hadith or take it seriously.[20]

With Islam currently under the microscope, Muslims have become extremely defensive, but instead of getting into an honest dialogue, many will shut you up, call you names, or accuse you of Islamophobia. They insist that the Prophet never meant to hurt women and treated them with great respect. To prove their point they pick one moderate point in the Qur'an and totally ignore the many hadiths, verses, and laws in question. Some degree of denial is one thing, but what about the following?

- "According to Mohammed, '. . . I looked at the (hell) Fire and saw that the majority of its residents were women.'"[21]

- "People ruled by a woman will never be successful."[22]

- "A woman advances and retires in the shape of a devil; so when one of you sees a woman, he should come to his wife and have intercourse with her."[23]

- "Women are more harmful to men than anything else."[24]

- "The husband may forbid his wife to leave the home."[25]

- "If the husband's body is covered with pus and blood and if the wife lick and drink it, still her obligation to husband will not be fulfilled."[26]

- "Women are domestic animals; beat them."[27]

- "Women are half devils."[28]

- "A woman has a crooked character, similar to the man's rib that she was created from. The woman is like a rib; if you try to straighten her, she will break. So if you want to get benefit from her, do so while she still has some crookedness."[29]

- "Ghazali said: 'If you relax the woman's bridle a tiny bit, she will take you and bolt wildly. And if you lower her cheek-piece a hand span, she will pull you an arm's length. . . . Their deception is awesome and their wickedness is contagious; bad character and feeble mind are their predominant traits.' Mohammed said: 'The likeness of a virtuous woman amongst women is like a red beaked crow among a hundred crows.'"[30]

It is clearly not just one troubling Bukhari hadith about women being deficient in intelligence and religion; it is the *totality* of Islamic teachings that treat women as evil and inferior. These teachings have also molded how Muslims view women and how Muslim women view themselves and their place in society. They have molded how Muslim children view their mothers and women in general. What's more tragic, some of these women have grown accustomed to their prison of guilt and shame and willingly end up taking the blame and responsibility for men's sexual misbehavior. Such a barbaric outlook on a woman's body runs deep in Muslim society and causes untold tragedies.

The Impact on the Muslim Woman

How does all of the above impact women and their relationships in Muslim society? Muslim women face a serious quandary. Whether she is devout or not, she must adjust to Sharia and she has the following three choices:

1. Reject Sharia

A Muslim woman can reject Sharia in two ways: in her mind without talking about it, or openly, making her a rebellious Muslim apostate. Most Muslim women who reject Sharia are silent about it and thus live as Muslims in practice only. They live the life of a Muslim in public and accommodate the appearance of obeying Sharia, but in private they have nothing to do with Islam. These are women who believe there is no escape route from Sharia.

However, very few Muslim women openly reject Sharia and demand equal rights to men. Rebelling against Sharia is viewed as a rebellion against Allah himself, or apostasy. Muslim women shy away from any association with such "apostates." Associating with and supporting Muslim feminists would only confirm the hadith cleverly accusing her of lacking in religion and brains.[31] In order to solve this problem, many Muslim feminists who have openly confronted Sharia have done so not by confronting the truth but by claiming that true Islam does give men and women equality and that currently Islam is a misrepresentation of the true Islam.

As for Muslim women living in the West who dare to openly demand equal rights for Muslim women and an end to religious laws, they are often the victims of fatwas and are ostracized, hated, and ridiculed. Some of their worst enemies are none other than a large number of Muslim women who want to appear as the good Muslims who obey Allah's law. The tragedy of Sharia is that it pits Muslim women against each other. Most committed Muslim women will tell you that Islam honors women and will themselves call Muslim feminists "apostates."

People outside the Muslim world look at women's plight under Sharia and assume that it is just a matter of time before Muslim women wise up, figure out what must be done, stand together in unity, and march for their equality and human rights. That happened to women in the West, so why not to Muslim women in the Middle East?

Many also believe that the reformation of Islam will come at the hands of its most oppressed group: women. That seems to be the logical conclusion, but I am not very optimistic regarding this view, partially because Muslim women are not united. But I do believe that if and when the power of Islamic Sharia ends, Muslim women may have a substantial role, but not the main one. The toppling of the Sharia sword must also come from Muslim men. Expecting Muslim women to bring in the reformation of Islam and Sharia is like asking slaves to end their own slavery or asking prisoners to leave their prison without the guards unlocking the doors. A Muslim woman's inferior status in society goes so deep and is so intertwined that many Muslim institutions are dependent on it. For Muslim women to simply revolt against Sharia would be regarded as anti-family, anti-man, anti-religion, anti-government, and worst of all anti-Allah himself.

A grassroots Muslim feminist movement is very hard to imagine happening today. The majority of Muslim women are consumed with their own survival, and the last thing on their minds is rescuing other women. Furthermore, there is the issue of trust. Women do not trust other women in the Muslim world. This is the legacy of polygamy. Consciously or subconsciously, other women are viewed as possible rivals, as potential second, third, or fourth wives for their husbands. Any single woman becomes an automatic threat, and thus friendships between women are strained and distrustful. Something as basic as friendship and trust is needed for a feminist movement to succeed, and this is lacking in Muslim women's relationships with one another. In order for Muslim women to live and function under Sharia law, they had to develop elaborate manipulative skills in their relationships with both men and other women.

2. *If you can't beat them, join them*

A large number of Muslim women have discovered that they can achieve power and respect by supporting Sharia and radical Islam. Thus, rightly or wrongly, they choose to become militant and aggressively support Sharia. Some become as radical, if not more radical, than men. They become guards of the Muslim woman's jail. Such women monitor the compliance of other women and take that holier-than-thou approach.

In the world of sudden Muslim wealth from petrodollars, being a devout Muslim woman can be a high-paying job in itself. It has been rumored that several Egyptian belly dancers took an early retirement after wealthy Saudis bribed them with millions of dollars to abandon belly dancing and appear on Arab TV preaching their newly found piety and virtue. These reformed belly dancers wear Islamic clothes (but cannot do without tons of makeup) preaching to the choir.

Perhaps the most repulsive and tragic of such women are those who openly celebrate the death of their suicide-bomber sons in the jihad against the Jews. Such women are called heroes in Arab papers and are set up as the ideal example of what a Muslim woman should be. These miserable souls have paid dearly to get respect, recognition, and a life pension. One example in Gaza is a woman who lost several sons to terror and was given a seat in the parliament. Other Muslim women perhaps just get their moment of fame when they advocate the return to the true Islam and lifestyle of the prophet Mohammed. An Egyptian woman by the name of Hiyam Darbak founded an Egyptian association for the promotion of polygamy. In an interview on Arab TV (MBC TV) aired on November 28, 2006, she said that every month she encourages her husband to take another wife, but he refuses. This attitude is not rare among educated Muslim women.

Saudi Arabia is financing Islamic studies and Middle East studies departments in the West, headed by very assertive Muslim female professors proud of their head scarves, eloquently defending Sharia, and denying that Islam is anti-women. One powerful Muslim woman in the United States told me confidentially that her Muslim head cover was a political statement and that the "ethnic look" in America brings with it power. Some members of the Muslim student organizations on American campuses say that the Islamic outfit is their way of jihad. One American-Egyptian student was interviewed on a CNN show about Islam. To the question of what it means when an Arab American woman regards her outfit as a form of jihad, she explained that her clothes are more than just a personal matter but a way to show the public her beliefs and support of Sharia.[32]

Muslim women in the West who are militant Sharia advocates are well organized and often generously funded. Such women have deadened their senses to the suffering of their sisters in the Muslim world and actively try to discredit critics of Sharia. Many of these women are looking after their own self-interests.

The only "feminism" allowed under Sharia is a unique kind—if you want to call it that—the self-destructive "feminism" of the assertive militant Muslim woman who herself acts like the "virtue police." Imposing the values of Sharia on all Muslim women around her makes her unique, virtuous, a hero for Allah's sake, and she takes that on as her form of jihad. This form of feminine jihad becomes even more glamorous in the West. Western feminists have achieved their rights by being anti-establishment; however, this strand of Muslim feminism is actually in support and in harmony with the Muslim establishment that enslaves them.

Muslim feminists find Western governments easy targets for their suppressed desire to rebel. They know that Western governments and police will not treat them as the virtue police back home would. Here in the West it is "safe" to rebel. Thus we see the Muslim women covered up in black demonstrating in rallies with their men carrying signs that say, "We want Sharia," and "Western Law is oppressive." As unbelievable as it seems, I witnessed that distorted call for justice at a Muslim rally in London by a black-nikab-wearing woman. That has become the replacement feminist cause of many committed Muslim women who live in the West: rebel against the hand that offers them dignity.

The call for Sharia law in the West has become the most common form of Muslim feminism in the West, the exact opposite of Western feminism, which seeks greater freedom and dignity for women. And to everyone's surprise, Western feminists are sometimes very understanding and supportive of Muslim women's form of jihad, willing to gang up against the "bad" Western governments for denying these women their Sharia.

3. Live in denial

This third group of Muslim women is probably the majority. They are idealists who live in denial. They judge Islam and Sharia by a narrow view, believing wholeheartedly in its ultimate goodness, which they derive by judging it by their own personal life and experiences. To them Islam is "my good father, mother, grandparents, uncles, and aunts" who were decent human beings, prayed five times a day, got along well, and treated us well. It is what I call "judging Islam by the nice Muslim family that lives next door." To them, Islam and Sharia are the goodness naturally found in the humanity of 1.2 million

Muslims in the world; the humanity that, regardless of religion or culture, exists naturally in any society. To such women, Sharia is their destiny, and they must accommodate it and adapt their lives to it however unjust or inconvenient it may be. These women feel comfortable with their bodies covered and, for some, even their faces covered. Concealment of the body has become for them a comforting boundary in a society that invades every aspect of their lives and respects no boundaries.

Living in their Sharia prison, these women have developed a tough, aggressive, and often manipulative outer shell. Since they cannot argue about how Allah has described their evil nature in Muslim scriptures, they tend to overcompensate by getting easily offended if Islam is criticized, projecting a rough demeanor and blaming society but never the religion. They do not actually have to go to a Sharia court to understand that their testimony could be worthless, thus they feel it is the duty of women to be the ones who always compromise, appease, are mature, and make peace in the family. They accept their inferior status as a badge of honor and even as a sign of virtue. They rarely venture out of their comfort zones, learn something new, read a challenging book, or seek to learn more about other cultures. They don't look at the larger picture or the human tragedy in Sharia courts. Their attitude is that women who go to such courts (and receive a raw deal) asked for it. They needed to prevent it coming to that. They do not see the link between the harsh life of Muslim women and Sharia, nor do they connect the dots of the ills of Muslim society to its theological roots.

Many of these Muslim women are convinced by what Arab media tells them—that the ills of Muslim society should be blamed on dictators in the pocket of the West, on past historical injustice, or on Israel. Daring to objectively examine and analyze the larger picture of Muslim society has never occurred to them, and what is worse, such analysis is prohibited by Sharia itself. They suppress their own doubts and obediently mold their lives around Sharia, convincing themselves that they are happy and proud to show the world the virtues of Islam. Obeying Sharia is their virtue, and that is all that matters. They do not want to be reminded of violence in the Muslim world. They have solved the problem in their own little world. They could care less about what is happening in Sharia courts; they refuse to even look at photos of the stoning, flogging, and honor killing of women. They live in denial and have convinced themselves that all of the anti-women verses in the Qur'an, Hadith, and Sharia laws are simply misinterpretations because Mohammed is "the perfect man" and could never have uttered any injustice.

More than that, they believe that critics of Sharia are misinterpreting on purpose because they are enemies of Islam who want to give Islam a bad name. They explain away polygamy by saying, "There is not one man in my family who has a second wife." They defend the hadith that describes women as deficient in religion and intelligence as being misunderstood. Their first reaction to a stoning of a woman is, *What has she done?* not, *How could that be?*

This third group of women, because they are the majority, are the ones standing in the way of a strong Muslim feminist movement and the reformation of Islam.

I understand this thinking; I was once in their shoes. Our religious education told us that Islam liberated and honored women and that it freed slaves, yet the truth is much the opposite. We constantly heard Qur'anic exhortations telling us to remain content and accept our destiny as Allah's will. We were told, "It is *maktoub*," meaning "it is written," and no one, especially women, can rebel against the destiny that Allah has chosen for us. Women who follow the maze Islam has created for them will not be noticed and will be safe. On the other hand, if anyone deviates and is noticed, she will get no mercy from anyone. Other women in society—mothers, aunts, sisters, cousins—were among those who reinforced such attitudes. "Respect your husband since his approval is your way to Paradise," and "Hell is the destiny of the rebellious woman."

As a result, Muslims in general and women in particular have not developed an awareness of human rights, political rights, or their God-given rights to life, liberty, and the pursuit of happiness. The concept of human rights is alien to nations who practice Sharia, so people have developed very little consciousness of their own oppression, shame, and the isolation and segregation of the sexes under Islamic Sharia. However, the internal anger that builds as a result does not go away; it is only transferred to other areas of life, which further complicates things.

What a scam has been foisted on Muslim women. They have been sold enslavement disguised as virtue! One cannot help but wonder why a half billion women in the Muslim world would put up with it. And I think there may be an answer.

A Worldwide Stockholm Syndrome

I believe that Muslim women have succumbed to none other than a massive Stockholm Syndrome. This well-known psychological phenomenon is named after a 1973 bank hostage incident in Stockholm, Sweden, when after six days of captivity, the hostages resisted rescue attempts and identified so fully with their captors that they refused to testify against them in court. In America, Patricia Hearst became a well-known example of this syndrome. She was kidnapped by a radical political group in 1974, and after months of captivity, she joined the group and even participated in armed bank robberies.

Stockholm Syndrome is caused by captives identifying with their captors initially as a defensive mechanism in fear of violence. Small acts of kindness by the captor are magnified because under such duress all perspective is lost. Survival is all that matters. The syndrome accounts for why many domestic abuse victims do not press charges against their abusers. It has also been seen in prisoners of war and concentration camp survivors.

The Stockholm Syndrome, on a massive societal basis, accounts for why millions of women not only put up with their abuse but also support and champion the very Sharia laws that imprison them inside their homes and inside their hijab.

The Effect of Polygamy

In the previous chapter we discussed polygamy as part of the marriage contract, but polygamy has a much larger dynamic. Polygamy comes at a price. Since a woman is much less valued in every way under Muslim law, she is also not worthy of being honored by one man. While Sharia says she is not worthy of fidelity, at the same time it demands of her complete obedience, loyalty, fidelity, and trust in the man. But no law on earth will make a woman trust a man who has three other wives. Polygamy, thus, does not come for free. It has consequences to the health and happiness of the Muslim family. Most of the ills and anger within the Muslim family are directly linked to the institution of polygamy.

Halide Edib, an early feminist in the waning days of the Ottoman Empire, described polygamy as "a curse, a poison which our unhappy household could not get out of its system. . . . The constant tension in our home made every simple ceremony seem like physical pain, and the consequences hardly ever left me. The rooms of the wives were opposite each other and my father visited them in turn."[33]

Polygamy causes polarization within the family as each wife becomes a separate center of power against the others, resulting in fierce competition, animosity, and rivalry between members of the larger family and wives. Children grow up in an atmosphere of continuous quarreling, routinely hearing raised voices, indecent words, and biting insults. Mutual distrust and disrespect become the norm. An Egyptian polygamist recently complained in a television interview of the constant inner fighting in his household.[34]

Muslim families often have terrible fights over inheritance, accusing each other of conspiracies over property. In such an atmosphere there is an absence of positive values and virtues in the home. Children grow up in such a poisonous atmosphere that they acquire a lifelong negative outlook on life and a victim mentality, always feeling they didn't get their share. And indeed many Muslim children in polygamous homes lack the special attention children need, especially from the father, and they end up lacking a compassionate and kind approach toward life and people.

Stepmothers are traditionally hated and conspired against by the children who also develop a silent hatred toward the father, who in their eyes is the one responsible for the mess. In the end, men suffer from polygamy as well. Because he has not earned love, respect, and loyalty, when the father is old and weak, he often becomes a victim, too, as he is abandoned by children and wives.

Furthermore, the chaos in the family caused by polygamy is transferred to chaos and corruption in society.

Polygamy is a source of embarrassment to Muslim apologists, as evidenced by the excuses they offer to soften its glaring presence. First, they must put down Western society in order to prove they are right. Thus they say that it is better to be married to multiple wives than have a mistress as is done in the West. It may be that if a man wants to cheat on his wife nothing will stop him, but the threat of a mistress and the threat of a legal wife are two very different things in the eyes of society and God. Under Islamic law, all wives will share the inheritance equally. This is very different from an affair in the Christian West where such relationships are socially and religiously unacceptable. A mistress in the West has no spousal rights, and if a Western man chooses to marry his mistress, he must first obtain a legal divorce from his first wife and settle all financial issues with her before he can marry his new sweetheart. That makes all the difference.

I know that most Muslim women, if they had a choice, would rather suffer a husband's side affair than have him acquire a second legal wife. As a child, I remember overhearing an argument between a husband and wife where the wife was begging her husband, "Go ahead and have affairs, but please, for the sake of the children, don't take a second wife." To the wife, a second marriage is a devastating blow to her stature, pride, and security, as well as to the stability of the entire family.

Another argument for polygamy is that there are more women than men. Does that mean in societies with more men than women, we then should allow *women* to have more than one husband? Women are 52 percent of the world's population. Does that mean that men should be allowed to marry a maximum of 1.2 women?

On a more health-related note, some argue that women can be infertile, thus men need to marry other women. Does the same thing apply to men who can also be infertile? Others argue that during a wife's pregnancy men can't have sex for a long time. But that presumes that men are mere animals. It also flies in the face of reality, since most men, including Muslims, build and maintain a happy family with one wife, regardless of pregnancies. And what of the Muslim belief that women grow old before men do? That is simply scientifically untrue.

The fact that there are good and happy Muslim marriages is in spite of, and not because of, Islamic Sharia. Supporters of polygamy must understand that women's deep fear of the institution of polygamy exists even among those in a happy monogamous relationship. That fear creates deep distrust in men-women relationships, and it does not matter how faithful and good the husband might be. The woman is forced to look after her own and her children's best interests and security just in case. That distrust creates unhealthy alliances within the family—between mothers and sons, a wife and her own family, and the husband and his own family who stand behind each of them as protectors of their respective interests. Thus, the wife still relies on her clan, and the husband also relies on his clan. The family camps often pull apart the family unit and can be extremely hostile.

This scenario plays out in Sharia courts across Muslim lands, where clans and families are in conflict with one another. Blood relationships are the only ones that matter in the Muslim/ Arabian culture. With time, and after her father dies, a new alliance for protection emerges between the mother and firstborn son or sons. Women who have no male relatives and no sons are in a very weak position in Muslim marriages and society.

A mother's close dependence on her son can complicate the mother's relationship with a daughter who feels left out by the mother's special treatment of the son. A Muslim daughter early in life, like all daughters, often has a special relationship with her father, but later when she sees him mistreat her mother or get a second wife, that special relationship is damaged forever. On an Arabic television show, I saw a young girl complaining that her father used to love her until she started defending her mother when she was mistreated and beaten. Later her father started calling her names, too, and told her, "You are just as crooked as your mother." Children, boys and girls, often secretly hate their father for taking a second wife and having a new set of children.

A woman's dependence on her son also results in deeply troubled relationships between women and their daughters-in-law, which often go so far as to be abusive. If the eldest son becomes his mother's protector, his wife must come second. It often goes much deeper than jealousy or competition between the two women. In extreme cases, the daughter-in-law may become the virtual slave of her mother-in-law and her husband's sisters and other close female relatives. Horrendous stories have surfaced from Pakistan of women being imprisoned, beaten, and severely disfigured by their husband's mother.

The sons of oppressed women also suffer consequences. Women's doting on their sons, who can do no wrong, often results in arrogant, spoiled young men. They grow up with a sense of entitlement, which fans the flames of anger on the Arab Street.

Sharia oppression of women also forces women into using manipulation, overreaction, and even oppression of other women. To stop the constant interference from family, she must develop an ability to get offended easily but never tell what the true reason is. She also learns to blame all her troubles on outside forces. When her husband beats her, she can't blame him, so she blames it on the evil eye of Aunt Fatima or her unmarried spinster neighbor.

A Muslim woman is financially insecure because there is no community property between husband and wife. She must worry about wealth inherited from her family because if linked to her husband, it can consequently go to the second, third, or fourth wife and her children. Thus in a Muslim marriage, the personal wealth of husband and wife are kept separate. She also could be financially devastated in case of divorce, which she has no control over. But if her husband dies, inheritance laws still discriminate against the wife and confirm the power of the man's extended family. A man's parents share in the inheritance with his wife and children. Financial survival is tough if the wife has no male children since daughters only get half of a son's share.

Because of all of the above financial insecurity, many women resort to subterfuge, hording and hiding money, gold jewelry, and other items of value behind their husbands' backs. As a child, I heard women advising each other, even in Arabic movies, "Hide some money for a bad day," or "Spend his money as fast as you can before he can have extra for more wives."

Oppression of women clearly does not come for free to the welfare of the whole family. But with all the distrust, oppression, and degradation, many Muslim women have managed to keep a proud façade, a characteristic of the Arabian desert that has not been taken away from her by Sharia.

In a society that belittles the intellect of the woman, it is very rare to see Muslim couples act as equal partners, especially intel-lectual partners. The distrust between men and women is also reinforced by the strict sexual segregation. They have little to do with one another outside of the bedroom.

But even inside the bedroom, given Sharia's highly regulated sexual laws, it becomes difficult for Muslim men and women to relate to one another. The relationship has been poisoned by the hostile and demeaning views of women. When Muslim women are stoned, flogged, honor killed, shamed, and dishonored, all because of sex, what could the view of sex be other than terror and fear? But after a life of segregation from the opposite sex, the day after signing a marriage contract, the couple is expected to practice normal, happy, and healthy sex? What was previously prohibited by law is suddenly allowed overnight. With payment of the dowry she must become a sexual toy to a man she hardly knows. It is a huge leap and a difficult adjustment not only for the woman but also for the man. The relationship gets even more complicated when Allah tells the husband he can use the same hands that embrace his wife to beat her if she says no.

Even in our twenties, many of my girlfriends and I were petri-fied of sex and what would happen on the wedding night. Both bride and groom must psychologically adapt to an act for which one day earlier a woman can be stoned to death. But one day later, after the marriage contract is signed and the dowry paid, she then must be obliged to have sex. Some Muslims go through this tran-sition with relative ease, but many find it a difficult transition.

Muslim Women in the West

As I have spoken on college campuses across America, Muslim chaplains on U.S. college campuses have tried twice to prevent me from speaking. That happened to me at the all-female Wellesley College when I was a guest speaker invited by Hillel, the Jewish student organization. Apparently, when they failed to cancel my appearance, the female Muslim chaplain on campus had warned the Hillel organization not to allow me to say anything critical of Islam. However, I am no longer the kind of person who can be silenced from speaking truth. The Muslim students who attended appeared hostile from the beginning, and I was reminded of the message that I heard in a mosque I once visited in Los Angeles where they preached: "Do not assimilate in America," and "You must wear your head cover with pride. It is your form of jihad."

At the Wellesley event, a large number of Muslim girls wearing head scarves were present. As I spoke, I began noticing that they were making faces at me. They rolled their eyes, with "disbelieving" facial expressions—did everything but stick out their tongues. And they continued to talk to each other in loud whispers while I spoke: "How can she tell such lies?!" "I was never, ever indoctrinated against Jews!" "Can you believe what she is saying?" "We do not call Jews pigs and apes! How can she lie about her own people?"

Then one by one, at least four to five times, these young women demonstratively got up to leave the room during my speech. This inconvenienced whole rows of the audience, as they had to physically twist aside to let them pass, causing distraction in the entire room. And then each girl did precisely the same thing as they returned a few minutes later, presumably from a bathroom break. All the while I could see the Jewish students' uneasy and frightened reaction.

During the question-and-answer period, some shouted out that I was telling lies about Islam. Some yelled, "We are free under Islam. How can she deny this?" When I spoke about the topic of women currently being stoned to death in Iran and apostates being jailed and killed, the Muslim girls had no comment and acted as though they could care less. They have lived in Western democracies most or all of their lives and have developed a disconnect from the reality of life under Islamic Sharia. These young Muslim women with chips on their shoulders were simply exercising the only power any Muslim is allowed to have: the power to enforce the reactionary status quo and to further the Muslim jihadist mission.

That night was a reminder of my fear of Sharia knocking at the doors of Western democracies. The West must understand the danger. I am frightened of my culture of origin, a culture that has managed to indoctrinate and desensitize women to the plight of other women living under Sharia.

But I am also happy to report that there were a few Muslim students who came to me after my presentation to thank me for opening their eyes to the truth in the Muslim world, and some even apologized for the disrespectful response of the majority of the Muslim crowd. I will never forget one Muslim girl called Samar who wrote to tell me, "You are giving me the hope and strength to stand against extremism."

However, most members of the so-called moderate Muslim student organizations walk with that holier-than-thou attitude in the hallways of Western learning institutions, trying to push the agenda of the clerics who control them and educate America about the "religion of peace"; but when I asked, not one of them had ever demonstrated in front of the Iranian embassy or the Afghani or Saudi embassies to spare the lives of Muslim women who are being stoned and flogged, or to spare apostates about to be killed.

The militant Muslims on college campuses, while vocal, do not represent the majority of Muslim women in the West who do not make noise and are quietly happy to have escaped Sharia—a bit like I once was. Bahraini feminist Ghada Jamsheer has called on oppressed Muslim women to leave for sanctuary in Spain since they cannot find protection in their own country and its Sharia courts. But Western protection of many Muslim women is now threatened by calls from radical Muslims to bring Sharia to the West. Where would a Muslim woman escape to if that goal is achieved?

When I moved to the United States and started working, I noticed a sign at my workplace that other employees passed by and probably hardly noticed. It was a statement hanging on the wall that said that it is an equal employment opportunity organization that does not discriminate in regard to sex, religion, race, or national origin. I remember standing in front of that sign and reading it once and then again. I took a deep breath, a sigh of relief that I was now in America. This simple statement meant a lot to me. It was a reflection of my new country's values, its sense of justice, and its level of civility, something most Americans take for granted.

Many people think that there is still discrimination in America, but as everything else in life, it is a matter of degree. The bottom line in every society—what makes it civil, what makes life livable—is the law. There will always be a portion of every society that discriminates, commits crime, and fosters hate. It happens in racially homogeneous as well as racially mixed cultures. What counts is whether the laws protect everyone equally—women, men, black, white, Christian, Jew, and Muslim. Law is the criteria measuring society's values.

Even in my case, it took me time to actually get used to my new freedoms in the West. After having lived for decades under fossilized seventh-century laws that protected the oppressors and punished the oppressed, I often pinched myself and wondered if I was really free. It takes a while for things to really sink in. Looking back at my life as a Muslim, I feel betrayed. Actually, more than *betrayed*—I feel angry about the devastating state of Muslim women under Sharia for fourteen hundred years, the hiding and misrepresentation of actual scriptures—trying to make them appear as something else, the lies, propaganda, the taboos, the glaring contradictions.

Even though I was very eager to become an American and had a Western education, a college degree, and wore Western clothes, I still carried baggage from my upbringing. In America, it felt so nice to see men treat me normally, equally, and with respect, courtesy, and dignity. Little things like men opening doors, smiling, or saying hello were remarkable events for me. Having come from a background where men walk like peacocks and both male and female treat each other with arrogance or fear, being treated as an equal or having friendly chitchat with a male coworker was a breath of fresh air. I no longer had to fear that a smile might be misunderstood as flirtation. In the West, a Muslim woman can finally let her guard down and start treating and be treated by the opposite sex as a human being, without the hostility, without the adversity, and without thinking of who has the upper or lower hand. But all of that is now being threatened by calls from Sharia seekers in the West who want to bring us back to our knees.

Now the Sharia enforcers in the West are becoming all the more bold and belligerent, showing no respect for the Western values they chose to move to and live under. They hate to see their wives, daughters, and female family members live in equality and dignity. Living like fish out of water, the men who promote Sharia in the West want Sharia to oppress their women so they can feel a sense of fake power. They want to continue to dehumanize and step on the female slaves that Allah has given them. However, as we will discuss in detail in the coming chapters, the West must never allow even limited Sharia marriage and family laws to be practiced in any Western democracy, simply because it is against basic principles of human rights and equality between the sexes. Sharia strips a woman of her God-given right to be a human being.

For all of my Muslim sisters, I ask: where will we go if Sharia keeps following us? The lives of Muslim women living under Western democratic law and the lives of those living under Sharia are a world—and centuries—apart. Bringing such laws to the West will be the beginning of the end of true Western democracy.

Will the West yield? I certainly hope not.

Four

Men:
The Illusion
of Power

NAGUIB MAHFOUZ, THE NOBEL PRIZE–WINNING EGYPTIAN
writer, wrote a magnificent epic trilogy of colonial Egypt, *Cairo
Trilogy: Palace Walk, Palace of Desire, Sugar Street*, published in
1957, which was made into the Egyptian movie *Palace of Desire* in
the 1960s. It follows the story of a Cairo family from the 1920s to
the 1940s. The father, Al-Sayyid Ahmad Abd Al–Jawad, was a
tyrannical patriarch, who rarely smiled at home and ruled his
household with a strict hand while living a secret life of self-indul-
gence. I remember being glued to the screen watching the family
interaction and dynamics: the feared father whom everyone waited
on hand and foot, especially the wife Amina who ran to take off his
shoes when he came home. She addressed him by "Si Sayyid,"
meaning Mr. Sayyid. At home and in the neighborhood, he was a
respected tyrant, feared by his submissive wife and children. As my
siblings, my cousins, and I eagerly watched the movie, we touched
the heart of the traditional family; we laughed and cried and identified with the family—especially the wife, who was a caricature of
many women we knew in real life.

One day the wife told her children that she wished to visit a
holy mosque for blessings, but the husband was not home to

give her permission. Her children encouraged her to go anyway, promising they would make sure the father would not know of her trip to the mosque. We rolled on the floor with laughter when the clumsy wife was almost hit by a car on the street and came home running short of breath, traumatized and riddled with guilt from such a daring excursion outside the home. She even blamed the close-call accident as Allah's punishment for her daring to leave the house without her husband's permission.

As the movie jumped to the next scene, the contrast in the lifestyle and rights between men and women became crystal clear. While his wife was agonizing over going to a mosque without permission, the movie suddenly showed us Si Sayyid's leisure time pursuits—not at home, but in the home of pleasure women. He was surrounded by a fun-filled atmosphere: belly dancing, singing, and laughing. The scene showed him drinking "Islam forbidden" wine from the high-heel shoe of the belly dancer, played by the Marilyn Monroe of Egyptian movies, Hind Rustum. He was engaged in the "rights" allowed to him as a man by Islam. Paying for a pleasure marriage night was all it would take to protect him and the pleasure women from any religious or legal crime.

This great movie hit a chord with everyone who saw it. I cannot count how many Muslim men I know who resemble this caricature. In every family there are varying degrees of the Amina and Si Sayyid characters.

The contrast between husband and wife roles under Sharia was hilarious, and the writer's sarcastic commentary was obvious in the film. In this human drama, Mahfouz captured a common trait of the Arab/Muslim man: a depressed and authoritarian patriarch at home, but outside he is cheerful, fun-loving, and the life of the party. Mahfouz's mild and honest critique of Muslim society brought him some criticism by radical Muslims. He actually survived a stabbing in Cairo in 1992 by an Islamist who believed that Mahfouz was insulting Islam.

Si Sayyid's character touched a chord in the minds of Mahfouz's readers because of his familiarity in Muslim society. The double life of some Middle Eastern men is especially noticeable when they travel to the West. The image of the Arab man who is prohibited from drinking or holding hands with a girlfriend on the Arab Street is suddenly seen going overboard with pleasure indulgence in Las Vegas or Monaco. Even with all the sexual privileges he's entitled to—four wives plus all the temporary sexual partners Sharia grants him—he becomes like a child in a candy store. In the West, he couldn't care less about the virtue police, his or his partner's sexual purity, reputation, appearances, what the woman he is with is wearing, or where she is going. Like Si Sayyid, he can now dance, sing, drink, and revel without restraint.

The extremes in the life of the Muslim male and even some females are especially noticeable when they leave Muslim society and travel; the serious, authoritarian, and oppressive need to protect his honor at home, and the cheerful, easygoing, fun-loving persona away from home. Even the 9/11 terrorists spent a few days in Las Vegas doing what Islam forbade them to do before that doomed final day of their lives.

Even though many Muslim men love Western freedoms, they do not want to let go of their rights and privileges under Sharia. They want to have their cake and eat it too, even if it leads to a double life.

Some Muslim men have a hard time adjusting to Western society's equal treatment of men and women, rich and poor, and upper and lower classes. In Colorado, a Saudi immigrant named Homaidan Al-Turki was sentenced to twenty-seven years to life for keeping a woman as a slave and sexually abusing her in his home. Al-Turki, who also had a wife and children, claimed that he was a victim of anti-Muslim bias. He told the judge: "Your honor, I am not here to apologize, for I cannot apologize for things I did not do and for crimes I did not commit. The state has criminalized these basic Muslim behaviors."[1] Both Mr. Al-Turki and his wife were arrested in 2005 on state and federal charges of forced labor, aggravated sexual abuse, document servitude, and harboring an alien. In short, he was keeping an Indonesian woman in her early twenties as a maid, baby-sitter, cook, and sexual slave, for little or no pay, under his wife's nose. Mr. Al-Turki was a graduate student and owner of a religious bookstore.

Sexual enslavement runs so deep in Muslim culture, that the job of maids has become a substitute for slavery. Several affluent Saudis and other Arabs have been caught in a legal predicament in the West simply because of the practice of slavery which still flourishes in certain pockets of Muslim society even if they no longer openly call it slavery. Saudi Arabia was among the last countries to abolish slavery in 1962. But until today, ranking Saudi religious authorities still endorse slavery; for example, Sheikh Saleh Al-Fawzan insisted recently that "slavery is a part of Islam" and whoever wants it abolished is "an infidel."[2]

This is not just a Saudi phenomenon. I once heard of a bizarre story of the sexual enslavement of an Israeli woman in Gaza. She was kidnapped from inside Israel by a man in Gaza, probably, in the early or mid-1950s. She was forced to become one of his wives, lived like a slave, and gave birth to a number of children. When the Israelis took over Gaza after the 1967 War, the Arab man approached the Israeli soldiers and told them the story of the abducted woman. In the end the woman, her children, and the man were transferred to Israel proper. He converted to Judaism and married the woman for whom he had secretly felt pity for many years and later grew to love and respect.

Sharia has been exceedingly "generous" to men at the expense of family cohesion and stability. And lest we think polygamy is a great gift to men, consider this: because of his right to polygamy, a man is deprived of a wholesome monogamous relationship, its emotional depths, and a satisfying life partnership, which is the cornerstone of Western civilization. Instead, Sharia has cursed him into believing that his wife is not to be trusted. A polygamous man, deep down in his psyche, knows that if he does not vow loyalty to one wife, he cannot count on her emotional loyalty either. If she cannot feel secure in their relationship, neither can he.

A man may decide to be faithful to one woman and never marry another, but in the back of his mind he always knows that his faithfulness to one wife is not required by God. While men may like fantasizing about having more than one wife, I believe that the majority of men do need the stability and intimacy of a relationship limited to only one woman. In the end, having many wives can have the same effect on a man as having none at all.

Obviously, not all Muslim men follow their rights under Sharia; the humanity of many has stood in the way of the temptation to be corrupted by it. There are many good Muslim husbands who stay faithful to one wife; they realize the blessings and the privilege of marrying one wife. Again, like many other situations under Islamic Sharia, many Muslims choose to rise above the corrupting temptation and reject their rights given to them under Allah's laws and the example of the prophet. They choose what their instinct tells them is right, not because of religion, but in spite of it. Yet the corrupting factor is always there, tempting him in times of trouble. It is there when members of his own family tell him, "You are spoiling your wife," or "You are not man enough," or "Your wife is not obedient." His corrupting rights are there when he goes to the mosque and hears a sermon telling him, "This is the right stick with which to beat your wife." The corrupting rights are there staring at him on the marriage contract where three spaces are waiting to be filled out if he wishes; they are there when other women tell him, "It is within your right to marry me."

So much is standing in the way of marital intimacy and a holy covenant between the Muslim husband and wife. Because of Sharia, men miss out on the best life can offer—genuine love, loyalty, and respect from his family.

The Illusion of Power

Sharia has given men the illusion of power, not over himself but over women. But outside the home is another story. He is the freest and happiest man on earth, the master of his destiny . . . or is he? First, let's look at his "power" in the home, where he rules as a king.

In a supreme irony, a man's very reputation—his "honor"—is not dependent on his own personal actions or integrity. Instead, it is directly linked to and dependent upon the sexual purity of his wife, his daughter, and any female relatives. Honor is a far different concept in the Muslim world than it is in the West; honor is directly connected with a man's ability to control his females and his ability to keep their sexual life totally restricted within marriage. Even the slightest rumor about his daughter or wife can hurt him. And so for the sake of honor, he must constantly monitor the women in his family. He must be preoccupied with how his wife, daughters, and female relatives dress, where they go, and with whom they associate. That is a burden made even more difficult by a religious environment that discourages trusting and respecting women. Muslim men, day in and day out, are reminded of this by mosque preachers who quote hadiths and Qur'an verses telling men never to trust a woman. "Women are to be feared most." Abu Huraira reported Allah's Messenger as saying: "Had it not been for Eve, woman would have never acted unfaithfully towards her husband."[3] The *Dictionary of Islam* says: "Let him not consult her on matters of paramount importance; let him not make her acquainted with his secrets, nor let her know the amount of his property, or the stores he possesses, beyond those in present consumption, or her weakness of judgment will infallibly set things wrong."[4]

It cites three things to be avoided by husbands concerning trust of their wives:

1) Excess of affection, for this gives her the predominance and leads to a state of perversion. When the power is overpowered and the commander commanded, all regularity must infallibly be destroyed. If troubled with redundancy of affection let him at least conceal it from her.

2) Let him not consult her on matters of paramount importance; let him not make her acquainted with his secrets, nor let her know the amount of his property, or the stores he possesses, beyond those in present consumption, or her weakness of judgment will infallibly set things wrong.

3) Let him allow her no musical instruments, no visiting out of doors, no listening to men's stories, nor intercourse with women noted for such practices; especially where any previous suspicion has been raised.[5]

Wives clearly are not to be trusted. A husband must even go so far as to withhold or hide his affection for his wife, because that gives her too much "power." What a sad thing that is, to deprive a woman you love of even the knowledge that you love her.

The following is a very telling hadith: "Narrated Ibn 'Omar: During the lifetime of the Prophet we used to avoid chatting leisurely and freely with our wives lest some Divine inspiration might be revealed concerning us. But when the Prophet had died, we started chatting leisurely and freely (with them)."[6]

The above hadith reflects how the gender apartheid managed to find its way even to the husband and wife relationship especially in public, poisoning it with feelings of shame, distrust, and hostility.

A man's role in the home has been narrowed down to that of the feared disciplinarian and controller. According to codified Islamic Law: The Prophet said, "Hang up the whip where the members of the household can see it."[7]

Sharia has ripped apart the base and core of trust and stability in the family and replaced it with hostility, alienation, and anger, which spread to every relationship within the family unit. If the husband/-wife relationship is compromised, all other relationships will be affected.

Giving excess rights to the man has drowned him in a role that constantly demands satisfaction of his ego, and pride and has prevented his elevation to the higher, more civilized role of the partner and lover at home. Smart Muslim men who opt out of that hollow "superior" role are not kindly regarded by Muslim society, which calls them weak and unmanly.

While the man is led to believe he is a master of his life and his women in the home, outside the home is another story. As soon as he steps outside of his power zone at home, he too becomes a slave—a slave of the brutal, dictatorial Islamic Sharia state. He must endure the hierarchical injustice, humiliation, and insecurity of living under the brutal totalitarian regimes of the Middle East. Corruption is everywhere, from ruthless and disrespectful bosses at work to cars that hit him and drive away as though nothing happened, from distrustful coworkers to corrupt policemen who openly demand bribery or brutally beat him.

The contrast between Muslim male power at home and helplessness outside the home is enormous. A Muslim man's anger, disappointment, and feelings of victimization are thus compounded not only by his mother's shame—which he subconsciously absorbed in childhood—but also by the shame of his treatment in the Muslim State. At home he enjoys the only respect he can get, but in the famous Arab Street, he is angry and oppressed. Is it any wonder that Muslim men desperately cling to their women's honor, submission, and obedience? Taking away Sharia marriage and divorce laws from men without reforming the oppressive dictatorial system under which they must live would bring down upon them an unbearable sense of failure.

This political reality also has an effect on family life and the treatment of women, children, and the poorer classes. This chain of oppression and brutality operates between all levels of social classes from top to bottom. Muslim men of power and wealth carry their authoritarian control from the home into the workplace. Arab bosses are commonly rude and brutal to subordinate workers. Some even carry this authoritarian style of work environment with them when they move to work in the West.

An American friend once told me about a Lebanese coworker who had been his supervisor, and not a very good one. My friend reported, "He seemed to concentrate more on getting me to respect his customs such as not sitting cross-legged or showing the bottoms of one's feet or shoes. He once asked me not to place my hands in my pockets while in his presence; he once pulled my hands out of my pockets from behind. He even asked me not to laugh and joke while on the job. He created a lack of trust and class-consciousness, making an environment that was suffocating. Against all modern management experts' advice, my supervisor could not develop a work environment that was based on teamwork." Indeed, the concept of teamwork is completely foreign to someone accustomed to viewing the workplace—and the world—in only dictatorial, authoritarian ways.

Some Muslim men who move to the West adapt to it and love it, but others cannot, and they insist on demanding the Sharia state that spoiled them rotten. Many Muslim men in the West feel weak without the laws that grant them the master-slave relationships in the home, so they demand Sharia in the West. Indeed, the West is a big challenge to some Muslim men. Those who do not measure up to Western male expectations end up full of anger against and envy of the Western system.

The Muslim man lives in two worlds: the world of the oppressor inside his family and the oppressed in Muslim society. But often his true anger is directed at the West, a culture that has long solved a problem he is incapable of solving—how to live in peace with himself, with his family, and in the world of the other. He is puzzled by the West—the culture that wants neither to oppress him nor to give him special privileges. That is when he feels he is at his weakest. It is an environment some Muslim men can never understand, and some who do understand it don't want to live under it because they would rather have the upper hand in Muslim society. A close Muslim friend in Egypt once told me, "I don't want to emigrate to America, with all of its freedoms, democracy, and human rights, because when I am in Egypt, I know how to milk the system to my advantage, and I don't have to work too hard." He then laughed and said: "I can get even more than I deserve."

The Angry Young Men of the Arab Street

With all the legal rights, privileges, and freedoms given to men, one would think they would be among the happiest in the world, but that is far from the truth. The much talked-about "Arab Street" is typically made up of angry men consumed with hatred and envy of the outside world, engrossed in self-pity and a victim mentality. Where does this all come from?

From birth until approximately age seven, the Muslim boy is brought up almost exclusively by women—his mother and women of the extended family. He starts his life as a male dealing almost exclusively with the half of society accused of severe moral and intellectual deficiencies, not to mention all sorts of physical impurities. In those crucial early years, he bonds with victimized women. Her identity becomes his identity, and her suffering becomes his suffering. He observes his father and other men treating his female protectors with suspicion, disdain, and derision. Then suddenly, as he reaches late childhood, he joins the world of men, a world of male pride, brutality, aggression, and power. He then is subjected to shaming and physical punishment, a customary Muslim disciplinary tool to transfer him to the world of men and the world of brutality. Yet he is torn, struggling with the same traits of helplessness, victimization, envy, and superstition from which his mother suffered. Hidden deep within the male image of pride he must now portray to the world lies a man who can easily become offended and shamed.

The worst insult to the Muslim man becomes his comparison with his mother. Once in a speech, President Gamal Abdel Nasser of Egypt attacked King Hussein of Jordan as *taale lummuh*, meaning "he turned out like his mother." The phrase and image was so powerful that the Egyptian public, composed mainly of men, started chanting, "Taale lummuh." This public insult to the king of Jordan is a shameful episode in Nasser's legacy.

A man's acquired characteristics from oppressed women early in his life end up becoming his curse, too, when he does not measure up to a world ruled by men. As he gets older, he must conform to the pride of his father while suppressing the early years of identifying with the victimization of his mother. But sooner or later the male character wins and the boy becomes another copy of his father. Eventually he starts treating the mother the same way his father did. Even though the Muslim male is ordered to love and respect his mother and be her guardian as he gets older, I have seen many Muslim men ridicule their mothers' opinions, chastise their cooking, and sometimes treat them like immature girls who cannot care for themselves. And if his father dies, the last thing he will allow is his mother remarrying. He is now her man and guardian, the guardian of a woman living under Sharia and whose honor is linked to his honor; the cycle is now complete.

Like Si Sayyid's extreme lifestyle, the Muslim man is torn between extremes of pride and shame. Muslim views of female and male are both molded together within him. On the one hand he could be a depressed, insecure, superstitious, envious, manipulative, and victimized man, and on the other hand, he could be proud, dominant, aggressive, angry, and easily offended. The struggle between the two extremes has become his destiny and his curse. He must struggle all his life from dissociating himself from women's shame, something he could never seem to rid himself of. He cannot blame himself, his father, or Allah's law for his shameful struggles. He cannot blame his mother for it either, since he and the rest of society want her to stay that way, the way Allah's law intended a woman to be. This is how Islam, he is told, honors and protects women.

In the end, the Muslim male is no winner. He cannot escape the victim mentality; he was breast-fed by a mother oppressed by the system. The same Sharia that gave him incredible power at the expense of women has indirectly oppressed him too. It has set him up for disappointment and unrealistic expectations from a society that does not treat him with the same respect that his women at home treat him.

The Numbers Game

Not only do the majority of Muslim men lack the power or wealth for polygamy, but there is also not a large enough female population to put into practice all their rights under Sharia. Polygamy has indirectly worked against most Muslim men simply because they cannot afford the wives and sexual options their religion allows. Poor younger men have to compete with the older married ones over single women. Even the temporary, few-hours-of-pleasure mutaa marriages require a kind of dowry. Thus the majority end up sexually repressed in a culture obsessed with virginity. You see them, in the famous angry Arab Street, filled with feelings of victimhood, anger, restlessness; always ready after a fiery Friday sermon in the mosque to riot, burn, and even kill.

In reality, Sharia's generosity to the Muslim male can only benefit the wealthy, powerful, and privileged. Polygamy is unfavorable to poorer, lower-class Muslims and contributes to an imbalance—a shortage of available brides—because many young women would rather become the second wife to an older, richer man than take a chance with a young, poor man who might eventually have a second wife on her anyway.

It is not easy to be a poor Muslim man—repressed, disaffected, unable to marry or afford an apartment. He can become a ticking time bomb against the Muslim State, but with the right programming and jihadist indoctrination, his anger can be channeled to the service of the Islamic State and not against it. His poverty must become a badge of honor, and his contentment with what little life brings must be rewarded in the afterlife— that is what he is told. "The Prophet said, 'I looked at Paradise and saw that the majority of its residents were the poor.'"[8]

Only the privileged and powerful Muslim males on the top of the food chain can make use of Allah's generous sexual Muslim laws allowing him four wives and limitless enslaved women (often maids). Even with today's Arabian wealth from petrodollars, the majority of Muslim men are poor. That leaves the majority of the Muslim male population unable to compete with the privileged wealthy men. Luring foreign poor women from other parts of the world such as the Philippines, Russia, and India have become a common practice in Saudi Arabia. But for the majority of poor Muslim men across the globe, they are told they must be content with their share in life. This principle is always stressed in Muslim preaching. Poverty and contentment with one's share in life is a virtue in Islam, and the men on the street have bought that scam.

Women have also been scammed into protecting their valuable chastity, waiting endlessly in their parents' homes to realize their aspirations for marriage, which is limited and controlled by those who can afford to pay the dowry for their enslavement. The Sharia marriage scam is perpetrated against all Muslims, male and female, except for the few powerful alpha males who can afford to milk the Sharia system to their advantage and eliminate the competition. Poor men's and women's needs must be channeled toward the afterlife while the wealthy Muslim alpha males are having a party right here on earth.

Sharia was created by the powerful to serve powerful males— from Mohammed in the seventh century who had the first pick of war-captive women, to the caliphs who kept endless harems, to Arabian kings and princes and Muslim dictators who satiate their every whim; from Bin Laden with his multiple wives to powerful religious leaders—sheikhs, mullahs, and ayatollahs— who have wives as young as their granddaughters. All of this is at the expense of women, the family unit, and the majority of Muslim men as well. The powerful have managed to protect Sharia and mold their religious system to their best interests for fourteen hundred years to protect their best-kept Islamic secret, their sexual club. They will never, ever give that up easily.

Jihad

So what do the poor and powerless males get? They get jihad. For the poor, angry young men, their dreams of sexual pleasure must be limited to the seventy-two *houris* heaven will provide when they do jihad. Convincing Muslim males of their sacred duty to do jihad keeps the whole system in place for the alpha males.

One of the results of jihad is fewer men competing over the female population, and that makes powerful and wealthy Muslim men very happy. Thus for polygamy to thrive, jihad must continue. But even with war and jihad, the population of women in Muslim countries is never four to one. Polygamy can never be equally available to all men since that would require that the female population must always be quadruple that of males.

Islamic texts are full of calls for jihad. Violence against infidels is central to Islamic scriptures and jurisprudence. This is what the good Muslim man must do to the unbelievers:

- "Your Lord inspired the angels with the message: 'I will terrorize the unbelievers (non-Muslims). Therefore smite them on their necks and every joint and incapacitate them. Strike off their heads and cut off each of their fingers and toes.'"[9]

- "Fight and kill the disbelievers wherever you find
  them, take them captive, torture them, lie in wait and
  ambush them using every stratagem of war."[10]

The above demands from Allah cannot be achieved by happily
married Muslim men who live in stable and loving relationships
in a relatively peaceful society. Thus Muslim men must remain
in their quandary of the competing feelings of pride and shame.
Being both oppressors and oppressed is the right balance for fuel-
ing the fire of jihad. A victim mentality and a need to blame the
other must be perpetuated as a pretext for jihad. Jihad is what
restores the Muslim man's pride against those who humiliated
him—that in addition to his many rewards in heaven.

Angry, envious, and hateful Muslim preachers must continue
breeding and perpetuating the victim identity. They curse the
infidels, yell and scream from the pulpit of mosques at Friday
prayer services. Ironically, many of the ills in Muslim society
serve the purpose of jihad. The famous Arab Street anger is thus
not a coincidence, but a necessary fuel for the purpose of a religion that requires jihad. And blaming a scapegoat is key.

Whose fault is it that the young men on the street can't find
jobs or have no access to women? Leaders successfully convince
the young men that their lot in life is the fault of the infidels, and
the Arab Street buys into the line. They cannot blame their circumstances on the Muslim culture—apostasy is punishable by
death. Even thinking about blaming the system is a dangerous
thing. So they listen to their leaders and fall back on the blame
game that has been going on since the days of Mohammed.
Their deep feelings of guilt and shame as well as their poverty
must be the fault of the enemies of Islam, the infidels whom the
Qur'an calls apes and pigs and enemies of Allah whom Muslims
must never befriend or sign treaties with. From the time of
Mohammed, they have caused Islam trouble and are still causing
Muslims trouble by daring to question and challenge Islamic

texts and ask why Muslim women are oppressed. What can
Muslims do when Western inquiring minds read, question, and
analyze and, what's worse, encourage ordinary Muslims to do the
same? That is not only shameful but also subversive according to
Islamic Sharia where everything must be accepted at face value
and never questioned.

Muslim religious authorities can bluff the ordinary Muslim
into believing the convoluted interpretations—which they are
not allowed to question anyway—but Muslims cannot hide
their texts from the world. Muslim shame comes from the need
to explain themselves to infidels. The mere existence of the
infidels' free system causes many Muslim youth and women to
ask questions that an obedient, submissive Muslim should never
dare to ask. The West is thus blamed for the Muslim man's
shame, a shame they have managed to live with and have camouflaged and suppressed for centuries. And so the thinking
goes: Allah was right when he called infidels apes and pigs and
enemies of Islam. He was right when he ordered us to subjugate
them and treat them as second-class citizens unworthy of our
friendship or respect. Mohammed warned Muslims of the *fitna*—Arabic for "sedition or schism"—from the enemies of
Islam, the part of the world that refuses to abide by Allah's laws
and treats their women equal to men. Those are the same
people who occupied Muslims in the nineteenth and twentieth
centuries—we proud Muslims who once ruled over them. This
shameful *fitna* can only be rectified through jihad. They must
also be ruled by Allah's law.

Angry Muslim preachers in the mosque become poor Muslim
men's inspiration and role models. They curse and blame the
world for the Muslims' failures and deeds. Thus 9/11, the tsunami, and even democracy are blamed on Jews and other
infidels. The solution is always retaliation, boycott, violence in
the street, or an uprising. The theme of the sermon is always,
"Who has wronged us today?"

Naturally, there are questions that come to mind: Who benefits from all of this? Why is the cohesion and trust in the Muslim family unit undermined and to what goal? What is more important than family in Muslim society?

The answer to all of the above is jihad. With Islam's inability to be flexible, it has retained the warring culture as the basis for its survival. Sharia has frozen the desert culture in time under penalty of death. At the center of that culture was the male role upon which the survival of the tribe depended. The ultimate goal is survival and increasing the power of the tribe.

After Islam arose, the power of the tribe was transferred to the power of Islam, and the conquering of the other tribe was transferred to conquering non-Muslims. Muslim society, even today, is perceived as unsustainable without jihad. The battle against the "other" still remains the number one priority for the survival of the system, at least in the mind of Muslims.

Consider the sheer number of jihad, war, and violence verses in the Qur'an and Hadith. Muslim scriptures are consumed with promoting extreme violence against non-believers. Jihad against the outside non-Muslim world is the ultimate and holiest objective, more important than women, children, men, the family, and even happiness of Muslim society.

Jihad is above the family. This is confirmed by every conflict in the Muslim world today. Women, even if only in front of the camera, must celebrate the sacrifices of their husbands' and sons' lives in jihad against the injustice of the non-Muslim world. There is no guarantee to heaven for the man who lived a life of sacrifice for the welfare of his family or his community. Islam does not tell the Muslim man he is guaranteed heaven if he makes the world a peaceful place, but it does guarantee him heaven if he blows up the marketplaces and houses of worship of non-Muslims, if he sacrifices his life to kill the perceived enemies of Islam. Heaven is at his feet not when he dies protecting his wife and children from imminent danger. Yet if he dies in the process of expanding the power of Islam, he is guaranteed heaven and its infinite rewards. Jihad is the ultimate honor, more important than the family.

Muslim men must sacrifice their wives and family to protect Islam and his prophet. In the following hadith, a man was forgiven by Mohammed for killing his wife for the sake of the prophet Mohammed.

Narrated Abdullah Ibn Abbas: A blind man had a slave-mother who used to abuse the Prophet and disparage him. He forbade her but she did not stop. He rebuked her but she did not give up her habit. One night she began to slander the Prophet and abuse him. So he took a dagger, placed it on her belly, pressed it, and killed her. A child who came between her legs was smeared with the blood that was there. When the morning came, the Prophet was informed about it.

He assembled the people and said: I adjure by Allah the man who has done this action and I adjure him by my right to him that he should stand up. Jumping over the necks of the people and trembling the man stood up.

He sat before the Prophet and said: Apostle of Allah! I am her master; she used to abuse you and disparage you. I forbade her, but she did not stop, and I rebuked her, but she did not abandon her habit. I have two sons like pearls from her, and she was my companion. Last night she began to abuse and disparage you. So I took a dagger, put it on her belly and pressed it till I killed her. Thereupon the Prophet said: Oh be witness, no retaliation is payable for her blood.[11]

This story is chilling. Yes, he killed her even if he had two sons like pearls from her, and she was his companion. Of course, not all Muslim men are like that, despite the ideals of this hadith. It all depends on how closely a devout Muslim wants to follow the example of Mohammed, how devoted he is to the unholy relationship between violence, misogyny, and jihad.

Jihad and Marriage Do Not Mix

Terrorists are desperate Muslim men who cannot relate to life and to the idea of human happiness as a right. They have perverted sexuality and connected it to violence. Jihad for the sake of Allah is essential to the growth of Islam. A man cannot love a woman, his children, or life and choose to die in the process of spreading jihad, which is not a defensive war. So to make the idea attractive, jihad became an honorable duty of every Muslim and the only guarantee for heaven. Do not worry that you will miss your wife on earth, he is told. Allah will reward you with seventy-two virgins, more beautiful and younger than your earthly wife.

It seems unbelievable that anyone would fall for this, but believe it or not, this is the basic doctrine of jihad. Since jihad needs men who want to die in the process of jihad, hating and mistrusting women thus becomes essential. A happy, stable married life with a loving, trusting relationship with one wife and one set of children will make a man value his life, and that would be the end of jihad. Thus men must be encouraged to escape life, and the sanctity of life on earth must be devalued, while seeking happiness must be portrayed as shameful. They are led to believe that achieving a satisfying, loving, wholesome relationship with women is not possible on earth but only in heaven. For the survival of Islam through jihad, a large rupture in domestic relationships must be enforced, and affection, empathy, and love must be left out of the picture.

The Sexual Rewards of Jihad

The concept of love was removed from the Muslim man's understanding of sexuality. Islam's rewards to the jihadist today remain the same sexual rewards men were accustomed to in seventh-century Arabia — the unlimited sexual conquest of women captured in battle. But for the modern-day jihadist, it is the deflowering of seventy-two virgins in paradise. Religious leaders, while enjoying their earthly harems at home, tell the naïve Muslim men at Friday prayers that they will get what is due them only if they do jihad, that dying in jihad is the only guarantee to permanent sexual bliss. Dying in jihad has become the way to achieve the desert mirage of taking the virginity of limitless dark-eyed houris all with the blessing of Allah as a reward for their sacrifices on earth, all for the sake of protecting a system that can only survive through expansion like the pyramid scheme. The connection of violence and sexual pleasure through jihad is better than any Hollywood film could conjure up.

The lustful heaven of Islam was created to guarantee the obedience of a deprived, oppressed, and enslaved Muslim man who lives and dies as an *abdullah*, meaning "slave of Allah," serving an expansionist jihad ideology that only serves the powerful and the wealthy. Jihad became their hope, duty, and aspiration to achieve what they could not dare achieve on earth.

For Muslim leadership, the duty of jihad shoots two birds with one stone. First, by keeping the majority of Muslim men preoccupied with jihad and its rewards in heaven, they have eliminated majority male competition on earth. Second, for the Sharia system to survive, it must be continuously strengthened and reinforced by spreading inwardly and outwardly.

That explains why, despite the Sharia privileges given to males, the majority of Muslim men are not happy-go-lucky, sexually satisfied men. Actually just the opposite is true since most Muslim women are not to be seen or touched. The bottled-up sexual rage of the Muslim male must explode in the faces of the foreign infidel. Ultimate happiness and sexual gratification exist in heaven after they blow themselves up before Jews, Christians, or atheists. For Sharia to survive, they desperately need to stop international calls for human rights from meddling infidels. With today's small and interconnected world, the shame of the Islamic system of injustice and human-rights violations is there for the whole world to see. Western culture's freedoms and respect for individuals is putting Muslims to shame. Western democracies, by their mere existence, are exposing the divine scam against Muslim women and men. It is also exposing the true meaning of jihad, which is nothing but a deceptive system of acquiring the wealth, land, and possessions of others and claiming it for Islam. Jihad, glorified in the Qur'an, numerous hadiths, mosque prayers, politicians' speeches, in media, in songs, in poetry, and in ordinary conversation is nothing but a murder of the innocent and a violation of human rights.

As it has been for fourteen hundred years, the system backed by powerful scriptures heaps shame on anyone who has second thoughts about jihad. The Qur'an encourages Muslims who are slow and reluctant to attack unbelievers: "Believers, why is it that when you are told: 'March in the cause of God,' you linger slothfully in the land? Are you content with this life in preference to the life to come? . . . If you do not go to war, he God will punish you sternly, and will replace you with other men."[12]

The Qur'an promises rewards in the afterlife for waging jihad in: "Believers! Shall I point out to you a profitable course that will save you from a woeful scourge? Have faith in God and his messenger, and fight for God's cause with your wealth and with your persons. . . . He will forgive you your sins and admit you to gardens watered by running streams; he will lodge you in pleasant mansions in the gardens of Eden. This is the supreme triumph."[13]

The message to men is: "The Prophet said, 'To fight in Allah's cause is better than the world and whatever is in it.'"[14]

"The Prophet said, 'Nobody who dies fighting and finds good from Allah (in the Hereafter) would wish to come back to this world . . . except the martyr who, on seeing the superiority of martyrdom, would like to come back to the world and get killed again (in Allah's cause)."[15] The Prophet said, "Know that Paradise is under the shades of swords."[16] Just in case heaven and its women might not be seductive enough as a lure, like a salesman who cries, "But wait, there is more," here is yet another perk: "If you are a murderer, you are forgiven by Allah for your murder only if you die in jihad."[17] If the man returns alive from jihad, the salesman will cry again, "But wait, there is more," there is the booty: "The Prophet said, 'Whoever has killed an unbeliever and has proof or a witness of it, then his belongings will be for him.'"[18]

Jihad can be directed both outward and inward. Even if the whole world is Muslim, internal jihad will turn Muslims against each other. The Prophet has said that Muslims will divide into many sects but only one sect will go to heaven. That means the majority of Muslims are infidels and apostates who do not deserve heaven. That is the next level of jihad to come to the Muslim State. The angry young troops of jihad have a permanent holy mission even within the Muslim State. We have only to look to the bitter enmity between Shi'ia and Sunni, and the work of death squads against each other to know that there would not be an end to jihadist fervor, even if the whole world were conquered by Islam.

While a minority of men is reaping the benefits of the Sharia Islamic State, the majority is kept enslaved to maintain it. Mohammed himself and most of his close followers (the Sahaba) did not die in the many battles they conducted, but instead died from assassinations and divisions among them after Mohammed's death. Throughout history, kings, amirs, sheikhs, ayatollahs, and princes have not themselves done the jihad, but mobilized their resources and their nation's wealth to promote it. In our day, a good portion of Saudi wealth goes to fund terror and jihad instead of improving the lives of Muslims worldwide.

Improving living conditions, valuing the family, giving women their rights, and learning to love life right here on earth would end jihad. If the day comes when Muslims start seriously preaching against violent jihad, the average Muslim male will finally be able to wake up from his fourteen-hundred-year illusion. He will start seeing where his oppression comes from. He will start asking for the first time: How can I achieve my marital and sexual rights right here on earth? Why should I be a slave to the Saddam Husseins of the world and the Muslim hierarchy of totalitarianism? Why should I sacrifice myself for a system that oppresses me, my wife, and my family?

Sharia, with its blatant injustice, is not sustainable unless jihad is constantly done. The end of Sharia will come when every Muslim—both men and women—stand up against jihad and end it. Jihad is nothing but a more dignified name for continuing the old tribal custom of raiding and battling the other tribe, winning slave females, and stealing their property. If Islam is to be reformed, the concept of jihad must be exposed for what it is: a dangerous commandment against world peace and human rights. It is a violation of life, liberty, and the pursuit of happiness for both Muslims and non-Muslims alike.

The grandiose pyramid scheme of protecting Sharia's power and sexual privileges for some at the expense of the healthy functioning of Muslim society as a whole is unnatural and inhumane. The Muslim system of total control through fear, terror, and the lure of sexual bliss in heaven is unnatural, unsustainable, and corrupt. If jihad ends, the pyramid scheme collapses.

The Driving Force Behind Sharia

The number one driving force behind Sharia is not the stability of the family; it is not human happiness; it is not even the happiness of the Muslim man who seems to be the beneficiary of most of Sharia's laws. The driving force behind Sharia is jihad, asserting the supremecy of Arabia, the never-ending restless expansion and enforcement of Islam worldwide. For that aim, Sharia has not just sacrificed the woman but has also sacrificed the man while giving him the illusion of control. The Muslim male's mission on earth is to die for the expansion of Islam and keeping the few male beneficiaries of the system happy and protected. That agenda is simple; it is the enslavement of the majority for the service and happiness of the minority of powerful males. But for that to be achieved without easily being exposed, an elaborate, complicated, extreme, and contradicting religious law was created. It is the most inhumane, cruel, and punitive system of laws practiced today by any secular or religious group on earth. It is using and abusing two major human basic needs—sex and man's need to be close to God—all for the sake of the enslavement of the majority of the population for the benefit of the few.

Part II

SHARIA:
The State

Five

Life Behind
the Muslim Curtain

"WE ARE CHRISTIAN."

That was the answer given by brothers Mario and Andrew Ramses, ages eleven and thirteen, on a test at an Egyptian public school. The purpose of the test was to "permit" the two boys to convert to Islam. Their answer was "wrong."

The two boys were told they must take the conversion test for Islam or lose their education credentials. Refusing to convert would also make them apostates, a serious crime punishable by death under Sharia. This is not some historical case from the seventh century; this happened in 2007 in a public school in Alexandria, Egypt.

The whole ordeal started when Egypt's ministry of education ordered the boys to take the test that would result in their conversion to Islam because their father, who left the family about five years earlier, had decided to convert from Christianity to Islam. The parents, Medhat Ramses and Camellia Medhat, were a Christian couple when the boys were born, but the father then divorced the mother, leaving his sons behind, and converted to Islam to marry a Muslim woman.

Islamic religious laws, adopted by the Egyptian government, require that children follow the faith of any parent who converts to Islam, since according to Sharia, Islam is the superior religion and abrogates all other religions. Children, according to typical court rulings, are supposed to follow the "better" (or more noble) of the two religions, and that is Islam. According to Sharia law, children do not have the freedom to follow the religion of a non-Muslim parent or the religion they were born into, but must follow the religion of the parent who converted to Islam. Muslim courts say that leaving the children to follow the corrupted religions (Christianity and Judaism) of the other parent would be condemning the kids to the doom of hellfire where Christians, Jews, and all other non-Muslims are destined.

Such cases in Egypt usually end up with Christian children yielding to authority and converting to Islam. But what brought this case to public attention was the categorical refusal of the two boys, who serve as deacons in their Christian church, to convert to Islam, who said they will not "deny their Christianity and convert to Islam no matter what it would cost them." Egyptian media attacked the mother and blamed her for applying pressure on her sons to not convert. The whole Coptic Christian community in Egypt as well as in the West were praying and pleading to all human rights organizations to stand up for the human and religious rights of the two boys.

The Egyptian government yielded to international pressure by making an exception for the two boys, exempting them from taking the conversion to Islam test as a requirement to their education. However, the laws remained the same for future cases. Christians would continue to suffer under such despotic Sharia laws that cannot be changed or amended and must remain carved in stone. Converting non-Muslims to Islam remains the primary goal of Muslim society, and that can be done through intimidation, fear, financial loss, jihad, or, as in the case of the two boys, the Sharia courts.

With radical Islam now on the rise, it is no longer safe for Jews and Christians to live in Arab and Muslim countries. They are not allowed to practice their religion peacefully in many Muslim countries, and in Saudi Arabia, they cannot practice any religion other than Islam under their Sharia laws. In one-third of the world—the Muslim world—Christians and Jews are not welcome.

In the London daily, *Al-Sharq Al-Awsat*, February 2, 2008, Saudi columnist Hussein Shubakshi discussed the phenomenon of Christian emigration from Arab countries. He criticized the fact that this trend was being ignored in the Arab world and added: "This forcible expulsion is evidence of the narrow limits of tolerance and acceptance of the other." However, the majority of Arab media ignore the topic, and actually many committed Muslim writers and columnists openly advocate denying the right of non-Muslims to be full citizens in Muslim societies. Several Muslim countries will not even give citizenship to an immigrant, even when it is through marriage, unless they convert to Islam.

We Are Sinners vs. They Are Sinners

After I moved to the United States, I began to learn about other religions, something I was not allowed to do in Muslim countries. I was struck with a new concept that I never heard before. Christian pastors often said, "We are *all* sinners" and only through the grace of God can we be forgiven. That statement was revolutionary. I needed days to think about the depth of its meaning, the premise of this concept, and how far it will lead me in how I view myself, others, and people who follow other religions. We humans are struggling, imperfect, and vulnerable, whether we are Christian, Muslim, or Jew. "We are all sinners" was one of the most comforting, liberating, uniting, and humbling expressions I have heard by a preacher. The notion that God is gracious and forgiving was an exciting revelation to me. That meant we don't have to die in bloody battles killing others—"the real sinners"—to guarantee salvation.

In Islam, my religion at that time, we looked at ourselves and others very differently. "*They* are sinners. . . . Non-Muslims are

sinners. . . . We are Muslims." They are guilty, but we are innocent. Muslims and non-Muslims were never considered as
equals in anything, not even in our imperfections as human
beings. The Qur'an and the Hadith were consumed with the
idea of *kaffir* (non-Muslim) representing "evil" and Muslim representing "good," which caused a split in how human beings
were perceived—as good and bad, superior and inferior, human
and sub-human. Our Islamic education stressed the inequality
between Muslims and kaffir. Kaffir is the dreaded word used
against others and also against Muslims who deviate or do not
follow Allah's commands to the letter. Kaffir means "infidel," or
a person who goes astray.

Muslim leaders, even in the West, teach that non-Muslims
deserve to be punished. In a question-and-answer session with
Imam Abdul Makin in an East London mosque, the imam was
asked why Allah would tell Muslims to kill and rape innocent
non-Muslims. The imam's answer was: "Because non-Muslims
are never innocent. They are guilty of denying Allah and his
prophet."

A top Muslim lawyer in Great Britain, Anjem Choudary, backed
up the imam's position, saying that all Muslims are innocent. "You
are innocent if you are a Muslim," Choudary told the BBC.
Choudary said he would not condemn a Muslim for any action.
"As a Muslim, I must support my Muslim brothers and sisters. I
will never condemn my Muslim brother." Choudary went on to
say, "I must have hatred to everything that is not Muslim."[1]

The semantic trick that some Muslims use when they condemn terrorism is their interpretation of the word *innocent*. So
when they say, "We condemn terrorism against innocent people,"
they actually mean "killing innocent Muslims." Omar Bakri
Mohammed, leader of the Saviour Sect, publicly condemned
the deaths of "innocents," after the July 7, 2005, London transit
bombings, but when speaking at the Selby Centre in Wood
Green, North London, on July 22, 2005, he referred to the 7/7

bombers as the "fantastic four" and explained that his grief for the "innocent" applied only to Muslims. His words were: "Yes, I condemn killing any innocent people, but not any *kuffar*."

As to Muslims who disagree with the above views, they are also considered kuffar. On March 15, 2008, two Saudi writers, Abdullah bin Bejad al-Otaibi and Yousef Aba al-Khail, each called for a reconsideration of the Wahabi notion that all non-Muslims are kuffar, prompting a top religious figure, Abdul-Rahman al-Barrak, to call for their deaths in a fatwa published on his Web site.

That is the great divide—the notion of innocence and guilt, sinners and non-sinners, Muslim and non-Muslim—that every Muslim is commanded to believe and act upon. It is how we were trained to perceive others and explains why the majority of Muslims today are silent about Islamic terrorism. The Muslim outlook regarding the rest of humanity shapes how Muslim society thinks and acts politically and culturally at all levels. That is why the two Egyptian Christian boys Mario and Andrew together with the Christian minority in Egypt have suffered for fourteen hundred years. And that is also why almost all Egyptian Muslims have been stripped of their empathy for and support of Christian Egyptians and therefore fail to stand up for their basic kaffir human rights.

Do Not Befriend or Trust Non-Muslims

Regarding friendship with non-Muslims, the Qur'an says in 5: 51, "O ye who believe! Take not the Jews and the Christians for your friends and protectors: They are but friends and protectors to each other. And he amongst you that turns to them (for friendship) is of them." Don't even think for a second that the above verse does not cause a major divide between Muslims and non-Muslims. Those apologists who claim it has little effect on Muslim society are in denial and are unable to see Muslim society objectively.

When I began my research for this book, I worried the most about Sharia's support of jihad and violence against non-Muslims, which is supported by verses throughout the Qur'an and Hadith and has become part of Sharia law. But what I find terribly divisive and with detrimental consequences were the many commands prohibiting Muslims from befriending non-Muslims. Qur'an 60:1 says, "You who believe, do not take My enemy and your own enemy as friends, offering them affection love while they disbelieve in any Truth that has come to you; they exile the Messenger as well as you yourselves just because you believe in God, your Lord. If you have gone forth to strive for My sake, seeking to please me, would you secretly show them your affection? I am quite Aware of what you hide and what you show." The above verse tells Muslims not to befriend or show kindness, respect, or affection to those who disbelieve, and that they are not only their enemies but also Allah's enemies. The Qur'an asks Muslims not to even try to guide disbelievers and hypocrites. Qur'an 3:118 says, "O you who believe! Take not as your intimates those (unbelievers) outside your religion. They will not fail to do their best to corrupt you." Qur'an 4:88 and 89 say:

Why should you take both sides concerning hypocrites? God has discarded them because of what they have earned. Do you want to guide someone whom God has let go astray? Anyone whom God lets go astray will never find a way back to Him. They wish that you disbelieve as they have disbelieved, then you become equal. Do not consider them friends, unless they mobilize along with you in the cause of God. If they turn against you, you shall fight them, and you may kill them when you encounter them in war. You shall not accept them as friends, or allies.

Mohammed himself often prohibited and punished his followers who communicated with his enemies. The Jewish tribe of Banu Qurayza was accused by Mohammed of befriending his enemies, and that was the reason behind their massacre in the battle of the Trench, in 627. With the relentless teachings and orders of the Qur'an, Hadith, and consequently its laws, we were told who to befriend, mistreat, reject, boycott, not talk to, and even kill. They were non-believers, especially Jews.

With such cruel teachings invading our minds, souls, and actions, Muslim society has suffered unintended consequences. The harsh divisiveness between Muslims and non-Muslims and ordering Muslims to mistreat certain others, ended up plaguing Muslim society with much cruelty, negativity, lack of compromise, and rigidity. The suffering of the other at the hands of Muslims poisons Muslim society, a severe price for advocating hatred.

Khesam is an important phenomenon in Muslim society. What is *khesam*? I tried hard to find a single English word for it, but failed. The word *khesam* means severing relationships, cutting ties, boycotting, making a relationship null and void, or acting like someone no longer exists. Khesam is a phenomenon common in the proud Muslim culture. It exists at all levels—the individual, family, group, and sects within Muslims society. It happens when people become easily offended by the behavior of others and sometimes could be the result of unintentional acts, ending in khesam. These acts could range from being a friend to two people who do not talk to each other and suddenly one or both accuse you of not being a good friend because you speak to the other. Khesam happens after an illness when a person who is ill suddenly stops talking to you because you did not visit him or her enough during their illness. Forgetting to attend a funeral will surely result in the deceased's family never talking to you again. It could be for reasons as silly as a dress you wore, a comment you made, or a belief that you have "the evil eye."

Khesam is also common between Muslim leaders and Arab nations who deviate from the agreed-upon behavior. As soon as a Muslim individual or group violates consensus, he or she becomes a pariah. When Saudi and Jordanian leaders disagreed with President Nasser of Egypt, Nasser would run a campaign of insults and visa versa.

When President Anwar Sadat signed the peace treaty with Israel, the response by Arab countries was harsh, resulting in a long-lasting khesam—the removal of Egypt from the Arab League and transferring the Arab League offices from Cairo to Tunisia. Befriending enemies is serious business in the Muslim world. Even today, all Arab countries are boycotting Israel, even after the peace treaty that led to Sadat's assassination. Egyptians are not allowed to visit Israel or fully normalize relationships between the two countries.

Like many Muslims who move to the West, I have noticed a major difference in how *us* and *them* relate to one another. Westerners, for the most part, do not take everything personally and do not allow minor matters, words, or comments to get in the way of a good relationship. I have seen normal corporate rivalries in American business environment, but the atmosphere rarely becomes as feudal as business relationships in the Muslim world. Of course, this is a matter of degree.

Shortly after arriving in America, I became friends with an American neighbor who later became ill for a long time, and I was too busy to visit her. When I finally went to her house with a small gift, I was fearful, wondering if she would ever talk to me again. I told her how sorry I was for not coming sooner. She was delighted to see me and considered my visit very kind. On my part, I was pleasantly surprised that she was even still talking to me! *How kind these "naïve," forgiving Americans are*, I thought, *and how I wish my culture could learn a little about forgiveness.*

Discrimination within Muslim Society

The teaching of cruelty, hatred, and the dehumanization of the other can only come out of a culture that is also cruel toward its own members. Racism and class discrimination are part and parcel of Muslim society. Several Sharia laws promote discrimination against lower classes, and certain professions. For instance, the following testimony is not admissible under Sharia:

- "Evidence of a slave, female singer or a person of low-respect (street-sweeper, bathhouse attendant, etc) is not admissible."[2]
- "Testimony of a non-Muslim that has been punished for false accusation is inadmissible. If s/he later becomes a Muslim, her/his evidence is then admissible."[3]
- "Evidence of a freethinker is not accepted."[4]

Needless to say, freethinking is needed to deny ludicrous, unjust, unscientific, violent, anti-women, anti humanity hadiths. That is probably why the testimony of a freethinker is not accepted.

The laws specifying discrimination against certain professions and trades can even deprive a mother of her children. According to Gaziri, a modern scholar in Islamic law: "The conditions of the custody of the children is as follows. First the wife should not reject Islam. . . . Second, she must be of good character for if it was proven that she is corrupted by illicit sex, or theft, *or has a low trade such as a professional mourner, or a dancer,* she loses her right to custody."

Even compensation for blood money is divided depending on the dead victim's religion or gender: "The indemnity paid for the death or injury of a woman is half the indemnity paid for a man. A Jew or Christian is one third of the indemnity paid for a Muslim. The indemnity paid for a Zoroastrian is one fifteenth of that of a Muslim."[5] The specifics on compensation in Saudi Arabia were reported in the *Wall Street Journal* (April 9, 2002) as follows:

"If a person has been killed or caused to die by another, the latter has to pay blood money or compensation, as follows:

100,000 riyals if the victim is a Muslim man
50,000 riyals if a Muslim woman
50,000 riyals if a Christian man
25,000 riyals if a Christian woman
6,666 riyals if a Hindu man
3,333 riyals if a Hindu woman"[6]

Discrimination also extends to protecting certain killers under Sharia law. In the classic manual of Islamic law, *Reliance of the Traveller*, the following are not subject to retaliation:

(2) a Muslim for killing a non-Muslim; (3) a Jewish or Christian subject of the Islamic State for killing an apostate from Islam; (4) a father or mother (or their fathers or mothers) for killing their offspring, or offspring's offspring.[7]

The above law does not mean that parents are encouraged to kill their children, but the laws of retaliation do not apply to parents who do. Something, however, feels wrong with the above law, which just adds to the general atmosphere of forgiving and excusing violence, as well as a lack of respect for life. It also seems to condone abuse of children, which is very prevalent in the Muslim world.

It is important to mention here that there are no Sharia laws forbidding abortion. I am not surprised that under Sharia (a brutal legal system that does not respect life) abortion is not illegal. Adoption, however, is illegal under Sharia. It was forbidden by Mohammed after he married the wife of his adoptive son who was required to divorce her so the prophet could marry her. In effect it could be claimed he was marrying his daughter-in-law, so adoption in Islam was thus made illegal after this incident.

As for the list of exemptions from retaliation, not only is retaliation not allowed against a Muslim if he kills a non-Muslim, but also: "Regard is also to be had to a difference of religion, so that a Muslim shall not be put to death for the murder of an unbeliever."[8]

Respect must also be given to Muslims by non-Muslims in the Muslim State. Among the list of enormities a non-Muslim can do to a Muslim is "showing others the weak points of the Muslims."[9] Also: "Prohibited is: 'Cursing a Muslim.'"[10]

Not only that, but Muslims are actually *encouraged* to mistreat non-Muslims and are protected by Sharia for doing so. The Sharia advocates "being unyielding towards the unbelievers, hard against them and detesting them."[11]

The above Islamic laws toward non-Muslims are worse than slavery. As for slavery, slavery—even of Muslims—has never been abolished by Islam, and Mohammed himself owned a black slave and traded in slaves.[12]

The Culture of Slavery

As Muslims, we were taught a lie that Islam abolished slavery. But the nation that founded Islam, Saudi Arabia, only officially abolished slavery in 1962 as a result of pressure from the West. My own grandmother, who was born in the early 1900s, remembered and witnessed the slave trade in the Arab world. At any rate, the *culture* of slavery is alive and well not only in Sharia books but also in real life. In their treatment of ordinary citizens, especially women, Muslim society and their Sharia-influenced governments practice a form of enslavement. On the streets of the Arab world, it is very difficult to ignore the inhumane and slave-like treatment of the poorer classes, maids, and people in need.

Muslims resist the West's efforts to end slavery even today in Sudan and other parts of the Muslim world. When the English ambassador to the Ottoman Empire tried to get the sultan to abolish slavery in 1840, he got this response from the Muslim leader: "I am amazed and I smile when I think you expect my people to abandon an institution that is interwoven in our beliefs and *religion*, from the sultan down to the peasant."[13]

Even the average Muslim wanted slavery so much that when the Christians succeeded in forcing Muslims to abolish it in 1855, the Muslims of Mecca revolted throwing the place into chaos. As late as the twentieth century, Muslims were raiding, capturing, and forcing people into slavery. In 1922, just before Britain abolished slavery in Tanganyika, Muslims were raiding more than any group. They captured millions of slaves in the nineteenth century alone, a time when Christians began abolishing slavery.[14]

Islam, as a law and as a religion, on its own did not abolish slavery. It was due to the impact of the so-called Western Christian "occupiers" who officially brought an end to slavery in the Muslim world. It must also be noted that when the British and the French were occupying the Muslim world, the rights of minorities and women were more protected—the Copts of Egypt can testify to that. Egypt saw a vibrant feminist movement in the early 1920s during the British occupation. The Egyptian feminist Huda Shaarawi stood in the main railroad station in Cairo, took off her hijab, and threw it away together with a group of several educated upper-class Egyptian women. That movement lasted until the British left in 1954 and survived until the 1970s when radical Islam came back with full force taking women back to the hijab. That is something never mentioned by those who blame "imperialism" for all the ills in today's Muslim society.

With all the above conditions in the Muslim world that perpetuated enslavement and discrimination on the basis of religion, class, and gender, the Muslims' psyche has been split between oppressors and oppressed, Muslims and kuffar, innocent and guilty, and pride and shame. The barbaric degradation and humiliation of Islamic punishments for trivial Islamic sins have succeeded in silencing Muslims and turning them into enslaved followers. Remember, questioning and doubting is treason to the Muslim State.

Allah said in Qur'an 3:104 and 3:110 "that Arabs are the best of people ever created. . . . You are the best community ever raised among the people." This notion of "best" is not similar to the Jewish expression "chosen," which brings deep feeling of obligation and responsibility; in the case of the Arabs, it brings pride and dominance. Arabs are the best, and the Qur'an is perfect.

The fastest way to offend a Muslim is to question or point out discrepancies in Muslim scriptures. This isn't just a personal offense. The Qur'an itself discourages Muslims from asking questions: "O ye who believe! Ask not questions about things which if made plain to you, may cause you trouble. . . . Some people before you did ask such questions, and on that account lost their faith."[15]

Muslims are taught that asking questions are from Satan. Allah's Apostle said, "Satan comes to one of you and says, 'Who created so-and-so?' till he says, 'Who has created your Lord?' So, when he inspires such a question, one should seek refuge with Allah and give up such thoughts."[16]

Allah's Enforcers, Vigilante Justice

In the late sixties and early seventies, I often heard the famous blind sheikh Abdel Hamid Kishk ranting, raving, yelling, cursing, speaking against any possible peace with Israel. He talked about the promises of eternal sexual pleasures and even pederasty (by mentioning boys like pearls in paradise) for Muslims who entered Paradise. Kishk's mosque was next door to a dear Christian friend of mine who often heard Kishk's insults to the kaffir unbelievers on the mosque loudspeakers.

Kishk was criticized by a few Egyptian intellectuals among whom was human rights activist and journalist Farag Foda. In 1992, Foda was shot to death by a radical Muslim who said he was proud to kill an apostate. In his trial, none other than the well-known Al-Azhar scholar Mohammed al-Ghazali testified before the court on behalf of the murderer by saying that it was not wrong to kill a foe of Islam. He said, "The killing of Farag Foda was in fact the implementation of the punishment against an apostate which the imam (the Islamic leader in Egypt) has failed to implement." In other words, the killer was merely doing what the state should have done. Sharia law against perceived Muslim apostates, in this case, was not executed by the state but by vigilante justice. Let us look at the Sharia laws that support this horrific crime and violation of Mr. Foda's life:

The following Shafi'i Sharia law puts punishment for the following crimes not only in the hands of the judiciary but also in the hands of the public: "There is *no* expiation (punishment) for *killing* someone who has left Islam, a highway man, or a convicted married adulterer, even when someone besides the khalifa kills him."[17] In other words, a killer—outside the authority of the state—of an apostate, a robber, or an adulterer cannot be punished, and is forgiven for murder under Sharia law.

The following is also Shafi'i Codified Law: "A criminal, even if repents, will not be spared from punishment *except for the crime of Hiraba.*" The explanation section states: "Hiraba means violation of public safety by disrupting law and order due to attack of a united group. Plunder of property, rape, murder, and bloodshed is included in this."[18]

The law simply and clearly means that criminals of Hiraba (genocide) are "spared from punishment" if they repent. An example of this is when the Danish cartoon riots erupted causing burning and killing on the streets in many Muslim countries. If they repent, there is no punishment for them under Sharia.

Crowds of Muslim murderers have gotten away with murder, torture, and plunder in genocidal rage that killed many Muslims and non-Muslims. The examples are many in Islam and are still being committed today in the Sudan: in 1971, when thousands of Bangladesh Hindus and Muslims were killed by radical

Muslims in the liberation war; in upper Egyptian villages, where dozens of Copts were killed in drive-by shootings while leaving church; and the list goes on and on for fourteen hundred years.

The one common thing in Muslim genocide is that the criminals go unidentified and unpunished, which I believe is no coincidence. Muslim countries are very tolerant to those who kill in the name of Islam. The above Sharia law is designed to protect jihadists and terrorists and such other criminals of genocide, and has done so throughout fourteen hundred years. "Allah's Laws" are their guaranteed and successful protectors.

Allah's Enforcers

Since vigilante killing is allowed under Sharia under certain conditions, a Muslim not only is required to adhere to Allah's law but is also entrusted to enforce them on others right here on earth. A good Muslim cannot mind his or her own business since the hadith tells him: "whoever sees something wrong and accepts it is as though he had committed it."[19] In Pakistan, a liberal-minded female government cabinet member (and wife and mother of two) was assassinated for not wearing a veil. The shooter reportedly said, "I have no regrets. I just obeyed Allah's commandment." Also in Pakistan, barbers received threatening letters warning them against continuing their "anti-Sharia work" cutting customers' beards. One barber told the Associated Press that two dozen barbers have responded by asking customers to not request shaves. In Gaza recently, TV female broadcasters who did not wear the Islamic head cover received death threats telling them to cover or else. That is the power of Islamic Sharia. The fear and distrust from each other is at every level in society.

Can you imagine the power Muslim leadership and self-appointed Sharia enforcers have over the ordinary citizen? A simple fatwa labeling someone an apostate, even if that person lives in the West, becomes a death warrant entrusted to any

Muslim willing to kill an apostate in the name of Allah, with the full blessing of Sharia. And remember, it only takes one committed believer out of the 1.2 billion Muslims worldwide to become the executioner. Such crimes are happening in the West, not by some shadowy al Qaeda-linked person, but by some ordinary religious zealot who decides on his own to kill the enemy of Allah. Right here in America, a Pakistani Muslim man, in 2006, walked into a Jewish Center in Seattle, Washington, and shot five people, killing one woman. Of course that Muslim shooter has the luxury of claiming insanity under U.S. law, but I believe in the heart of that man he was simply killing infidel Jews, as the Qur'an orders him to do.

This and other Muslim scripture-motivated murders are often treated in Western courts as simple murders committed by people who often plea insanity, and the religious motivation behind their actions is not recognized by a naïve, politically correct West. That leaves many people vulnerable to such religious crime in the West. Liberal Muslims, Jews, and critics of Islam are often the target.

The West doesn't get it; they can't understand this kind of crime. They cannot call it "terrorism" because the individual Muslim is not linked to al Qaeda. But it is a special kind of terrorism that can be perpetrated under Islamic Sharia by just one individual who feels he is killing in the name of Allah. When he dies, he is hailed as a martyr and a hero of Islam for doing Allah's work. The West needs to understand that this kind of crime is not an *ordinary* crime. It is an act of terror allowed and encouraged to the individual Muslim under Sharia, and it is empowering radical Islam inside Western democracies.

A Muslim does not have to live in Saudi Arabia or Iran to fear Sharia's harsh punishments. That problem has been solved by the ingenious worldwide stranglehold of Sharia over ordinary Muslims. In the more secular Muslim states, the public must look over their shoulders not just for the official "virtue police" who can be easily bribed, but more importantly for fellow

Muslims who might see them acting like apostates and simply kill them thinking they are doing the right thing. You do not need the whole population to believe this, but even if 10 percent follow Sharia literally, that is plenty of prospective killers waiting to see a violation of Sharia on the street and causing a lot of fear, suppression, distrust, and chaos.

A Muslim preacher in London once said that if a non-Muslim walks in Muslim land, either he can be sold to a slaver or a muslim may just go and kill him. That "religious" leader spoke about the murder of a non-Muslim like speaking about killing a bug on the ground. That is what Muslims hear day in and day out from their religious leaders.

Do people in the West actually understand what a fatwa is and how far it can go? I have recently seen a list of fatwas against thirty-three Muslims and former Muslims issued in Egypt by radical Muslims. On that list is the name of my dear friend, the courageous Wafa Sultan. Some of the names on the list are people who still live inside the Muslim world. I cannot even imagine the fear a person who lives inside the Muslim world must feel when his or her name is on a death list telling any Muslim on the face of the earth to kill them. Again that is where Islam gets its power; it is not the power of conviction, but the power of fear.

When justice is left in the hands of people on the street, not only is it bound to be abused, but more importantly, the execution of justice is transferred to the streets and homes and not necessarily in courts. When I lived in the Middle East, I rarely heard of people going to court, but I heard of a lot of fear from the public and what self-appointed vigilantes can do to you. The pressure to conform to Sharia was stronger on the streets. That gives a lot of power to the Muslim religious leaders who can use the power of the fatwa to threaten people into conformity. Muslims have been turned against each other. They all must watch their backs. Distrust in the Muslim world does not only exist in the family, between husband and wife, but also between Muslims in society as a whole. People can kill each other for any reason and then lie or exaggerate claims to make it fit the allowable reasons to kill. Thus a man who kills his wife can say she was cheating on him; a Muslim who kills another can say he was an apostate or a robber.

The examples are many in seventh-century Arabia where people are forgiven for killing under certain conditions: "A Jewess used to abuse the Prophet. A man strangled her till she died. The Apostle of Allah declared that no recompense was payable for her blood."[20]

The murderer was *forgiven* by Mohammed because he claimed that the victim "abused," or spoke ill of the Prophet. Vigilante justice is especially acceptable if the victim is Jewish, and that is what is going on today when Muslims celebrate their son's death for killing Jews. That is the legacy that Mohammed left to the Sharia enforcers to use and abuse.

So in the end, it really does not matter if a country is ruled by 100 percent Sharia, 50 percent Sharia, or 0 percent Sharia. If Muslims take the actions of Mohammed as their ultimate honor to emulate, then Sharia can be 100 percent applied wherever Muslims live.

And if the above mess is not enough for Muslim society, the Qur'an itself promotes retaliation among people: "O ye who believe! *Retaliation* is prescribed for you in the matter of the murdered; the freeman for the freeman, and the slave for the slave, and the female for the female. He who transgresseth after this will have a painful doom. And there is life for you in (the law of) retaliation, O men of understanding that you may guard yourselves."[21]

And to those who think there is not enough suffering in the Muslim community with Sharia, Mohammed condemned the fate of his community to strife, instability, and bloodshed when he said in a hadith: "This community of mine is a community blessed with mercy. It is not punished in the Hereafter. Instead, it is punished in this world with strife, instability, and bloodshed."[22] Life on earth for the Muslim community has been condemned to one of strife, instability, and bloodshed. That is very true even today.

A Religion of Peace?

In my research for this book, I tried my best to find that peace is a major theme taught in Islamic scriptures, but the opposite is the truth. The Prophet himself set the sects that branched out of his own community against each other, forever. The strife began immediately after his death. This is what the Prophet said in the following hadith: "'My community will divide into 73 sects, and all of them will be in the Hellfire *save one.*' The people asked him: 'And which one will that be?' He replied: 'The one that follows what I and my Companions are upon right now.'"[23]

The impact of the above hadith on Muslim nations can be seen today among the different sects of Islam, especially Sunni and Shi'ite sects, who all call each other "apostates."

Radical Muslims believe that peace in the Muslim world will come when all the world has become Muslim, but how can that be when all the sects are fighting and killing each other—making good on the predictions of Mohammed. The Muslim State was never a peaceful state.

Even when Muslims tried to define the meaning of "Muslims," they forbid each other from asking questions. Questions will expose the discrepancies in Islam, so they must be stopped by Sharia itself.

That is the state of Islam internally, inside the Muslim State. A peaceful Muslim caliphate has never existed. It is even amazing that with all the contradictions and abrogation in the Qur'an, Muslims one hundred years after the death of their Prophet were able to reach some sort of agreement to produce Sharia law itself.

Peace inside Muslim society is very fragile. As Muslims,

especially women, we learned early in life to take what we are told very seriously, deal with it while appearing obedient, then move on with our lives without asking many questions. It is like living with a permanent maniac or in a hostage crisis. We must not anger the Sharia maniac who lurks about ready to kill those whom he thinks has violated what he thinks is right. The chaos can only be stabilized a little if we take care to "not rock the boat."

Criticism Is Blasphemy, Punishable by Death

Mohammed himself ordered the killing of those who criticized him, so that became the law of Sharia for blasphemy. Blasphemy, criticizing, or defaming Islam and the Prophet is punishable by death in all the different Sharia schools, no exception. The problem is that the word "criticizing" is not defined. So, anybody can claim anything as *criticism*. So effectively, the door of constructive criticism is blocked, and too many people are killed or harassed by this law. Blasphemy is virtually an act that makes a believer an unbeliever. In Shafi'i Law, there are 442 acts in section w.52 that are classified as "Enormity" (horror acts). Sharia law against criticizing or defaming of Islam, which is "blasphemy"— which therefore amounts to apostasy—is deserving of death. This includes the following Shafi'i law numbers:

- o.8.(7): to deny any verse of the Qur'an

- o.8.(19): to be sarcastic about any ruling of the Sacred law

- o.8.(20): to deny that Allah intended the Prophet's message to be the religion followed by the entire world

Criticizing Mohammed even by merely quoting a true historical story or hadith about him can cause Muslims to be extremely offended. Repeating certain hadiths that embarrass Muslims can immediately tag the person who mentions them as an "Islam hater." Such hadiths are regarded by sensitive Muslims as not for public consumption, especially in front of a non-Muslim. Only ulama (scholars) of Islam can appreciate them. In June 2007, the Egyptian Mufti (top Muslim scholar of Sharia), Dr. Ali Gum'a, claimed in the book *Religion and Life—Modern Everyday Fatwas* that the companions of the Prophet Mohammed would drink his urine to be blessed. He issued a fatwa titled: "The Companions of the Prophet Blessed Themselves with His Urine, Sweat, and Saliva." In his book, Dr. Ali Gum'a described the following incident of urine-drinking from a hadith: "Umm Ayman drank the urine of the Prophet, and the Prophet told her: 'This stomach will not be dragged through the fire of Hell, because it contains something of our Lord the Messenger of Allah.'"[24]

Immediately, there was a public outcry and media uproar in Egypt following publication of the above fatwa, and a complaint was filed against Gum'a demanding that he stand trial for harming Islam, the Prophet, and the Companions of the Prophet. Some argued that there was no point in raising such issues from the past even though the fatwa was based on true Islamic sources. They argued that it had nothing to do with public life today. Others stated that the fatwa was for Islamic scholars, not for the masses, and still others said that it was a tool for those who sought to harm Islam. Some also called on Gum'a to resign from his post as the Mufti of Egypt.

That tells us that the majority of Muslims do not know what is in their scriptures. For some it is better and safer not to know or be tempted to ask questions. Thus, here is a huge discrepancy between what is in Muslim scriptures and what Muslims perceive their religion to be. There is also the attitude that Muslims can secretly read such hadiths about Mohammed and how he treated his followers, but if a religious leader exposes this to the public in a book, it becomes an unforgivable insult and a major embarrassment to Islam that can be used by the enemies of Islam to discredit Islam.

Ordinary Muslims must never venture into the secret texts that only the learned Muslims can understand and appreciate— and then are obligated to conceal from the rest of the world. Only what can bring *honor* to Islam can be revealed, but what brings *shame* should be concealed.

Living in Denial

With today's sudden interest in Islam and the ideology that brought worldwide Islamic terrorism, causing huge government and private budgets for protection from Muslim jihadists, the world is exposing Muslim texts. Believe it or not, as these texts come to light, many Muslims are among the first ones to hear about their scriptures. Ignorance of Muslim scriptures is not confined to the less-educated Arab Street, but exists at all levels. I have encountered many Muslims in Ivy League universities in the United States who don't know or refuse to know the basic tenets of their religion. Denial of the truth of Muslim scriptures is the only solution for many, since acknowledging the tragedy is regarded as apostasy. The doors and windows are all locked around the Muslim mind preventing him from looking outside the box of Sharia.

Muslims, especially those who live in a Muslim State, often must choose denial for the sake of their own sanity. Even those who live in Western democracies must be careful not to say a word that might make them appear as apostates. For them, facts must not stand in the way. They must put up a front and report on each other, because everything must be sacrificed for the protection of Islam, Allah, and Mohammed.

The Evil Eye

Muslim society is plagued with distrust, anger, envy, and superstition. The phenomenon of envy—"the evil eye"—was discussed in detail in my previous book, *Now They Call Me Infidel*, but I cannot stress enough how detrimental that phenomenon is to Muslim society, and how deeply this concept is rooted in Islam. In Christianity, envy is one of the seven deadly sins and is considered something that hurts the person who envies. But in Islam, jealousy and envious feelings are actually believed to physically affect and hurt others. It is very common in the Middle East to see people attribute miscarriages, illness, and accidents to the envy of others. This phenomenon adds one more layer of distrust and paranoia and requires always being on guard against other people.

The belief in the evil eye has existed in many societies, especially in the Bedouin culture, long before Islam came about. But once again, Islam came in and reinforced this superstition instead of eliminating it. The Qur'an and Hadith often mention the evil eye.

The Qur'an warns against "the evil of the envier when he envies."[25] In one hadith the Prophet says, "The influence of an evil eye is a fact; if anything would precede the destiny, it would be the influence of an evil eye."[26] In another, "The effect of evil eyes to cause sickness is true."[27]

Muslim scholars tell us that a Jew had thrown a curse on the Prophet of God, and as a result the Prophet kept forgetting and became absent-minded. Then God sent him this well-known surah: "Say: I seek refuge in the Lord of mankind, From the evil of the sneaking whisperer, Who whispereth in the hearts of mankind, Of the jinn and of mankind."[28] The word *jinn* in the Qur'an refers to creatures with free will, made from "smokeless fire" by God.[29]

The Curse of Cursing

The culture of Arabia was rooted in poetry, much of which was used for insulting and cursing, called *hijaa*. Cursing against Jews, Christians, unbelievers, America, Britain, and the West in general is common practice. However, I have never once heard a

Muslim preacher curse communists or Hitler. The words *kaffir* and *fight* are perhaps among the two most common words used in Muslim scriptures. Most of the emphasis in Islamic scriptures is not aimed internally at believers, but externally toward those who do not believe. Cursing the "other"— the outsider, the unbeliever—is intrinsic to Muslim culture.

Mohammed himself cursed some people around him, and he was also cursed by some who did not believe in his message. According to Bukhari in the book of Al Maghazi, Mohammed cursed his enemies in his dawn prayers. Below are some examples of such curses:

- "The Prophet said, 'O Allah! Curse Shaiba bin Rabia and Utba Bin Rabia and Umaiya bin Khalaf as they turned us out of our land to the land of epidemics.'"[30]

- "The Prophet said, 'O Allah! Be very hard on Mudar tribe. . . . Afflict them with years (of famine) similar to the (famine) years of the time of Prophet Joseph.'"[31]

- "The Prophet said, 'O Allah! Destroy the chief of Quraish. . . . Destroy Abu Jahl bin Hisham . . . Shaiba bin Rabia . . . Utba Bin Rabia . . . Umaiya bin Khalaf . . . Uqba bin Abi Muait.'"[32]

- "Allah's Apostle invoked evil upon the infidels, saying, 'O Allah! The revealer of the Holy Book, defeat these people and shake them. Fill the infidels' houses and graves with fire.'"[33]

- Narrated Abdullah bin Mas'ud: "The Prophet faced the Ka'ba and invoked evil on some people of Quraish, on Shaiba bin Rabi'a, 'Utba bin Rabi'a, Al-Walid bin 'Utba and Abu Jahl bin Hisham. I bear witness, by Allah, that I saw them all dead, putrefied by the sun as that day was a very hot day."[34]

In one scripture, Mohammed himself tells that he cursed someone because of his quick "human" temper.

> Anas b. Malik reported that there was an orphan girl with Umm
> Salaim (who was the mother of Anas). Allah's Messenger saw that
> orphan girl and said: O, it is you; you have grown young. May you
> not advance in years! That slave-girl returned to Umm Sulaim
> weeping. Umm Sulaim said: O daughter, what is the matter with
> you? She said: Allah's Apostle has invoked curse upon me that I
> should not grow in age . . . . Umm Sulaim went out wrapping her
> head-dress hurriedly until she met Allah's Messenger. He said to
> her: Umm Sulaim, what is the matter with you? She said: Allah's
> Apostle, you invoked curse upon my orphan girl. . . . She states
> you have cursed her saying that she might not grow in age or grow
> in life. Allah's Messenger smiled and then said: Umm Sulaim,
> don't you know that I have made this term deal with my Lord.
> And the term with my Lord is that I said to Him: I am a human
> being and I am pleased just as a human being is pleased and I lose
> temper just as a human being loses temper, so for any person from
> amongst my Umma whom I curse and he in no way deserves it,
> let that, O Lord, be made a source of purification and purify and
> nearness to (Allah) on the Day of Resurrection.[35]

Mohammed died with extreme bitterness against the Jews who
refused to abandon Judaism and convert to Islam. He cursed
them more than any other group in the Hadith and in the words
he delivered from Allah in the Qur'an. In fact, the last statement
that Mohammed made was: "O Lord, perish the Jews and
Christians. They made churches of the graves of their prophets.
There shall be no two faiths in Arabia."[36]

The presence of Jews and Christians in Arabia ended with
that. Jews were a people with a firmly rooted history and heritage
in the Middle East. They were busy promoting their lives and
businesses in Arabia while Mohammed was busy making war,

raiding, and winning booty for Allah's sake. Those are the people who contributed greatly to Middle East culture, ethics, religions, and society. They are the people whom Islam chased out of their own holy temple location, first destroyed by the Romans, who at least did not build anything on top of it. As a further "curse," Arab Muslims built their mosque above the temple ruins to end all traces to Jewish culture, heritage, and history.

When Jews in 1948 created their state again, a state so small you can hardly see it on the map of vast Muslim lands, the old animosities were brought back to the front of the Arab mind, a mind that could not tolerate seeing Jews rule themselves in their own holy land. During the last sixty years, 99 percent of the Jews who lived in Middle Eastern and North African Muslim countries have been evicted or killed, with over a million of them taking refuge in Israel, minus their property and bank accounts.

Is it any wonder that cursing has become a tradition and a common phenomenon in mosques and in Muslim society as a whole? It might sound strange to the Western mind that the most common place of cursing is inside the mosque. As a Muslim I lived most of my life watching many angry, vindictive preachers on TV who never missed a chance to curse the infidels. It felt repulsive, but I never saw anyone in my family or society comment in any negative way about this kind of preaching, and thus I grew up thinking it must be okay; not only okay, but also good and even *holy* to hate and curse. I never learned in my culture of origin that a place of worship should be holy and cursing is not holy. It took me a long time to learn this simple truth, but it was not Islam that taught me this.

It is often very hard to have a logical discussion without making Muslims feel offended. This is very noticeable when one watches Arab TV debates that often deteriorate into exchanges of insults, cursing and calling each other the dreaded words "infidel" or apostate.

The phenomenon of cursing has become a tool often used by

Muslims to silence hard questions that are taboo to honestly answer to non-Muslims. In early 2007, I was invited on *Hannity & Colmes* to comment on an incident that occurred on Hannity's radio show in which a Shi'ite Iraqi American imam cursed, yelled, and raved at Sean Hannity for insisting on a yes or no answer as to whether the imam thought Hezbollah was a terrorist organization. Instead of answering the question, the imam screamed and accused Hannity of causing divisions by insisting on such questions.

My comment on the show was that Muslim imams are not accustomed to being questioned, and when they are, that is what happens. They live in a world where there is no intellectual honesty, no dialogue, and no respect.

The Great Satan

Muslim preachers describe the West and the Jews as the personification of Satan and therefore deserving of being cursed, humiliated, deceived, and killed. To many Muslims, the non-Muslims—and especially Jews—are no longer regarded as human beings with human rights like everyone else. They have become Satan, and Satan has become them. They are the source of evil and temptation that Muslims must avoid by any means. Is it any wonder that Muslims call America "the great Satan" and Israel "the little Satan"? That is what Islamic scriptures have done to the Muslim mind. Day in and day out, preachers tell Muslims that the West and the Jews are using pornography and drugs to destroy Muslim society. In my last visit to Egypt, I read in Islamic literature that Israeli Viagra is aimed at sterilizing Arab men.

Such outrageous propaganda is the only way a population can be prepared for jihad against non-Muslims. To scare the hell out of them is the fastest way to prepare generation after generation for jihad; fear is the most powerful motivation used by Islamic teaching to produce a population ready to accept violence and terror as a solution.

Permission to Lie

The teaching of cruelty, hatred, and violence by many Muslim preachers has a major function in preparing people for jihad. But beyond that, Sharia and education tells Muslims it is acceptable to lie, when it comes to non-Muslims, if it is in the best interest of Islam. Non-believers, especially Jews, don't deserve befriending, mercy, respect, or even life; but there is one more thing they do not deserve—it is the truth.

According to Sharia law r8.2: "Lying is obligatory if the goal is obligatory."

Some of the Shafi'i laws say lying is a sin and/or crime. But according to Islamic Sharia, there is such a thing as "permissive lying." In law r8.0, "Umm Kultum added, 'I did not hear him (Prophet) permit untruth in anything people say, except for three things: war, settling disagreements and a man talking with his wife or she with him (in smoothing over differences).'"

The above law tells Muslims basically that they can lie under certain conditions in international relationships during war in Muslim-to-Muslim relationships to settle disagreements inside the family. I guess that covers it all! The notion—lying to non-Muslims in time of "war"—can be conveniently stretched to anything they want, including killing non-Muslims, invading the West, or killing Muslims who reject or resist Sharia.

From the book *Towards Understanding Islam*, by Islamic scholar Sayyid Maududi: "In real life, telling a lie is not only allowed, in some circumstances it is decreed to be mandatory."[37]

The above order to Muslims to lie under certain conditions is not just something on the books, but has infiltrated Arab and Muslim culture thoroughly. I learned this from personal experience when I started speaking out against radical Islam after 9/11. The main reaction I got from many Muslims was, "How dare you say what you say [the truth] in front of Americans, Jews, and non-Muslims!" Some Muslim students would point-blank tell me,

"You do not have to say what you say publicly. We Muslims and Arabs should discuss these matters privately." Few of their questions to me were about the content of what I said, but most of their comments were, "How dare you?" I know and they know what they mean by that.

Even the most knowledgeable Americans in the audience probably never realized the threats I was hearing publicly: subtle threats because I would not "lie," deny, or cover up to my fellow Americans about Islam's jihadist and expansionist agenda in the West. According to Islamic Sharia, I am obligated to lie if the goal is obligatory, and Muslim expansion is obligatory.

The politically correct crowd in the West must understand that Sharia laws themselves demand that Muslims lie to them. Although difficult for a Western culture to comprehend, dishonesty is encouraged in children from early on. In 2007, I was watching a children's show on Arab TV where a Muslim preacher was speaking to children, all boys around age ten. He told them that lying is not allowed under Islam except to non-Muslims and Jews and in time of war, or when you lie to settle a problem between two Muslim groups or people, or to lie to your wife for the sake of not creating problems. Imagine that! This is being told to Muslim children today.[38]

Is it any wonder that Muslims will look Western media in the eye and say, "Islam is a religion of peace," and then turn around to their own Muslim people and say, "God bless the Magnificent Nineteen," meaning the nineteen 9/11 Arab terrorists?

Believe it or not, Sharia law also tells Muslims that it is sometimes permissible to conceal witnesses in Hudud cases! Sharia law tells Muslims that under some circumstances, it is okay to fool the system. "One may conceal or give witness in Hudud cases." (Explanation section: "It is not obligatory to give witness voluntarily.")[39]

The explanation section of another law states: "There is difference of opinion about false witness. Says if a person gives false witness s/he will not be punished in anyway except his/her face is to be blackened and s/he will be forced to walk in (the) market with a declaration: 'this person gave falls witness.' In some cases concealing witness is encouraged."[40]

With all of this, truth and lies often become indistinguishable in the Muslim and Arab mind. The truth has become what Muslim leaders want you to believe in a world where the end—the triumph of Islam—always justifies the means. The penalty for telling the truth in some instances under Islamic Sharia can be hazardous to your health, and with the passage of time Muslims have developed a fear of speaking the truth. With the huge number of Muslims living under a religion they do not understand and are not allowed to understand, their whole life is a lie, but they dare not say it. Muslims are molded from birth to simply play the game of lying, *taqiyya* (in Arabic), and hold back what their true intentions are, *kitman.*

Any wonder why a large number of Arab media, Muslim religious leaders, and Arab politicians after 9/11 insisted 9/11 was a Jewish conspiracy? Similarly, from the pulpits of mosques, religious leaders after the 2004 Indian Ocean tsunami said that it was probably the doing of the Jews because many of the affected nations were Muslim.

Taqiyya and kitman serve the aims of the Muslim obligation to kill in the jihad. The commandment to do jihad runs so deep in Muslim society that lying about the jihad objective is no longer a problem for many Muslims who no longer connect the dots. Jihad is camouflaged as self-defense, and lying is the only tool to do it. Nothing supercedes jihad, not even honesty. Human happiness or the well-being of one's family does not even come close. Golda Meir was right when she said, "The Arabs will stop fighting us when they love their children more than they hate Jews."

Golda Meir figured it out.

I simply cannot quote all the commandments for jihad—they are so numerous, but one can simply read Sharia books, the

Qur'an, and Hadith to understand the enormity of this obligation. Just a sampling—one that anticipates possible believers' resistance—from the Qur'an 2:216: "Fighting is prescribed for you, and ye dislike it. But it is possible that ye dislike a thing which is good for you." The wishes of Allah for followers to do jihad delivered by Mohammed through the Qur'an has thus become Islamic law: "Our Prophet, the Messenger of our Lord, ordered us to fight you till you worship Allah alone or pay us the Jizyah tribute tax in submission. Our Prophet has informed us that our Lord says: 'Whoever amongst us is killed as a martyr shall go to Paradise to lead such a luxurious life as he has never seen, and whoever survives shall become your master.'"[41]

The Problem of Guilt

The extreme, contradictory, and barbaric system of control that Sharia represents is unnatural, and the basic humanity of Muslims, who are just human beings like everyone else, often stands in the way of their becoming the robots they must be. How do Muslim men and women who follow the ideals of Sharia view themselves? Is guilt inevitable? How do Muslims process this guilt when their humanity does not allow them to treat non-Muslims and even each other like that? How do they psychologically handle commands by Allah to hate, lie, deceive, enslave, and even kill for the sake of Allah who is supposed to be the god of all creation?

The only way to resolve the guilt is to confess that Islamic violent teachings are wrong, but that is simply not a realistic choice for many Muslims who want to remain Muslims. So what the system of Islam does—on both the state/society level, and individual/personal psychological level—is to fabricate an excuse for violence. Today, in a world that values human rights, some Muslims don't wish to admit that their religion wants to take over the world and create a one-party Fascist state called the Caliphate. But believe it or not, many other Muslim leaders openly say so and think it is their right as Muslims. But for "reasonable, modern" Muslims, especially when they speak to the West, their humanity tells them this is a violation of the human rights of others. The only solution for Muslims is to think of themselves as victims. The reinforcement of Muslims as victims is a primary objective of Muslim preaching and Arab media. The majority of Muslims have bought it. Some Westerners have bought it as well. Not a bad strategy if the objective is to conquer the unsuspecting, guilt-ridden West.

Perhaps everyone should watch a short film on the Internet called "Pallywood," showing a number of Palestinians, with the help of media, stage scenes of violence and war with Israelis with no real Israelis present to fight. The film shows a satellite view of a funeral of a man supposedly killed by Israel. The corpse keeps falling off the wooden board they are carrying it on, but miraculously stands up and jumps back into the coffin being carried by the mourners. What would propel a large number of Muslims to go through all of this—a big enactment and web of lies for the purpose of showing Israel to be a villain? Why the lies if the truth is supposedly bad enough? The lies and the truth have become indistinguishable in my culture of origin where the end justifies the means. The majority of Muslims never stop to think: *Why do we hate? Why must we be intolerant of other religions? Why do we have to take the life of others simply on the basis of religion?*

The terrorism against Israel must be constantly justified to the West, whom the Muslims desperately need for their support against Israel. Jihad against the Jewish State is not over land or because Jews are monsters and kill Arab babies and rape Muslim women; it is because in the seventh century Mohammed ordered Muslims to eliminate Jews. But such truth cannot be said, not even to the average Muslim who cannot connect the dots. Do you think Muslims will honestly tell that to the world? I don't think so. Muslims have robbed the Jews of a life of peace in their homeland, of their holy temple, expelled them from Arabia and limited them to second-class *dhimmi* status. Just the sight of Jews ruling themselves in an area that was once ruled by Muslims drives Muslims crazy. When Jerusalem was in Arab hands, Jewish religious sites were desecrated and Jews were not allowed to visit them—something that Israel does not do to Muslims and Christians who have free access to their holy sites.

I cannot forget the famous photo of three young Israeli soldiers looking in awe when for the first time they touched the remains of their holy temple—the Wailing Wall in Jerusalem—after their troops liberated their holy sites in 1967. To the Jews the Wailing Wall is like Mecca is to the Muslims. But Muslims don't want to see Jews rule themselves; they must remain slaves and *dhimmis* like their Jewish ancestors in seventh-century Arabia. How can the United Nations only blame Israel for violating human rights? The world is upside down; it is scary.

The Number One Obsession

Going back to my people, how do Muslims process the guilt from their obligation for constant jihad against Jews, a group of people who, for fourteen hundred years, have suffered terror, humiliation, and oppression cleverly concealed as retaliation for "the occupation." (I wonder who is occupying whom?) With every act of terror against Jews, a claim of victimhood must precede it and must be sustained with shouting until the next act of terror.

In an interview with a Hamas member of Parliament, Ahmad Abu Halabiya, which aired on Al-Aqsa TV on December 5, 2007, he said that Israel uses artificial earthquakes to shake the foundation of Al-Aqsa Mosque (which sits on the Temple Mount in Jerusalem). When many Israeli tourists were killed by Egyptian terrorists affiliated to the Muslim Brotherhood and al Queda at Taba, a resort in the Egyptian Sinai, Muslims blamed it on Israel. Egyptian preachers and even media started spreading the rumor that this was done by Israel in order to embarrass Egypt. The deception is phenomenal. I am often speechless when I hear of the in-your-face audacity and ease by which lies flow against Israel by my people. Do they really want the world to believe that the Israeli government is killing its own citizens in Egyptian resorts for the purpose of embarrassing Egypt, the only country to initiate a peace process with them? Such lies are often for internal consumption only, to assuage Muslim guilt feelings when it comes to Jews. The lies must continue to explain away fourteen hundred years of jihad against the Jews, and amazingly much of the world is buying it today in the twenty-first century.

Accusing other groups of one's own acts is a basic sin in any religion, but not to Sharia, which permits and encourages lies during war. According to the Sharia logic of injustice, Jews don't deserve the truth, justice, or mercy. As far as Islam and its Sharia laws are concerned, Jews are not human; they are apes, and Christians are pigs who deserve to die if they stay faithful to their religion. The Jews that Arabs describe in their mosques, Arab textbooks, and media don't exist. Arabs are fighting an imaginary Jew of their own creation.

Israel is not perfect; no society is. But the way minorities, such as Jews and Christians, are treated by my people is embarrassing. It is tragic and a disgrace. The hateful venom spread from mosques, media, and schools against the Jewish people is frightening, and the world must wake up before another holocaust happens.

The holocaust against the Jews is going on right now but not all at once. It is done bit by bit through acts of terror. And the world is buying the propaganda that it is done because the Muslim world loves the Palestinians so much they are willing to sacrifice their own children for the cause. Tens of thousands of Egyptians have died in wars initiated by Egypt against Israel, and I lived through all of them. At an early age I lost my own father to the cause of killing Jews. Nasser proclaimed him a *shahid*—a martyr. I lived through the sick euphoria of the Egyptian masses during Nasser's time, who were worked up to go to war to eliminate the

Jews from the face of the earth at a time when Egyptian land was already free of Jews. That was the sentiment then, and it still is.

The Palestinian "excuse" comes in handy when it is the Arab world that pushed them against the fence of Israel and gave them nothing but weapons to fight and terrorize. For sixty years they have been shamed and told they are not worthy of being called Arab and Muslim if they don't fight and destroy Israel. Muslim nations have told the outside world, "We love the Palestinians and want to help their suffering," but never financed improvements of the infrastructure and economy of the West Bank and Gaza. Funds instead go to financing terrorism. To this day, Palestinians live and die in various Arab countries but are never given citizenship other than Palestinian, and that is done by design to keep the pressure on Israel and sustain the so-called refugee problem.

Why did the Muslim world and its media not protest when Saddam Hussein killed fellow Muslims? Why would they cover up for him? Why did they close their eyes to the genocide in Algeria and the Sudan? The reason is simply because if the genocide is done by Muslims, it is ignored or forgiven. But Jews must never kill Muslims, even in self-defense. Sharia laws that were created long before the State of Israel came into existence explain it loud and clear. Is the world that naïve to buy all of that?

The Arab-Israeli war is a religious war against any religion other than Islam that dares rule itself in the Middle East. That is the problem in a nutshell, period. Muslim society's hatred of Jews is simply a reflection of Mohammed's hateful obsession against them. Very few people recognize this. It is embarrassing and sad.

Very few people understand that Mohammed himself issued a fatwa against the Jews in the seventh century, and this is the root of it all. For those who think that Muslim hatred of the Jews only started in 1948 with the creation of Israel, or as a result of the so-called occupation after the 1967 war, I must remind them of the following fatwa. Mohammed said in his hadith: "The

Hour Resurrection will not take place until the Muslims fight the Jews, and kill them. And the Jews will hide behind the rock and tree, and the rock and tree will say: oh Muslim, oh servant of Allah, this is a Jew behind me, come and kill him!"[42]

The world must demand that this hadith be taken out of Muslim scriptures and never be taught again to any Muslim child.

This extreme, hateful obsession against Jews dominates Muslim society, and at the source of this hateful propaganda another propaganda machine must process the guilt. Make no mistake, there are deep feelings of guilt that must be processed so Muslims won't be psychologically destroyed when their religion commands them to kill without mercy.

This is how the process goes to reduce the guilt and impossible pressure to stay faithful to Mohammed's commandment to brutalize, do jihad, terrorize, conquer, and expand Islam around the world: Muslims must become the *victims* of the groups who are the object of their jihad. The same thing was done by Mohammed himself. When the Jews refused his message, they were accused of all kinds of treason, assault, and violations. Using these claims, Mohammed mobilized his men to kill eight hundred Jewish men and take their women and children as slaves. The same tactic still happens today, and it works all the time, not only on Muslim citizens but, unbelievably, also on the international community.

The rewards to Muslims who kill the People of the Book (the Jews and Christians) was clear then inside Arabia. Qur'an 33:26 and 27 says, "He has tossed some People of the Book who had backed them up, out of their strongholds and cast panic into their hearts; one group you killed while you captured another group. He let you inherit their land, their homes, and their property, plus a land you have not yet set foot on."

Today, the purpose is also clear; it is to erase everything Jewish in the land of Israel and Jerusalem and claim everything to Islam. As Muslim children, we were always told that Jerusalem was a

Muslim city taken away by foreigners, the Jews. We believed it. With the creation of Israel, Muslims once again are reminded of Mohammed's shame when Jews found his religion a bad attempt to imitate their religion and replace it. The Banu Qurayza Jewish tribe must be killed again and again.

This is the obsession that drives Muslim society. The Muslim world lives in its own reality, one that is very different from the reality of the outside world. The propaganda of the Arab world resonates well with those who are attracted to conspiracy theories. Being prone to conspiracy theories is very prevalent in the Muslim world. Perhaps 80 percent of Arabs believe that 9/11 was perpetrated by Jews, even after the Arab Street went out to celebrate the event, and even while they hail the Magnificent Nineteen!

Rising above Hatred

Qatari reformist Dr. Abd Al-Hamid Al-Ansari, former dean of the Sharia and law department at Qatar University, has recently published several articles in Gulf papers in which he discusses the baseless excuses for terrorism and how the Arab world ignores and denies the phenomenon of terrorism. He uses the term "split personality" for some people who call terrorists martyrs. He says,

Hatred is a culture of prohibitions, and the result of our viewing the world as an enemy lying in wait for us. Many factors have played a part in shaping this world view, including the religious messages anchored in fears of plots against us, the educational messages that have produced in young people alienation from the modern era, and a great number of publications by the Muslim Brotherhood and by the nationalists, which have, for the past 50 years, spread hatred of the other and conspiracy theories against the Muslims.[43]

And finally, what does a Muslim do if he wants to rise above the hatred?

How did I do it? I didn't want to hate, lie, or perceive the non-Muslim world as my enemies; I did not want to befriend, humiliate, abuse, kill, or defend killers. I left Islam because I felt secure enough in America to dare to leave the culture of hate, the prison of Islam. Without America I could never have done it; I could not have escaped from the claws of Sharia and seen the light. I learned the other side of the story, a story untold in my Muslim society of origin, which enabled me to complete a picture, a picture of people who wanted to remain faithful to Judaism and Christianity and are suffering every day in the Muslim world. I learned truths about them from the Bible, the Old and the New Testaments. And I am grateful.

There is nothing that the impotent sword of Islam can do to change my mind; it can only scare people, kill, and terrorize. That sword is flying high on the flag of the Arabian nation that brought us the culture of stoning, beheading, and amputation of limbs—Saudi Arabia. Sharia's total disregard for human rights continues its quest for total control through fear, terror, and beheading inside and outside Muslim countries. What kind of religion wishes to hold 1.2 billion people hostage? Arabia has achieved the support of one-third of the world to repel any penetration inside the nucleus of Islam, Saudi Arabia. The expansion of Islam surrounding Arabia was necessary padding to fend off the impact of Judaism and Christianity. The doors to escape from Islam are all closed tight by a law that can never be holy. What kind of a so-called religion or ideology kills those who leave it in this day and age? What kind of religion relies on vigilante justice by the man on the street to keep its followers within?

The Ultimate Punishment

Why do not more Muslims break away from the insanity and rise above the hatred, as I and a few others have done? There is good reason: the fear of death, a very real fear. Let's look at the fact of the ultimate punishment in Islamic law. The following are Sharia laws for apostasy:

- Apostates are to be given three days to repent and return to Islam. If s/he refuses, s/he is immediately killed. All Sharia books agree unanimously on this point. (Hanafi law in general, Shafi'i law fl.3, Hanbali law from Al Mughni, Maliki law, and Codified Islamic law).

- It is obligatory for the caliph to ask him to repent and return to Islam. If he does not, it is accepted from him, but if he refuses, he is immediately killed.[44]

- There is no indemnity for killing an apostate (or any expiation, since it is killing someone who deserves to die).[45]

- Testimony of apostates is not admissible.[46]

- An apostate does not inherit from Muslim parents.[47]

- Marriage of an apostate is immediately dissolved if the spouse is and remains Muslim.[48]

According to Sharia, leaving Islam is the ugliest form of unbelief and the worst. It may come about through sarcasm, as when someone is told, "Trim your nails, it is sunna," and he replies, "I would not do it even if it were."[49] Acts that entail leaving Islam are many, but they are mainly the denial of the Qur'an, Allah, the Prophet, or anything which by consensus of Muslims is believed to be part of Islam.[50] Even "denial of any hadith turns a Muslim to a kaffir,"[51] or denial of the existence of angels or jinn.[52]

To be a Muslim is to have a relationship not with Allah but with the Sharia-run State. And to be a loyal member to a Muslim State is like being a member of the Mafia—the similarities are many.

But membership in the Mafia is usually by choice, while membership in the Islamic State is by birth. The majority of Muslims were born into the religion and are not converts. In both organizations, one must obey orders to commit acts of terror or at least do everything to support the killers and even give them glorious names.

The wealth of both the Mafia and the Islamic raiders depend on extortion. In the case of the jihadists, it is from booty from the land of *Dar al-harb* (the non-Muslim house of war). In both, breaking the vows of silence that protect the organization is punishable by death. In the case of Islam, lying is an obligation to protect Islam. It is the same with the Mafia.

And finally, in both, if you choose to leave, you must be killed. Islam is perhaps the only religion on earth today that meets the qualifications of the Mafia, where having a religion is not a personal matter and a relationship with God, but it is a personal relationship with the group; it is a group identity and a contract with the rest of the Muslim world. It is being part of the Muslim ummah. The violation of that involuntary contract is punishable by death. That is what being a Muslim is.

By killing apostates, Islam produces followers and *not* believers.

Minds Closed Shut

A society of oppressed, angry, and blind followers is not the kind of society that can thrive. Blind followers worry more about survival than innovation, discovery, and research. Because Muslims are forbidden from doubt, analysis, and thinking for themselves, discussion among Muslims often deteriorates into insults and name-calling. The angry mind of the Arab Street values retaliation and self-pity more than finding ways to work hard for prosperity. The accumulation of centuries of intolerance to free thinking has resulted in a paralyzed brain and has killed normal initiative and innovation. Because Sharia allows no choices, people accept their destiny without trying to change it, giving in to fatalism. The expression "*In Shaa Allah*," meaning "if Allah wills," is the most commonly used expression by Muslims. Other commonly used expressions that reflect the societal fatalism: *"Maktoub"* — "everything is written," and *"Elquesma"* — "this is my destiny or my share in life." Society becomes fatalistic, static, stagnant, and rigid. Just look at the difference between India and Muslim Pakistan.

While Muslim scholars are busy trying to prove to themselves and the world that all scientific discoveries and innovations were originally in the Qur'an, the Judeo-Christian cultures of the "kaffir" are busy doing the hard work for such scientific discoveries. Only on Arab TV can you find an actual Arab researcher defying scientific axioms by saying such outrageous things as "the earth is flat and much larger than the sun (which is also flat)." That debate actually took place in October 2007 on Al-Fayhaa Arab TV. Fadhel Al-Sa'd, an Iraqi researcher on astronomy, said, "The Qur'anic verse that I have just recited—'The breadth of Paradise is as the breadth of the heavens and earth' attests to the fact that the earth is flat." For him, there was no further discussion since that is what the Qur'an says.

Can anyone even imagine a Madame Curie, a Thomas Edison, the Wright Brothers, or a Sigmund Freud working their experiments in Saudi Arabia, Iran, or even less-oppressive Egypt? Working to find solutions to society's problems cannot happen in a tightly controlled intellectual climate that prohibits questioning. That is why the Egyptian peasant's life has not changed drastically since the time of the pharaohs. Islam has sedated them. The thought processes of a Muslim must come to a halt at every step to first check whether or not such thinking is allowed under Sharia.

There is only one direction that a Muslim's thought process is allowed to venture: *I am right, and you are wrong; I am superior, and you are inferior; Islam and the Arab culture is the only way, and yours is evil and I must do everything I can to change you. You are sinners, and I am a Muslim—the only true religion—and through jihad I must change you; if I die without accomplishing my goal,*

other Muslims behind me will succeed, and I am guaranteed heaven.
That is the only kind of thinking allowed.

Muslim Society's Contributions to the World

Every time I watch the Olympic games, I wonder why the
Muslim nations are hardly represented. I see worldwide talent—
China, South Korea, Japan, both Western and Eastern European
countries, Russia, America. Where are the talents and contributions of the Muslim world and "the religion of peace"? Even in
soccer, which is the number one sport in the Arab world, they
don't even come close to Britain or South America in international competition.

Every time I see the list of countries winning Nobel Prizes, I
wonder, *Where are the Muslims? What are they dreaming about?
What are they aspiring to?* The people they hate the most, the
Jews, are amply represented in all categories of innovation and
talent. Is that what Islam wants—to destroy talent and the people
who are contributing the most to the world? Muslim societies
have not contributed much to humanity, but have actually
destroyed and sucked away the talent and innovation bit by bit
from the nations they conquered. Contrary to conventional wis-
dom, it is not Arab talent that came out of the Middle East, but
the talent of the great civilizations conquered by Arabs and their
swords. Established great civilizations and great religions such as
the Assyrians, the Egyptian Copts, and others have been practi-
cally eradicated. Just look at what happened to Egypt.

Muslim society has been a taker for a long time and not a
giver. All they have given the world are memories of their old glory
days when they took over Spain, Egypt, Persia, Mesopotamia,
and the Ottomans and then called them "Muslim and Arab
contributions to the world." The Arabian Peninsula, obsessed
with preserving their way of life and exporting it to the rest of the
world, must look closely to the sword on their flag and see the
destruction they left behind when they forced Islam and Sharia

on great civilizations, sucked the life out of their brilliance and greatness, and left them in poverty, chaos, and destruction. Just as the desert-raiding tribes of history did to each other, they did and are still doing that to the world.

If it was not for the discovery of oil—even that was discovered and developed by the West—I do not know what the Saudis would have contributed to the world other than terrorism, fanaticism, injustice, and Fascist states under the guise of religion. They hate the infidels and want to kill them, but love the infidels' technology, their dollars, their air conditioners, their cars, and their many gadgets. They love it so much, they have created huge American-style indoor shopping malls with all the American stores; they have used their oil wealth to fabricate tropical islands off their coasts and create indoor Alpine-style ski slopes in the desert, snow and all. Yet they curse the infidel they love to imitate.

The Great Satan in Muslim Closets

Sharia has failed to preserve and protect what the Arabian Peninsula culture feared the most: the corruption of their citizens by outside influences. But what they did not calculate was that the corruption was happening internally due to the horrific repression. After all, there is also a "great Satan" in Muslim closets, but unlike the West, theirs must be hidden. A report on the Arab Internet Web site Al-Arabiya, which was pulled due to readers' outrage, said that fifty incest births have occurred in Saudi Arabia recently. We can only imagine what happened to the girls who were incest raped. There are also reports that homosexuality is on the rise. As to the oppressed Saudi women, it is reported that when they travel abroad, many of them simply do not come back. What Arabia feared the most is now coming back to haunt them with a vengeance.

It is time for them to embrace the rest of humanity and join their fellow man. It is time for a change from inside Saudi Arabia; time for them to use their wealth to help their brethren in times of disaster and need; time to pull their own lower classes out of abject poverty; time to pay proper wages and provide minimal living conditions for foreigners they bring in to build their soaring hotels and office towers; time to take a positive role in undergoing positive change from within and set themselves as an example to the nations and cultures they ruined with their most oppressive form of Islam, the Wahabi sect. It is time for Saudis to wake up and see what they have done to the world around them and take urgent measures to calm the constant Islamic volcanic eruptions instead of condemning the world to permanent war, terror, and suffering. They must acknowledge the elements of Islam and its Sharia that defy universally accepted norms of human rights; time to put an end to denial and obfuscation. Saudi Arabia, the time is now.

Six

A Dictator's Dream

A COMMON VIEW AMONG MANY ARABS IS THAT WESTERN governments back Arab dictatorships, and that is the main cause of their oppression. It is the British and the French occupation or America's foreign policy's fault that we have dictatorships, the complaint goes, even among the most educated Arabs on U.S. college campuses. Such views have even managed to convince some Americans that Arabs having undergone a colonialist period or that U. S. foreign policy is the problem.

The premise that the brief historical period of colonialism or America's working relationship with the Saudi or Egypt governments is behind the existence of Arab dictatorships is faulty. What about Syria and Libya? America does not support them and actually treats them as a threat to world peace, yet both countries are long-time dictatorships. Claims that America for some "evil" reason wants Arab dictatorships to stay in power persist even after America took out Saddam Hussein, the most oppressive dictator of the bunch. You would think that those who blamed America for backing dictatorships would kiss America's hand for taking out a horrific dictator who was a threat not only to his citizens but to other surrounding Muslim countries as well. Saddam Hussein's army actually raped many Kuwaiti women, following in the tradition of the old seventh-century Muslim battles. But the people who blamed America for backing dictatorships still want to blame America. They simply turned their anger at America for "backing dictators," to anger at America for daring to interfere in the internal affairs of Arab countries and take out a dictator, even if he was a butcher like Saddam.

The perpetually enraged Arab Street does not really know what it wants, but it will remain offended at the West whether Western countries work with Arab dictators or take them out.

Arab media claimed they wanted the well-being of the Iraqi people, but covered up Saddam's atrocities and kept the Arab Street unaware of what was happening to the Iraqi people for decades. However, when America liberated Iraqis from their tyrant, instead of doing everything they could to make the transition to a freer society easier, the Arab Street and media were cheering for the terrorists who mostly came from surrounding Arab countries to blow themselves up along with a lot of Iraqi citizens. They are more concerned with causing America's mission of bringing peace, unity, and democracy to Iraq to fail.

The whole premise of Arab claims doesn't make sense to the West and is fraudulent. But the last thing Arabs want to see is freedom and democracy planted in the Arab world by an "infidel" superpower. That is why everything is being done to make Iraq an impossible mission for the West. Do Muslims want or do they *not* want their dictatorships? When it comes to the Arab world, nothing seems to make sense.

Let us examine what is really behind Arab and Muslim dictatorships. What is the nature of the Sharia-ruled Islamic State, the Caliphate? And what is the role of the Islamic leader, the caliph?

I give you the words of Sheikh Maulana Maududi, one of Islam's eminent scholars:

"A state of this sort cannot evidently restrict the scope of its activities. Its approach is universal and all-embracing. Its sphere of activity is coextensive with the whole of human life. It seeks to mould every aspect of life and activity in consonance with its moral norms and program of social reform. In such a state no one can regard any field of his affairs as personal and private. Considered from this aspect the Islamic State bears a kind of resemblance to the Fascist and Communist states."[1]

Maulana Maududi's comparison of the Islamic State with Fascism and Communism was not meant as a negative and was not disputed by other Muslim scholars as an unfair comparison. In fact, Sheikh Maududi was making an accurate description of the Islamic State in his book *Islamic Law and Constitution*.

The Prophet Mohammed was not only a prophet but also head of state, which he became after he moved to Medina. His example as a leader became the model for Muslim leaders who followed him, called *khalifa* (in English, caliph), meaning a Muslim head of state, but the word in Arabic literally means "one who replaces someone else who left or died." The Muslim caliph is the successor (in a line of successors) to Prophet Mohammed's position as the political, military, and administrative leader of the Muslims, but not in Mohammed's prophetic role. According to Islam, Mohammed is the last of the prophets.

A Muslim State must be ruled by a caliph, and the establishment and continuation of the Islamic Caliphate (by force, if necessary) is a *fard kifaya*, meaning a "communal obligation" of the Muslim *ummah* (nation). In that system, the Muslim head of state, the caliph, is the representative of Allah in order to execute his laws.

Qur'an 2:30 says, "Behold, thy Lord said to the angels: 'I will create a vicegerent (a Khalifa) on earth.' They said: 'Wilt Thou place therein one who will make mischief therein and shed blood? whilst we do celebrate Thy praises and glorify Thy holy (name)?' He said: 'I know what ye know not.'"[2]

According to the above verse, Allah calmed the fears of the angels who were worried about abuse of power by Allah's representative on earth, who might cause mischief and shed blood. The caliph has been entrusted as Allah's representative on earth to implement the laws of Allah. The caliph's role has thus become divine in order for Sharia to be implemented.

Mohammed died without naming a successor, and that was the start of a long period of bloodshed, assassinations, revolutions, and counterrevolutions among Muslims over who would succeed him as the caliph of Islam. Like the last ten years of Mohammed's life, the period of the caliphs that followed was anything but peaceful but on a much larger scale. Perhaps the fears of the angels in Quran 2:30 came true. Sharia also defined how a caliph should come to power and how to legally rule the Islamic State. The use of force is one of the three ways for a Muslim caliph to come to power:

According to Shafi'i Law o.25.4, a caliphate may be legally effected:

1) by oath of fealty (being chosen or selected);

2) by the caliph appointing a successor; or

3) through seizure of power by an individual possessing the qualifications of a caliph. Thus a takeover (by force) is also legally valid by someone with moral rectitude or knowledge of Sacred Law.

Thus, under Sharia, the three ways of choosing the caliph are by selection, by nomination, and *by force*. Is it any wonder that the majority of Muslim leaders today, as well as historically, come to power after a coup d'etat or an assassination? And is it any wonder that all Muslim leaders are constantly under the threat of an assassination or a coup d'etat?

I was a citizen of a Muslim country for thirty years and never voted or even understood what voting was at the time. I also noticed that it matters little to a Muslim leader if he assumes power through peaceful means, like inheriting it through his father, or by revolution—the two most common means of assuming power in the Muslim world. It also matters little to Muslim citizens themselves if their leader came to power through revolution, coup d'etat, or by assassinating the prior leader. All is forgotten by the ordinary Muslim citizens, who are told to celebrate the new leader. And amazingly they do.

In fact, sometimes acquiring power through revolution makes a Muslim leader even more popular in the eyes of his subjects who are trained to admire such a gutsy act. His revolt becomes their revolt. That was the situation with President Gamal Abdel Nasser of Egypt who, together with a number of military officers, seized power in a coup, which they later glorified as a necessary revolution for the sake of Egyptian freedom and Pan-Arabism. It also mattered little that such a revolution brought in a one-party tyrannical dictatorship replacing a more democratic multi-party parliamentary kingdom. No one in the Egyptian media ever dared to make a comparison between the two systems to inform the public what they got for their glorious revolution—nothing but more poverty, food shortages, and defeat after defeat in unnecessary wars with Israel. The same kind of military dictatorship is still controlling Egypt today. Since 1952 Egypt has had only three leaders.

Absolute Power Corrupts Absolutely

Muslim leaders also follow the example of Mohammed himself who was in many ways above the law. Qur'an 33:36 reads: "And it becometh not a believing man or a believing woman, when Allah and his messenger have decided an affair (for them), that they should (after that) claim any say in their affair; and whoso is rebellious to Allah and his messenger, he verily go astray in error manifest." Obeying Allah alone was not sufficient. According to this verse, Muslims have no right to decide and must completely surrender brainlessly—like sheep—to Mohammed. This verse also confirms that independent thinking is not allowed in Islam.

No other religion makes such a demand of its followers. Consider this hadith: "I heard Allah's Apostle saying, 'He who obeys me, obeys Allah, and he who disobeys me, disobeys Allah.'"[3]

Sharia law, very generous to the Muslim male in general, is even more generous to the caliph. Sharia law protects the Muslim head of state from being charged with Hudud crimes (the most serious under Sharia): "Head of Islamic State cannot be charged with Hudud crimes (Murder, adultery, robbery, theft, drinking and in some cases of Rape)."[4]

Exemption of the Muslim head of state from serious crimes can explain the actions of the likes of Saddam Hussein and others who got away with genocide, rape, murder, theft, and plunder of wealth—both of their own country's as well as others'. Muslim leaders have been corrupted by such exemptions from the barbaric Sharia laws they must enforce. Is it any wonder that not one Arab or Muslim country wants to see democracy succeed in Iraq? Democracy, which cannot exist under Sharia, will not only expose them all but also expose Sharia itself.

That is not all. Following the example set by Mohammed, critics of Mohammed, the Qur'an, and the Sharia must be killed. Sharia has made rebellion against the caliph an enormous sin, even if the ruler is unjust: Ibn Hajar Haytami's "List of Enormities" includes: "Rebellion against the caliph, even if he is unjust, where there is no mitigating pretext or one that is patently false, or betraying one's fealty to him because of some worldly disadvantage in remaining loyal."[5] And under Sharia law o25.5: "It is obligatory to obey the commands and interdictions of the caliph, even if he is unjust."

Some Muslim jurists even go as far as saying that it is better to support a Muslim unjust ruler than supporting a non-Muslim just ruler. In his book *A Short History of the Revivalist Movement in Islam*, Mawlana Mawdudi writes: "The moral condition of the religious leaders of those days can be gauged from the fact that when Halaku Khan asked for their verdict as to who was superior between an unbelieving just king and a believing unjust ruler, they pronounced unhesitatingly in favor of the Former."[6]

This is a recipe for disaster. It has resulted in tyranny, chaos, and internal and external genocide throughout fourteen hundred years of Islamic history. "Allah's Laws," which were created under the caliph one hundred years after Mohammed died, gave Islam the muscle and the backbone to create a totalitarian state, where the laws became the guaranteed protectors of the caliph.

Jihad, the Duty of Caliphs

Sharia also defines the main duties and responsibilities of the caliph. The following are three among many of the caliph's responsibilities:

1) To safeguard Islam in its original form, and to protect against the introduction of new things (*bid'a*) into Islam.

2) To defend the rights of Muslims abroad, and to see to it that Islam can spread freely in non-Muslim lands (including the use of force).

3) To organize jihad against any non-Muslim government that prevents Muslim *dawa* (proselytizers) from entering its land.[7]

Jihad is not just the duty of the individual Muslim but also the duty of the Muslim head of state and the Muslim State itself. Numbers 2 and 3 entrust the caliph to take his people into war and command offensive and aggressive jihad. Muhammad Zia-ul-Haq (1924–88), the former president of Pakistan and Pakistani army chief of staff, said that jihad in terms of warfare is a collective responsibility of the Muslim ummah and that it is not just a personal duty of individuals.

According to Shafi'i law o9.8: "The Caliph makes war upon Jews, Christians and Zoroastrians until they become Muslim or else pay the non-Muslim poll tax provided he has first invited them to enter Islam or pay *Jizya*, the non-Muslim poll tax, (in accordance with the word of Allah Most High Chapter 9 verse 29)."

The Muslim caliph must promote the jihad Muslim military institution that encourages the plundering and looting of the lands of non-believers, also according to law o25.9 (8): "(When the caliph appoints a ruler on a region, his duty includes) if the area has a border adjacent to enemy lands, (he will) undertake jihad against enemies, dividing the spoils of battle among combatants and setting aside a fifth for deserving recipients." Mohammed himself lured Muslims with promises of booty from jihad: "Mohammed promised that we would enjoy the treasures of the Persians and Romans."[8]

Just vs. Unjust

Some Muslim apologists tell the West that jihad is only for just causes, but they don't explain what a "just" cause means in Islam. It is injustice if non-Muslims do not allow *dawa* (proselytizing) in their countries. However, the reverse is forbidden under Islamic Sharia; Muslims prevent kuffar from proselytizing in Muslim land. To proselytize in Muslim countries is a major crime that goes against the first duty of the caliph, which is to safeguard Islam from any change or new ideas. "The Prophet said that anyone who tries to disrupt the unity of the Muslims should be killed by the sword."[9]

The bottom line: the concept of justice and injustice to Muslims is very different from the Western perception. Under Sharia, there are two different sets of justice—one for Muslims and one for non-Muslims. To Muslims, it is always a "just" war if the end goal is to spread Islam. If the war is waged by non-Muslims to stop Muslims from marching in to spread Islam inside their land, it is an "unjust" war. The Egyptian religious scholar and jurist Mohammed Abduh

(1849–1905) published an article in 1903 evaluating Islam's early military campaigns and determined that Islam's early neighbors "prevented the proclamation of truth" engendering the defense of Islam. "Our religion is not like others that defend themselves . . . but our defense of our religion is the proclamation of truth and the removal of distortion and misrepresentation of it."[10]

Many Muslims call for *dawa* in the West, which technically means "an invitation to Islam." They present it as a peaceful invitation, but they do not tell the West that this is the first step before outright war if their *dawa* is rejected. So when Muslims say *dawa*, the West should be warned, because what they do not want you to know is that *dawa* is merely the "make nice" first step preceding outright jihad, according to Sharia. Muslims who believe in *dawa* also believe in the totality of Sharia and demand it even in the West.

To many Muslims, the words *peace, tyranny*, and *oppression* are also very different from the West's perceptions. Peace will come only when everyone accepts Islam; otherwise Muslims must be in a permanent state of war and unrest. To Muslims, the terms *tyranny* and *oppression* describe Muslims who live in a pluralistic society under a kaffir government that equates Islam with other religions, thereby depriving Muslims of the superior status given to them by Sharia. It is not uncommon for Islamists to carry signs in London or New York telling the West it is the British or American constitutions that are tyrannical because it does not give them all the advantages over non-Muslims and women that they have under Sharia.

Thus the good Muslim leader must go to war against non-Muslim countries if they do not allow him to freely proselytize, forcing others to convert to Islam or pay the *jizya*. According to Sharia, Muslims must have total access to proselytize in non-Muslim nations, but they will not allow equal access to non-Muslim countries. Non-Muslim countries that refuse these conditions will suffer from organized jihad. On that basis and under that logic, no nation is sovereign enough to reject Islam. Sovereignty is only given to *Dar al-Islam* (house of Islam), which must never be desecrated by the existence of non-Muslims. Do you see the logic?

Bottom line, the Muslim head of state must wage and/or allow jihad against non-Muslim nations in order to facilitate Arab and Muslim imperialism. This is not a secret; it is in Muslim scriptures. As Mawdudi notes, "Islamic jihad is both offensive and defensive."[11]

This principle of Sharia is clear in today's Muslim relationships with any non-Muslim countries even with superpowers such as the United States. Arab governments have access to proselytize, build mosques, finance Islamic Studies and Middle East Studies departments on American college campuses, but they criminalize the reverse. Non-Muslims who proselytize in Muslim countries are arrested, jailed, or killed. Not one university in any Muslim country today has a Christian Studies or Judaism Studies department; only Islam is taught. Most Americans do not comprehend that this is a one-sided access relationship.

State-Sponsored Terrorism

Many Muslims deny that suicide missions are allowed in Islam. It is true that Islam, like many other religions, forbids committing suicide out of (personal) desperation, but the Qur'an orders Muslims to kill and get killed in jihad. "They fight for God's sake; they kill and are killed as a rightful promise from Him."[12] In fact, the Qur'an is replete with such horrifically inciting dictums. It is full of orders to kill the kuffar (enemies of Allah and his messenger) and promised dreadful punishment in hellfire for those who refuse to kill kuffar.

One of the enormities (major sin) in Sharia is: "Fleeing from combat with unbelievers, unless one is falling back to regroup or separating to join another unit to reinforce them."[13]

The Muslim State is in a permanent state of war with non-Muslims who refuse to accept Islam. According to Qur'an 60:4,

"And there hath arisen between us and you hostility and hate for ever until ye believe in Allah only." Thus, Islam is at perpetual war with the non-Islamic world. According to leading Islamic authority, Majid Khaddur (1909–2007), "Jihad is a doctrine of a permanent state of war, not continuous fighting."[14] Muslim schools in Egypt taught jihad as a permanent war institution against non-Muslims, period.

In time of military weakness, Muslim states often refrain from going into actual war and instead choose state-sponsored terrorism as an alternative, which in fact has become the preferred form of jihad. This is the form of jihad going on today with some Muslim states masking their involvement and financing of terrorism.

The treasuries of the Muslim states throughout history have been dependent on wealth from jihad battles. Even Mohammed, the first head of the Muslim State, admitted he was made wealthy from terror: "The Prophet said, 'I have been awarded victory by terror, so the treasures of the earth are mine.'"[15]

Both Mohammed and the caliphs that succeeded him filled their treasury with money and wealth taken from jizya and ransom in jihad wars. "Allah's Apostle said, 'I have been made victorious with terror. While I was sleeping, the keys of the treasures of the world were brought to me and put in my hand.' Allah's Apostle has left the world and now we are bringing out those treasures."[16]

The followers of Mohammed are still reaping the treasures acquired through terror.

However, the majority of today's Muslims are in denial, especially after 9/11. Today's jihadists cannot be as honest about their intentions as jihadists were fourteen hundred years ago or even just a few decades ago when jihad was their pride and joy. I sometimes receive e-mails from Muslims who insist that dying in jihad "is our pride" and that "the most glorious word in the vocabulary of Islam is *jihad*." In today's world of international law and human rights, things such as violent jihad, extortion of war spoils, jizya money for protection, and giving "temporary peace" in exchange for ransom, are major international crimes similar to the barbaric actions of mafia gangs and lawless pirates. These are acts that the whole world has defined a long time ago as against international law. But committed jihadists and Islamists do not seem to get the message.

Barbaric laws, which until very recently were considered normal, are now suddenly putting the so-called Muslim moderates to shame, but they do not know what to do with their jihad and Sharia. They try to redefine jihad as an inner struggle and something peaceful, but by doing so they become deceptive. Violent jihad has become their dirty little secret that they can neither explain away nor get rid of.

After 9/11, the mask of Islamic jihad has been lifted and the ordinary Westerner has been rudely awakened. For the first time, many people are trying to understand this thing called jihad. They are trying to see just what is in this Qur'an that is the motivation behind such terrorism. They are shocked and in disbelief at a religion that orders their followers to engage in piracy and mafia tactics against those who refuse to join them.

The politically correct Western kuffar are often even embarrassed for Muslims and don't discuss their worries of Muslim demands for Sharia in the West lest they offend the highly offendable Muslim community. But that is what many Muslims are counting on.

How did such religious laws govern one-third of the world for fourteen hundred years without being exposed for what they are? They're merely a scam to suck the world's wealth just as the proud Arabian Bedouin heroes—terrorists by today's standards—plundered, looted, and robbed the wealth of the other tribes while committing the most heinous human atrocities in the process, beheading men and raping and enslaving women.

To resolve the fourteen-hundred-year-old Sharia fraud, a small number of Muslims, mostly in the West, have chosen to leave

Islam very quietly, myself included. But the vast majority of Muslims are still locked in the mental prison and believe in their own peaceful illusionary vision of Islam, which never existed in Muslim texts or the actual history of Islam.

The Hazards of Governing and Being Governed

With all the Muslim laws protecting the Muslim leader, he is still among the most vulnerable and insecure leaders in the world, constantly prone to backstabbing, assassinations, and coup d'etats. Sharia's requirement that Muslims must tolerate even an unjust Muslim leader does not produce happy citizens. Muslim Sharia could care less about an individual's right for life, liberty, and the pursuit of happiness. As a matter of fact, such Western-style rights are condemned and discouraged in the Muslim State. That causes a lot of built-up anger and repressed hostility inside the Muslim population. Ironically, jihad itself counts on that anger to fulfill its mission. Many Muslim institutions are built around the existence and promotion of Muslim anger. The anger resulting from cruel and dysfunctional Sharia must be channeled toward the outside world through jihad. Without anger there could be no jihad. The clever Muslim leader is the one who keeps the anger in proportion with jihadist activities.

But he must be very careful. Muslim countries that do not promote jihad are vulnerable to the anger turning inward. If a Muslim leader in today's world abandons jihad, he is confronted with one of the angriest populations on earth, a population that will become a major threat to the Muslim State and its leader. That is why the Arab Street is ungovernable if the outlet of jihad is taken away, while at the same time Sharia laws remain intact. Sharia's inhumane laws must be coupled with jihad if the pressure cooker of the Muslim State is not to explode in the face of Muslims themselves.

Thus, the reasonable Muslim leader, after 9/11, found himself in a terrible quagmire, since under Sharia one of his duties is both offensive and defensive jihad. When they face the international community, they condemn violent jihad and terrorism, counting on the West's ignorance and naïveté.

But when leaders face their own people, they cannot deny it or declare jihad illegal. What the West considers aggressive jihad—such as 9/11, the Madrid and London bombings, and the Russian school massacre—are viewed by Islamists and even many ordinary Muslims as defensive acts. A huge number of Muslims have been indoctrinated to believe they are victims regardless of the situation, therefore offensive terrorist jihad is justified. The thinking is: "We are entitled to it because we are victims." In such a situation, the Muslim leader cannot condemn even 9/11 as an act of Islamic terrorism. So he resorts to denial, blames the Jews for it, or engages in double-talk. Thus we often see the Muslim leader stand before Western cameras and condemn violent jihad and terrorism, but as soon as he confronts his citizens, he speaks about his pride in his jihadists.

A Muslim leader, who cracks down hard on jihadists and terror groups and refuses to support them even "discretely," will be considered in violation of his basic duties of jihad under Sharia, at least in the eyes of Islamists. That is the reason why reasonable Muslim rulers like Musharraf of Pakistan and Mubarak of Egypt are trying to "hold the stick from the middle" (to quote an old Arab expression), trying to please both the West and their Islamist war mongers. The one thing they do not want is to be perceived is being anti-Islam.

But moderate or not, Muslim leaders also understand that their power and bargaining position with the West is enhanced by Islamic terrorism even if they have nothing to do with it. They must always hold the stick from the middle, for both their own safety and power. No Muslim leader wants to be perceived as a kaffir who supports the West. Let us examine what happens to such Muslim leaders.

According to Sharia, there is only one exception to the obligation of a Muslim citizen to obey the caliph, even if he is unjust,
and that is if the caliph is a kaffir: ". . . unless the ruler has Kufr
(disbelief)."[17] That means that Sharia lifts its protection over the
Muslim ruler if he becomes kaffir or a disbeliever in Islam. Thus
citizens are no longer required to obey him, and he must be
toppled and/or assassinated. Many Muslim leaders have been
named kaffir simply for respecting and cooperating with the
West on equal footing. Signing a peace treaty and ending hos-
tilities with Israel will certainly do it for any Arab leader. That is
exactly what happened to President Anwar Sadat of Egypt after
he signed the peace treaty with Israel. Some people close to
Sadat said that when he signed the treaty with Israel, he was signing his death warrant. They were right. In the eyes of Islamists
he became a kaffir, a leader who should no longer be obeyed
and must be killed.

The Uses of Terror

It is true that 9/11 was primarily intended to "strike terror in
the hearts of the unbelievers" and earn "respect" (fear) in the
minds of Islam's enemies. However, 9/11 was also aimed at
teaching a lesson to Muslim leaders who are often accused of
becoming allies of the West and the United States, which is
considered to be an abandonment of their jihad duty. Such leaders "profess the faith but are treacherous in their hearts." Osama
bin Laden regularly issues death threats to Arab leaders for their
"complicity" with the West, and that makes him very popular on
the Arab Street.

Tyranny in the Muslim world not only flows from the top to
the bottom, but also often comes from the bottom up. Many
Muslim preachers and Islamists have no respect for the legitimacy of any government that is not based totally on Sharia, and
no constitution is ever Muslim enough for them. In this dynamic,
only tyrannical governments can survive. Muslim leaders who

want to promote some level of democracy, civility with the West, peace with Israel, and an open society while at the same time stand up to Islamists and terror groups are branded sellouts to the West. They are called traitors and thus have no protection from an assassination.

Underground Islamist groups exist in almost all Muslim countries even in countries like Saudi Arabia that follow full Sharia. Sharia by its nature is very hard to follow 100 percent, and because of that, underground Islamist groups cause constant turmoil and instability even to the most conservative Muslim State. Such groups sometimes go dormant as the Muslim Brotherhood did under Nasser, only to come back later with a vengeance, which is the case in Egypt now.

Islamist Sharia-enforcer groups do not see the reason for Sharia's failure as intrinsic or that it is inhumane, cruel, barbaric, or against human nature. Since they were trained to never doubt or question, they blame the many dysfunctional aspects of Muslim society on other factors but never on Sharia itself.

Many blame the failure of Sharia on the evil Muslim dictators. I was once told exactly that by the head of a Muslim student organization right here in America. They often express the wistful belief that perhaps in America they can accomplish their ideal Muslim State. You see, the restless Islamist is always looking outward to solve problems and never inward—and certainly never in their scriptures. They believe in the great rewards by Allah awaiting those who spread Sharia across the globe in yet another attempt to accomplish their perfect peaceful and harmonious caliphate.

Muslims are often unhappy with their Muslim countries of origin, but instead of looking within to make them better, they want to force an "ideal" Muslim State on other civilizations, especially those that are unsuspecting and peaceful. That being a commandment from Allah is mixed with their greedy desire to take over other people's accomplishments. Greed blinds their logic. They want to take over a ready-made civilization and claim it for themselves and Islam. Sharia gives them permission to do so, setting them supreme above all those they robbed. There certainly is a lot of booty and spoils of war in America; it is the ultimate prize for the Islamist mafia.

Many Arabs, even the so-called moderates, perceive all Arab leaders as traitors who are pandering to the West at the expense of their Islamic duty. They don't want to consider that perhaps there is something wrong in their leaders' divine Sharia inheritance, and they refuse to consider the impossible situation Muslim leaders are faced with. I am personally not a fan of Arab dictators, but I believe that they are the best you can get under Sharia. You get the leaders you deserve, and what your culture produces.

Former chairman of the Islamic Center in Los Angeles, Dr. Maher Hathout, an Egyptian-born former cardiologist regarded by some as a moderate Muslim, gave a speech at an MPAC Jerusalem Day Rally in Washington DC on October 28, 2000.

In his speech, Hathout sounded more like the typical Muslim imam giving an angry and condemning Friday *khutbah* (sermon). He urged the assembled Muslim demonstrators "to take your message to the streets of America." Then he said: "We are not here to talk about the dynamics in the Middle East, particularly after the two summits of shame that exposed completely the Arab and most of the Muslim governments. . . . What we must tell them is 'you are answerable to your people, you are a shame on the face of our nation the Muslim Nation, and you will be flushed down in the cesspool of the history of treason.' . . .We are awaiting for them a general intifada that will get rid of them and restore to the ummah its dignity."[18]

Mr. Hathout was calling for "a general intifada," a revolution, against Arab and most Muslim leaders who failed the ummah (the Muslim State). More radical Muslim preachers in the West have preached: "We will take over U.K., we will take over U.S.A., and we will take over Egypt" (accusing the Egyptian president of being an infidel leader). Even an educated Muslim cardiologist believes that the problem with the Muslim world lies with their tyrannical leaders without questioning the premise of the ideology behind the institution of the ummah.

I must admit that I do not understand how a Muslim scholar can read the Qur'an, Hadith, and Sunnah of the life of Mohammed and emerge with such denial of the failed fourteen-hundred-year history of Sharia, a history that brought down great civilizations such as Persia and Egypt and replaced it with misery, poverty, stagnation, terror, and turmoil. To them it is never the fault of Sharia or Islam, but the inability of Muslim leaders to bring us the heaven of the Muslim Sharia state that never existed in the first place.

Muslims today blame Muslim leaders but still demand to live under Sharia and refuse to see the connection. When Sharia laws were written in the early days of Islam, every greedy desire of a dictator was met and fulfilled through an Islamic law that gave his totalitarian rule legitimacy and stability. With Islam's tools of Sharia, the Muslim leader can now rule with an iron fist over subdued people, submissive warriors, who are made to believe heaven is better than this life. Muslim leaders today not only must abide by Sharia's harsh laws but cannot be blamed for them either. They would be correct to say, "I did not create them; Allah did," according to those who wrote the Sharia.

Sharia, even if partially applied, can only produce tyranny and dictatorships. Sharia is more than a dictator-friendly law. It is a dictator's dream handed to him by Allah. One of the reasons Islam spread and was adopted so quickly is because it provided the ideal equation for a dictatorship to function under, where everyone must obey or be killed. I do not believe that lands conquered by Arabs in its first century are totally innocent—their rulers found something valuable in the new "religion"—a quick solution to disobedient citizens who threatened them. Islamic Sharia gave them the perfect solution to many of their troubles. It also transferred culpability. They could say, "Tyranny is not my fault; it is Allah's wish." Best of all, Islam's divine laws legitimized taking

over the property of others. Arab Imperialism through the sword
has become the right of every Muslim dictator since. Mohammed
himself regularly raided caravans and made war for profit. His
actions were taught as something admirable and a badge of honor
in Muslim schoolbooks; it was all done for the sake of Allah.

Merging War, Religion, and State

Mohammed created the "nucleus" for the power of Islam—
waging war. When Mohammed started preaching his message
in Mecca, he gained only about one hundred followers in a
period of thirteen years, a relatively peaceful period that did not
include violent battles. But when he migrated to Medina, in just
a ten-year period, Mohammed conducted seventy-four raids or
full-scale wars between 622 CE until his death in 632 CE.
During that violent period, Mohammed became extremely powerful and wealthy and was able to unite the Arabian Peninsula
for the first time in its history. Through violent jihad, Mohammed
accomplished the establishment of Islam and gained thousands
under his command.

Mohammed perfected a formula for totalitarian rule, one that
has lasted for fourteen hundred years after his death. Islam made
its top priority the running of the state under an elaborate legal
system. Sharia became Islam and Islam became the state and the
state became Sharia. Where is the religion in all of this? Only
Allah knows.

What imperialist tyrants across history could have only dreamed
of was accomplished by bedouins of the Arabian Peninsula when
they merged religion with the running of the state, thus turning
everything the state does into a Divine Law from Allah. With a
sword in one hand and a holy book in another, they marched to
spread their get-rich-quick formula for wealth and power. The formula had little to do with religion and everything to do with taking
over the wealth of the conquered. They needed to feed the poor,
rugged desert tribes with the plentiful wealth of the Egyptians, the

Persians, the Assyrians, and others. Any Muslim leader who abandons the continuing march of that jihad would be doomed, even today. The oppression, cruelty, brutality, and barbarity were all a means to an end and "blessed by Allah." An Arabian Peninsula warring culture that excelled in little other than poetry, used the rhythmic, hypnotic, but contradictory book that no one around them really understood because the civilizations they conquered did not speak any Arabic at that time.

The cutthroat desert environment produced men who understood what makes people surrender and submit in desperation. They understood the dark side of human psyche and how to manipulate and enslave it, because they had been doing it to each other for generations and their physical environment had been doing it to them for a longer time. But soon they discovered that Mohammed did not give them enough power to rule with the authority he did; he was a prophet, and they did not have the "divine power" he had. They had to act quickly to secure the legal power to be and act as Mohammed did. Mohammed's life and actions had to be codified in law as the perfect example for a Muslim ruler. The early caliphs gave Islam the arms, legs, and backbone through a code called Sharia, which protected the Arabian culture and declared it superior to any other culture they conquered. If Mohammed exempted himself from laws, they, too, were exempted. But as we detailed in chapter 1, the early caliphs first instructed the imams to write the laws of Sharia, and then quickly discarded the scholars after they gave them absolute rule. Now Muslim caliphs can exercise their nearly absolute power, and even if they are "unjust" they must be accepted—because it is written.

Under Sharia, new dictatorial laws and fatwas are popping out every day to crack down further on any attempts for change or demands for freedoms, especially of other religions. Recently in Malaysia, a fatwa was issued banning Christians from using "Islam-related words," such as "God," "prayers," and "house of

God," in the Malaysian language because they are considered words used in reference to Islam only. The Malaysian government also restricted the circulation of Christian publications and banned evangelical Christian programs on TV. Foreigners are put on trial and punished by jail time and flogging for crimes such as sitting on the Qur'an by accident or naming a teddy bear Mohammed.

The laws against non-Muslims go beyond those created by the original Sharia, as Sharia continues to "renovate" itself. For example, in Saudi Arabia, a fatwa was issued recently banning women from surfing the Internet without a male family companion. Sharia's additions and "renovations" are never done to make the laws more human friendly, but always more cruel. The endless dictatorial arrogance of Muslim Sharia enforcers has no end.

Both Muslim leadership and Sharia itself close their eyes to vigilante crimes if and when it is in the interest of Sharia and the empowerment of the Islamic State. So if a parent kills a son who left Islam and converts to Christianity, the parent's crime is ignored. If terrorizing neighboring non-Muslim countries (like Israel) helps pacify and distract Muslim citizens from endangering the dictatorship under which they live, then terrorism is an obligation.

Some Muslim leaders do not even try to mask their jihadist ambitions. Ahmadinejad wants to conquer the top of the mountains to Islam. Sheikh Qaradawi and many other Muslim leaders have declared they want to conquer Rome, Western Europe, and America. Note that they are fixated on wealthy Western nations more than other less-wealthy and sophisticated nations. One Muslim expert told me that early Muslims were more interested in conquering Europe than Africa for the wealth and the white slave women.

To the likes of Ahmadinejad and other jihadist Muslim leaders, the following scripture is their example: "The Prophet said, 'Khosrau will be ruined. There won't be a Persian King after him.

Caesar will be ruined. There will be no Caesar after him. You will spend their treasures in Allah's Cause.' He proclaimed, 'War is deceit.'"[19] Even Allah shared Mohammed's spoils of war after every battle. "Spoils of war are for Allah and Mohammed."[20] "One-fifth of booty belongs to Allah."[21]

Considering the above, it is not unreasonable to ask: Is Islam a religion or a state?

Is Islam a Religion?

I appreciate Maududi's honest evaluation in equating the Islamic State with Fascist and Communist states. I would like to stress one major element of resemblance with the Communist state: like Communism, Islam is against religion. Islam is terrified of Christianity and Judaism and wants to mask the eyes of Muslims from ever seeing them or their holy books, and in that they have actually succeeded.

When I was a Muslim in Egypt, even though we had a large Christian minority, we never really knew what or whom they were worshiping; we never saw Bibles anywhere. Islam has so little confidence in itself that when it comes to Christianity and Judaism, it wants them eliminated from the face of the earth and does not even try to make a secret of it. Just read the Qur'an.

Mohammed began his life as a prophet trying to establish a new religion that would fit his Arabian world better but still linked to the Abrahamic faiths surrounding him. However, after thirteen years of failure in Mecca, his message changed from religion to power when Mohammed installed himself as a political head of state who used brutal and violent jihad to achieve his goals of expansion. While concentrating on jihad and submission, the concepts of love, trust, and compassion were neglected. The word *love* is never mentioned, not even once, in the Quran. When Jews and Christians did not willingly follow him, Mohammed abandoned every moral standard of religion to pursue them and eliminate them from existence. Toward the end of his life, he even declared a whole group of people as illegal to live—the Jews. His message turned into a violent obsession to eliminate non-Muslims. At that point, such violent messages abrogated any previous tolerance he taught. Religions and people who did not yield to his authority became Islam's number one enemy. That is when Islam turned from a religion into a political system, one that kept Muslims inside the prison of Islam under penalty of death.

The ruler who embraced Islam was given a gift of the most potent and all-embracing tool and formula of control imaginable. That totalitarian political formula had to remain under its original name "religion" in order to remain credible and enforceable in a seventh-century world that only understood the power of religion.

Statistics on Muslim scriptures have been brilliantly compiled by Bill Warner, the director of the Center for the Study of Political Islam. His survey revealed that at least 75 percent of the Sunnah (life of Mohammed) is about jihad. About 67 percent of the Qur'an written in Mecca is about the unbelievers or politics. Of the Qur'an of Medina, 51 percent is devoted to the unbelievers. About 20 percent of Bukhari's Hadith is about jihad and politics. Among those in Bukhari, 97 percent of the jihad references are about war, and 3 percent are about the inner struggle. Religion is the smallest part of Islamic foundational texts. According to Warner, even hell is political. There are 146 references to hell in the Qur'an. Only 6 percent of those in hell are there for moral failings, such as murder or theft. The other 94 percent in hell are for the intellectual sin of disagreeing with Mohammed, a political crime. Hence, Islamic hell is a political prison for those who speak against Islam.[22]

Yes, there is a minor part of Islam that is indeed religion, which consists of what a Muslim does to avoid hell and go to Paradise, described as Islam's Five Pillars—prayer, charity to Muslims, pilgrimage to Mecca, fasting, and declaring Mohammed to be the final prophet. Those who confine their observance to the Five Pillars become what the West calls "moderate" Muslims. Many Muslims, including many of my relatives, fall into that category; they practice the ritualistic side of Islam and barely know what is in their scriptures. But what a Muslim says in his prayers and time of prayers is not a choice for a Muslim who must recite what is ordered at the specified times. The Five Pillars of Islam by themselves cannot sustain themselves in the market of religious ideas. That was discovered early on by those who inherited Islam from Mohammed and saw mass defections. That is why they had to create Sharia, but what they created was a political and legal system of totalitarian control.

The most glaring evidence that Islam is hardly "religion" is in its apostasy law—the order to kill those who leave it. That immediately moved Islam from the realm of religion to the realm of totalitarian political ideology. One of the blessings of religion is that it gives people a sense of freedom and comfort from the cruelty of life and the harsh reality of man's political institutions; it doesn't add to such cruelty. By that standard, Islam has failed miserably.

The conclusion that I—and others who have studied it—have reached is that Islam as a whole is not a religion. It is Arab Imperialism and a protectionist tool to preserve what they believe to be a supremacist Arab culture. Without violent jihad, Mohammed could not have empowered himself in Medina; without the Reddah (bringing back to Islam) wars by his followers against the people of Arabia who left Islam as soon as Mohammed died, Islam could not have sustained itself in Arabia; without the violent jihad by the sword, Mohammed's followers could not have conquered the great civilizations around. Without death warrants (fatwas), vigilante crimes, injustice allowed under Sharia, and turning Muslims against one another, Sharia would be ineffective. And finally, without the death sentence for apostasy through the most barbaric means (stoning and beheading), Islam would have been forced to compete in the realm of ideas, religion, and ethics.

Is Islam perhaps too afraid of honorable peaceful competition to enter the marketplace of religious ideas? To protect its own survival, Islam instead chose to eliminate the opposition through its concept of jihad—war, killing, terror, lying, intimidation, threat, and defamation.

Islam owns one-third of the world's land but is ready to sacrifice several generations of its children, women, and men over Israel, an area of the Middle East that is smaller than the size of New Jersey. To accomplish that "holy" mission, taking away the land of "unbelievers," everything dear to the human soul and the beauty of life itself had to be sacrificed. To achieve Arab Imperialism, Sharia has given Muslims the right to use any means to achieve their goals. The goal of the jihadist ideology is to place every inch of land on earth under Muslim control and Sharia. While doing that, Sharia gave Muslims the right to violate human rights, eliminate Jews, subjugate women, and subject its children to horrific indoctrination in fear of the other, hate-mongering, and even lying.

The Qur'an, which is Allah's words, talks about how he took the lands of the unbelievers:

See they not how we aim to the land, reducing it of its outlying parts?[23] And how many a community have We destroyed. . . . And We, even We, were the inheritors.[24] See they not how we aim to the land, reducing it of its outlying parts?[25] And verily We have destroyed townships.[26] And He caused you to inherit their land and their houses and their wealth, and land ye have not trodden. Allah is ever Able to do all things.[27] He it is Who hath caused those of the People of the Scripture who disbelieved to go forth from their homes . . . while they deemed that their strongholds would protect them from Allah. But Allah reached them from a place whereof they recked not, and cast terror in their hearts so that they ruined their houses with their own hands and the hands of the believers.[28]

While some religions cater to the side of humanity that seeks fairness and the golden rule—to treat your neighbor the way you want to be treated—Islam discovered and preserved the side of humanity that wants to take from others, subjugate others, and perhaps even be subjugated to reinforce the feeling of victimhood. Islam exploits the dark side found in all of us to different degrees.

Tragically, many Muslims and Arabs are still incapable of seeing what causes their subjugation, poverty, backwardness, dependency, and brutal dictatorships. If they only look objectively in their scriptures, they will understand the sad truth. Only in an atmosphere of hatred and bigotry can a radical government survive. And only when they accept the truth about their own religion and culture can they be set free and advance—advance to what they are truly capable of achieving. Until then, they are simply pawns and prisoners of their own Sharia state and programmed to blame others for their misery and enslavement.

Instead, some Muslims want to solve all this misery by embracing ever-stricter Sharia and conquering the world to Islam. Every Islamist group is motivated by dreams of the return of the "peaceful" and "just" Muslim Caliphate they have learned about from their religious books. They long for a state that never was—and certainly never was peaceful or just. It was sheer bloody power politics: backstabbing, assassinations, conspiracies, revolts, counter revolts, rebellions, and mass-murders. One can just imagine how many millions worldwide have been killed in the last fourteen hundred years as a result of Muslim commandments to kill non-believers. And one can hope that the Muslim State is not headed to World War III and even more spilled blood.

Seven

Egypt:
A Case Study

A SAUDI RELIGIOUS AUTHORITY RECENTLY ISSUED A fatwa prohibiting Muslims from visiting the Egyptian pyramids because they are tombs of "infidels." The fatwa says that it is forbidden to linger among the ruins, or to enjoy viewing them. I wonder what the destiny of these great Egyptian monuments would have been if dynamite had already been invented at the time of the Muslim military conquest of Egypt in 639 CE. Might the Egyptian "infidel tombs" have received the same explosive treatment that has recently befallen the huge pre-Islamic Buddha statues in Afghanistan? The Islamic Afghani Taliban government explained away such crimes against one of the world's most spectacular historical artifacts as stopping the worshiping of "false idols."

Obsessed with the sword, death, and heaven, the warriors of Islam appeared on the world scene in 630 CE taking the region by surprise. The Arab invaders had only envy and contempt for existing religions and cultures. Their unwavering mission was to wipe out other civilizations and replace them with theirs. Because of the cruelty of Sharia, their culture could not survive if compared with other free and more humane ones, thus other cultures must be wiped out. It could not peacefully co-exist with more free cultures.

This attitude still reigns fourteen hundred years after the first wave of conquests. The present-day leader of the Muslim Brotherhood, Sayyid Qutb, wrote: "Islam cannot accept any mixing with the society of unbelievers Jahiliyyah. . . . Either Islam will remain, or the society of unbelievers: Islam cannot accept or agree to a situation which is half-Islam and half-infidel. . . . The foremost duty of Islam in this world is to depose the infidels from the leadership of man, and to take the leadership into its own hands and enforce the particular way of life which is its permanent feature."[1]

Qutb's above description of Islam is honest and unblinking. That fear of mixing with infidels was behind the Arab destruction of surrounding great civilizations, paving the way to Arab imperialism—then and now.

Make no mistake, Muslims entered nations not as missionaries, but through violent military conquests they called holy jihad. The Qur'an itself asks Muslims to not only highly tax but also disrespect, disgrace, and degrade those who refuse to convert to Islam. "Fight them [unbelievers], Allah will punish them with your hands and disgrace them. He will grant you victory over them and heal the chests of a believing nation."[2]

The diverse and indigenous populations of the Middle East were subjected to Islamization and Arabization through brutal jihadist genocide, forcible conversion, and severe humiliation. While brutalizing the "inferior" cultures, Muslim Arabs also needed to appear as liberators by convincing the ordinary people that Islam was freeing them from their evil leaders and old corrupt political and social systems. Thus it is holy to surrender to Islam—the word *Islam* itself means submission. The conquered populations were required to submit to the will of Allah, which means submit to Arabs and their religion and culture, and at the same time feel grateful and liberated; this is what ultimate takeover means.

Bedouins of Arabia moved with incredible speed to fulfill the dream of conquering the ultimate booty—wealthier lands and more accomplished nations with plenty of water, fertile agricultural lands, and beautiful women.

Perhaps the best way to understand what happened is to look at one region—one great, conquered culture: my country of origin, Egypt. The collapse of the Roman and Byzantine Empires left a vacuum in Egypt and all the Eastern Mediterranean area which created the perfect timing for Muslim invaders. Egypt and Persia were the two true superpowers of the seventh century. In the 639 CE they were both invaded, and by 641 CE both were under the total control of Arab Muslim forces. Muslim invaders met any resistance with extreme brutality. In the town of Nikiou, Egypt, not one soldier resisted them, yet the Muslims slaughtered everyone they met in the street and in the churches, sparing no one—man, woman, or child. They looted the villages and enslaved the people.

Muslim invaders dictated Arabic as the superior language of the Qur'an. So gradually, Egypt lost its national language—a Coptic language that was partially derived from Ancient Egyptian—and adopted a foreign language, Arabic. Forcing the Arabic language and Muslim legal system on the Egyptian population sped up the eradication of the old culture and the adaptation to the new. The nomadic Bedouin tribal culture instinctively understood the power of language and culture in their takeover.

Egypt's name was also changed to *Misr*, which is the Arabian name given to it in the Qur'an. The name *Egypt* was originally derived from the Egyptian word *Agbat*, meaning Copts, and is a reminder of the six-hundred-year Christian history of Egypt.

Few people today, including many Egyptians, know that Egypt was once a Christian nation. The Egyptians were predominantly Copts, an orthodox sect of Christianity. Today, Copts, one of the few remaining indigenous groups, represent only 10 percent of the Egyptian population. They and a few other groups, such as the Assyrians in Iraq, stand as a symbol of the forced eradication of the Middle East's former diversity of cultures, languages, and religions. Remnants of the great civilizations of the Middle East—the Copts, Jews, Assyrians, and the Armenians—stand as a reminder of what happened to the old civilizations of the region.

As noted in earlier chapters, those minorities who live under such a condition in Islamic countries were traditionally called *dhimmis*—people of different religions allowed to exist in virtual servitude by paying excessive taxes (*jizyah*), but prevented from enjoying the rights and protections of normal Islamic citizens.

Qur'an 9:29 says: "Until they pay the Jizyah with willing submission, and feel themselves subdued." According to Islamic scholar Ibn Kathir, dhimmis must be "disgraced, humiliated, and belittled while paying the jizya."

Egyptian Copts who survived the brutal genocide had to pay the jizya and live with extreme humiliation. Protection of the dhimmis is abolished if they rebel against Islamic law, give allegiance to a non-Muslim power, refuse to pay the jizya, entice a Muslim from his faith, harm a Muslim or his property, or commit blasphemy.

According to the discretion of the caliph or his representative, punishments imposed on non-Muslims for violating these rules are as follows: (1) death, (2) enslavement, (3) release without paying anything, and (4) ransoming in exchange for money. These punishments also apply to crimes of exercising free speech—even repulsive speech—and freedom of religion or conscience.

The moment their protection is removed, non-Muslims are back to being subjected to jihad, and that means Muslims can take both their property and lives. Egyptian Copts who today no longer pay the jizya tax are considered by some Islamists as having forfeited their "protection." The original inhabitants of Egypt are treated as aliens.

The jizya tax on Egyptian Copts lasted until 1855 when Islam weakened. During the colonial era under the British and French, dhimmi laws were abolished. However, colonial powers did often give preferential treatment to the Muslim majority who became very unhappy with the removal of the laws of dhimmitude—which deprived them of their semi-slaves. During that time, Jews and Christians, who had suffered greatly when Muslims were their rulers, took the opportunity of their equal status to raise their standard of living, seek education, and acquire properties and businesses. The colonial era also saw some improvements in women's rights, which produced feminist movements in Turkey and Egypt during the early 1920s. However, as soon as the British left Egypt in 1954, the Jews of Egypt were expelled, and the Coptic Christians started to suffer the effects of the gradual return of radical Islam and the reemergence of the power of the Muslim Brotherhood.

Devout Egyptian Muslims of today and even many Copts are unaware of and oblivious to the brutal history of the Islamic invasion and how it caused great suffering for their Egyptian ancestors. Terrorism worked in Egypt and in all the conquered nations. It accomplished its intended objective: the submission of citizens to Muslim takeover. Egyptians, like many conquered Islamized and/or Arabized nations, have gone beyond submission. Gradually, they began to carry the flag of Arabism, Islamism, and jihadism as their own. The desert bedouin Arabian culture, with all its brutality, misogyny, and discrimination, has become the predominant culture in most fifty-plus Muslim countries of the world. Like Dracula's bite, Islamic-forced submission was dark and contagious. While they had no choice at the beginning, those who were inflicted with that poison would later want to spread it and even become holders of the flag of Islam and proud to call themselves Arab. Now, sadly, some of the most radical Islamist groups in the world have originated from Egypt. Egypt paid a huge price to become Muslim and Arab.

And now, Egyptian history itself would be turned on its head.

Egyptian history before Islam was to be regarded as the era of *Jahiliyyah*, meaning the age of ignorance. Egyptian Muslims were taught to view their glorious history as having started only with Islam. The Islamization of Egypt reduced Ancient Egyptian history to "infidel history" that should not be appreciated or respected.

After the Islamization of Egypt, many of their glorious ancient monuments were buried in the shifting desert sand, as was the very spirit of Egyptians. I have a copy of an old painting of the Egyptian Pyramids and Sphinx, by the Scottish painter David Roberts (1796–1864), depicting how the French and British saw the sphinx and pyramids, as well as many of the great temples. In the painting, the pyramids were partially buried in sand and the sphinx was buried to its neck allowing only the head and neck to appear from a distance and with its nose chipped as it is today. A striking image of neglect of the monuments of pre-Islamic times—now instead semi-buried monuments to "ignorance." Thousands of years of history of a great civilization have become just a memory.

After the Islamization and Arabization of Egypt, Ancient Egyptian history was also buried in the minds of Egyptians. For me, looking at the painting was a sad reminder of what has happened to Egypt itself. The world's first true empire and superpower of the ancient world was conquered by a brutal force that erased its history and buried its greatness in the sand.

Ironically, the French and British "infidel" invaders of Egypt were the ones who gave utmost respect to Ancient Egyptian heritage and monuments. Napoleon's expedition in Egypt discovered the famous Rosetta Stone in the Egyptian Delta, a discovery that revived the knowledge of the ancient hieroglyphic language. The three-year French expedition had a tremendous political and social impact on the country. The British were in Egypt officially from 1882 to 1936 but lingered until 1952, a period of seventy years. The British were behind the extensive study of Egyptology and the discovery and preservation of many of the tombs of the pharaohs. Thanks to the efforts of the West, Ancient Egyptian history was revived, preserved, and given the respect it deserved.

There are definitely positive aspects to British and French colonialism that are rarely mentioned. The British never imposed their religion and culture under penalty of death, and bottom line, their positives were often greater than their negatives. But ironically,

Arabs until today blame their victimization on colonial powers and are unwilling to consider whether Islam and Sharia have anything to do with it. Egyptians never look back far enough to see what really prompted the drastic change from a great civilization to an oppressed, poor, virtually third-world nation.

Guilt over their colonial period causes the West to be especially susceptible to all the Arab victimization stories. It also increases Arab cries of victimhood in their attempt to blame others for their declining conditions.

Conversely, the colonial period of Muslims, as when Muslims colonized Spain for eight hundred years, is viewed not as a source of guilt but as a source of pride. Arabs are proud of their imperialism and eradication of other cultures in order to install Islam, but Western European countries are never forgiven for their colonizing, and they do not seem to want to forgive themselves either.

It is hard to imagine that pre-Islamic Egypt was ruled by several powerful, ambitious women, loved and respected by the citizens, and who actually ruled as pharaohs including Nefertari, Nefertiti, Cleopatra VII, and the great Queen Heshepsut, one of the most successful female pharaohs, who organized ship expeditions and exploration of the known world. Her mummy was recently identified in Egypt. To accommodate the heat, both women and men in Ancient Egypt covered little of their bodies. That did not bring any shame to the queens who sometimes wore chiffon gowns, makeup, and hair dyed with hennah. Almost 99 percent of Egyptian Muslim women today, under the hot sun, choose to wear the Bedouin style hijab, and many are covering their faces by choice.

In comparison with the past, today's Egyptian women have lost many rights under Islamic Sharia, which is Egypt's official law under its constitution. Perhaps the best way to understand how Sharia is affecting the culture of Egypt is to look at some of the cases now in Egyptian courts.

Case Nº4: Egypt Jails Christian Woman for Father's Conversion

In 2007, an Egyptian Christian woman, Shadia Nagui Ibrahim, 47, was sentenced to three years in jail on the charge of fraud for stating she was a Christian on her marriage certificate. Unbeknownst to Shadia, her father had converted to Islam for a brief period of time when she was around two years old. Her father's brief conversion in 1962 made her legally a Muslim despite her official papers stating that she is a Christian. Three years after he converted, he reconciled with her mother and returned home and wished to reconvert back to Christianity, but that was prohibited by law. So he had someone forge his document's ID back to Christian.

Under Egyptian Sharia law, converting to Islam is easy and encouraged but converting to Christianity is against the law. When the father's forged ID was discovered, they detained him and informed Shadia that on paper both she and her father were still Muslim and must remain Muslim. That complicated things, especially for Shadia who had lived all of her life as a Christian and married a Christian man. Under Egyptian Sharia law, it is illegal for a Muslim woman to marry a Christian man. Even though Shadia was unaware of her father's brief conversion, she was charged with "providing false information on official documents" for stating on her marriage certificate that she was Christian. The father was sentenced to three years in 2000. Later in 2007 she was rearrested and sentenced to three years after one brief court session. That case brought a huge outcry by the Coptic Christian community in the United States and Canada, which embarrassed the Egyptian government into pardoning and releasing her after serving several months in jail.

Case Nº 2: Conversion to Christianity Is Illegal under Egyptian Law

Mohammed Ahmed Hegazy is a twenty-five-year-old Egyptian convert (unofficially) from Islam to Christianity. According to Hegazy, he was detained in 2002 and tortured by Egyptian police for three days after they found out about his conversion.

Hegazy said that both he and his wife converted to Christianity but were forced to marry the Muslim way because they are both considered legally Muslim by the state. Hegazy said that his unborn son is the inspiration for wanting to officially change his religion, because only if the couple's religious status is officially changed will they be able to enroll their son in Christian religious classes at school, marry in a church, and attend church services openly.

So, in early August 2007, Hegazy and wife became the first Egyptians ever to formally demand from the government a change in their status from Muslim to Christian. When their demand was rejected, they sued the Egyptian government for rejecting their application. This unprecedented lawsuit threw Egypt in an uproar.

Hegazy, his wife, and their newborn son were forced into hiding, and their lawyer was forced to drop the case when he received several death threats. Since the case started in August 2007, Hegazy has gone through several lawyers whose lives were also threatened.

Hegazy, his wife and baby, and one of his lawyers are all now in hiding after several fatwas of death were issued against them by top Muslim clerics. A survey of Egyptian public showed approximately 56 percent of Egyptians want the death penalty for apostates like Hegazy.

The final court decision is that Egypt will not issue a change of legal status from Muslim to Christian. Period.

It has been reported by some Egyptian churchgoers that if a Muslim is caught going to a church while his or her ID card says Muslim, he or she could be arrested, questioned, and tortured. That is what happened to a twenty-seven-year-old Egyptian woman by the name of Shereen, mother of two from Alexandria, Egypt. She died in police custody on January 3, 2008, after five hours of torture for refusing to renounce her conversion to the Christian faith and return to Islam.

Case Nº 3: "Playing" with Religion

In April 2007, a lawsuit was filed by twelve former Coptic Christians who had converted to Islam but wanted to revert back to Christianity, and who were now demanding that the Egyptian Interior Ministry issue them new official documents in their original names and with "Christian" in the "Religion" entry field.

The Egyptian administrative court rejected the case. The lower court had argued that recognizing such a case would be considered apostasy under Islamic law and actually did charge them for being apostates.

The Egyptian Christian community was disappointed to see the final decision of Egyptian courts: "The court has uprooted the game of moving between religions, by ruling that the Interior Ministry has the right not to permit conversion in the official personal documents of Christians who converted to Islam and then converted back—because this should be seen as a toying with religion."

It is also important to emphasize that converting to Islam is made very easy by Muslims. All that a Christian has to do is to confess the *shahada* (declaration of faith) by saying, "There is no God but Allah, and Mohammed is his Prophet." When conversion to Islam happens, there are no questions asked. I find this very strange. Islam is a way of life, and if one is to embrace this religion, one should be required to study it in depth. But no education in Islam or Sharia is required or suggested, and the new convert simply joins the ranks of the majority of the Muslim population who themselves know very little about Muslim scriptures. This does not seem to be fair or logical in light of the fact that those who convert into Islam are not allowed to convert out.

In an effort to educate young Copts, the Coptic Church in Alexandria, Egypt, showed a documentary film on the premises of their church in 2005, advising their parishioners as to the facts behind converting to Islam and discouraging them from doing so. News of such a documentary film reached Muslims who decided that the privately shown documentary was an insult to Islam. An offended, outraged crowd that numbered in the thousands went on a rampage of burning churches, killing one priest, and stabbing a nun.

I have personally heard several chilling audio-taped confessions in Arabic of Egyptian Muslim men who participated in the kidnapping, rape, and forced marriage of Coptic girls. In these confessions, they claim that there is an Islamization movement of Egyptian Copts funded by people from Saudi Arabia. The men on the taped interview described in detail how they lured and drugged the Coptic girls with the help of Muslim girls wearing the hijab. After the forced marriages took place, they lived with their Coptic "wives" for a while and had a couple of children, all while receiving a huge salary they claimed to have come from Arab funds for Islamization of Copts in Egypt. The man on the tape said that he was eventually told to leave the Coptic young woman and her children. In Egypt her children would now be Muslims under the law. And as to her, she will have a very hard time remarrying again in Egyptian society.

❋ ❋ ❋

In the last two decades, attacks have been increasing on Egyptian Christians, and the same scenario keeps repeating itself especially after the Muslims come out from their Friday prayer sermon.

On Friday, May 11, 2007, right after the Friday Prayer, angry young Muslim men (whom the Egyptian media called extremists) attacked Christian-owned homes and shops in Bamha village, Al-Ayat, Giza district. Twenty-seven homes and shops were set on fire. This is just one incident in a long recent history of similar assaults and attacks that began in November 1972 with the setting on fire of the Holy Bible Publishing House (Dar al-kitab al-moqadas) in Al-Khanka, Egypt.

The Egyptian newspaper, *Al-Masri Al-Yom*, reported an incident in February 2007, of a number of Christian-owned shops being set on fire in upper Egypt as a result of a rumored love story between a Muslim girl and a Christian young man. The attackers used kerosene to set fire to twenty-five homes and five shops, all owned by Christians.

On Friday, December 31, 1999, the Egyptian village al-Kosheh experienced a horrific attack, which lasted for three days, spreading terror in the village and ending with the death of twenty-one Copts and the destruction of dozens of Christian-owned houses and shops. No one has ever been convicted or punished for this massive crime.

One of the latest is the chilling massacre that took place on May 31, 2008, at the desert monastery of Abu Fana, about two hundred miles south of Cairo. More than sixty Islamists, some of them women in full hijab, viciously attacked the monks. The monks were tortured for twelve hours, some hung upside down from trees. Their attackers ordered the monks to spit on their crosses and were forced to convert and confess, "There is no God but Allah, and Mohammed is his prophet." Two of the monks were killed. The monks, together with the workers of the monastery, were mistreated in the hospital and by the police, who so far have not arrested anyone for the crimes. The church and surrounding buildings were burned, and the agricultural land of the monastery, their beehives and fishing lake, were all destroyed.

The list of incidents of violence, killing, and burning of Christian homes and businesses in Egypt is too long to mention here. But the scenario is always the same: false rumors are spread against Christians, then a leaflet is circulated among the mosque worshipers calling on them to attack and reminding them of their duty of jihad and bringing back the honor of Islam. Some of those orchestrating the incitement tell the crowd that Copts should no longer be a protected minority since they no longer pay their jizya. After the Muslim crowd gets their dose of incitement at the Friday sermon, they are then ripe and ready to rush out of the mosque to commit madness, mayhem, and destruction against peaceful fellow citizens who are branded "infidels" by their religion. It must be noted here that many of the Danish cartoon riots also happened after the Friday prayers in mosques.

The sad truth is that there is hardly any ill in Muslim society that is not confirmed by scriptures: The Prophet said: "Then go to the persons who do not join the congregational prayer and order their homes to be burnt."[3]

The genocide against Christians and other minorities taking place in the Muslim and Arab world right now is mostly ignored or at best treated as insignificant news that only merits a few lines on the back pages of Arab media. Misleading and confusing coverage is the norm, giving a muddled account that leaves the reader unable to tell who was the aggressor and who was the victim. The Muslim armed attackers are described as a fringe extremist minority who have hijacked Islam, and Muslims have no prejudice against Copts. Or they say that it is a freak, isolated incident done by mentally unstable individuals who do not reflect on Islam or Muslims. Some media outlets sink as low as spreading despicable lies, claiming that the Copts provoke the Muslim majority, are exaggerating their suffering and claims, and are blaming the extremists on both sides since according to their twisted logic, the Copts who object to an injustice are counted among the extremists!

That same familiar explanation is given by Muslims when it comes to worldwide terrorism. After 9/11 the world heard the same excuse in defense of Islam: the attackers are not "real Muslims" but persons who have "hijacked Islam." This comes from Muslims who demand tolerance, understanding, and compassion from the victims of terror and that others not judge all Muslims with the actions of a few misguided hijackers. If this is the case, I am sure that many want to know how many misguided "hijackers of Islam" are out there. And does it make any difference to the victims of terrorism if the perpetrators are moderate, radical, or "hijacker" Muslims?

The part that the West does not understand is that Muslims do not apply the same logic to themselves. The demand for tolerance by Muslims is a one-way street. When one Danish cartoonist offended Muslims, all hell broke loose. Muslims in the thousands went on a rampage—burning, killing, and rioting. Christians were killed in Gaza, Nigeria, and other places in the Middle East. In the eyes of Muslims, every non-Muslim person from Denmark was responsible; the government of Denmark was responsible. The crisis was not limited to the streets of Pakistan and the Arab world; even Muslim governments demanded an apology from the Danish government. These are the same Muslim governments who call for tolerance of Muslims and have never apologized for 9/11 or taken any responsibility for Muslim worldwide terrorism.

It is astounding how Muslims in general have been desensitized to feelings of guilt toward victims of jihad. They tend to look at what the jihadists do and say, "So what? Every other religion has terrorists too." Muslims have been trained for generations to never sympathize with the suffering of non-Muslims who lived as dhimmis for centuries among them.

While Muslims are demanding understanding and compassion, some of their schools are teaching some verses in the Qur'an telling Muslim kids that non-Muslims are unclean and setting them up for a lifetime of resentment and conflict. Qur'an 9:28 says: "O you who believe! the idolaters are nothing but unclean." In another verse, 9:95, it says: "Unbelievers are unclean, impure and filthy." The Qur'an dictated how Muslims should perceive non-Muslims—as filth. I remember how some Muslims in Egypt viewed the Copts—as *nagas*, Arabic for "filth or unclean." On April 20, 2006, *The Times* of London reported that Muslim students are being taught in their schools that non-Muslims are filth. This belief also influences how Saudi Arabia treats non-Muslims, who are not allowed to set foot in their holy cities of Mecca and Medina.

This teaching is at the root of why many Arabs believe that the existence of non-Muslims on Muslim land is a desecration.

When U.S. soldiers, at the request of Kuwait and Saudi Arabia, sacrificed their lives to protect Kuwait from Saddam Hussein, it was not met with gratitude by the Arab Street. Instead, their reaction was, "How dare the infidels desecrate Muslim land." That is why America's defense of the Muslims against the Serbs, the Afghani Muslims, and the Soviet Union; the feeding of Somali Muslims starved by their own leadership—none of it earns the United States any credit in the Muslim world, just the opposite. The more America or the West tries to help stabilize the region, the more it is despised. They do not want to be rescued by infidels. This is a proud culture that looks down on the "other" and is easily shamed by feelings of dependency and inferiority.

Unlike the repentance of Americans regarding slavery, Germans regarding the Holocaust, and the British regarding the colonial era, Muslims have very little awareness of the impact of their fourteen hundred years of jihad, slavery, and abuse of women and minorities. There is no commandment in Islam to treat the other the way you want to be treated, what the West calls the golden rule. The majority of Egyptian Muslims have no idea about what their ancestors the Copts went through. They have been hardened and made rigid and insensitive toward them.

Muslims get extremely offended and even outraged when anyone even hints to the plight of Christians and women in Muslim countries. They are also sensitive to the topic of jihad, now that the world has begun to hear about it. Some Muslims claim that jihad is an inner struggle, but what kind of inner struggle is it that does not start with self-examination of being unjust to others? As a group, Egyptians and Muslims in general are immersed in feelings of self-pity and are incapable of feeling compassion toward non-Muslims. Acknowledging compassion to non-Muslim oppressed minorities is grounds for apostasy. A Muslim must stay hardened and unyielding. Only Muslims are the victims. You can find an Egyptian who befriends a Christian one day, but the next he might have no use for the friendship anymore and will call the Christian "blue bone," a derogatory term for Christians arising from their abuse in the seventh century, which caused blue marks on their necks. This lack of regret or sorrow is what can be expected from a civilization that was built on a dual system of ethics—one for Muslims and another for non-Muslims.

Current Conditions in Egypt

Egypt has never been as close to becoming a full Sharia state as it is today. The absolute supremacy of Sharia was upheld in the Cairo Declaration of Human Rights in Islam (1990). The Declaration, which was signed by forty-five Muslim countries, said that Sharia overrides any other law of human rights including the UN 1948 Universal Declaration of Human Rights. It is significant that Article 24 of the CDHRI states that it is "subject to the Islamic sharia," and Article 25 confirms that Sharia "is the only source of reference for the explanation or clarification of this Declaration." It is thus clear that Sharia has supremacy, and that the 1990 CDHRI has primacy.[4]

The situation in Egypt at the present is very tense. The country is wracked by strikes, demonstrations, and food riots. Indications are that things might get a lot worse in the coming years. There's a very real risk of an explosive situation, and perhaps a total uprooting of the system. Mubarak, one of only three presidents to rule since 1952, is now eighty years old and has been in office for twenty-seven years. The Muslim Brotherhood is threatening a takeover, a very real possibility.

Egypt is facing a huge challenge from religious tensions, inequality and divisiveness, exclusion, poverty, and religious zealotry. There is a lot of discussion over who will succeed Mubarak.

Qur'anic recitations are heard from several mosques all at once through loudspeakers wherever you go and at all hours. On every mile along the way to the Red Sea resorts, you will find a sign, not to tell you the mileage left for your destination, but giving one of Allah's ninety-nine names. Some of the names are "the deceiver," and *Al Muthil*, meaning "the one who humiliates, oppresses, or puts down."

On my last trip to Egypt, I was shocked by the economic and social deterioration. Conditions in poorer Cairo neighborhoods are deplorable—pollution and garbage everywhere, neglected and broken infrastructure, three and four families living together in one apartment causing a lack of personal and psychological space. The crowded quarters foster aggression and unwanted intimacy sometimes with perfect strangers. The crowded city of Cairo is hard to live in even if you are a millionaire. All these factors weigh heavily on the millions of Egyptian citizens. Yet the majority walk with signs saying, "Islam is the answer."

On Arabic-language TV, one sees a constant parade of religious leaders and commentators saying, "Islam will conquer Rome, Europe, and America," and that since Spain was once ruled by Muslims it must be taken back; that Israel should be wiped off the map; that America targeted and killed one million Iraqi citizens (no mention of Sunnis and Shi'ites killing each other). These pronouncements do not come from lower-level Muslim leaders, but from top leaders such as the Egyptian sheikh Yousuf Al-Qaradawi, who on July 28, 2007, said on Qatar TV that Islam's "Conquest of Rome" will save Europe from its subjugation to materialism and promiscuity." Egyptian celebrities continue to tell the public that 9/11 could never have been done by Muslims. Even some Egyptian journalists claim that the CIA and President Bush planned and executed September 11, and that Israel is flooding Egyptian markets with contaminated Viagra to sterilize Egyptian men.[5]

Lots of intellectuals and educated Egyptians are demoralized and in fear of what will happen to Egypt in the coming unpredictable period after Mubarak leaves office. Egypt is fast approaching a crossroads. The Muslim Brotherhood is gaining seats in the Parliament and plans to make Egypt an Islamic Sharia state. If Egypt is taken over by the Muslim Brotherhood, what will be the destiny of the Copts of Egypt? Will that bring the end to the peace treaty with Israel? These things could happen sooner than we think.

This is bad news even for Muslims because, unfortunately, the more the Islamization, the less the stability and harmony in society. When it comes to Islam, more religion does not mean more tolerance, compassion, and kindness between people. More Islam means more violence and religious intolerance. Many Egyptians come back from visiting Egypt with the same observation: with more religious expression and symbolism in Egypt, there is less civility, compassion, and tolerance between Egyptians. An Egyptian intellectual I know once asked, "Why does religiosity in Egypt bring with it ill manners? Why with Egyptians becoming more religious and observant was there also an increase in social tension, aggression, violence, and a reduction of politeness and courtesy between people? What kind of religiosity is this?" he exclaimed, but did not give an answer.

The case study of Egypt is an example for Western democracies to learn from. There is a lesson about appeasement that must be told. The attempt by many dhimmis to appease Muslim authority—a quite natural reaction to their subjugation—empowered the Arabian Muslims.

History keeps repeating itself, and the example of Egypt proves that the passage of time does not necessarily mean positive progress. The West should look at the example of Egypt seriously, because Islamic history also keeps repeating itself and the warriors for Islam keep using the same tactics. Egypt is an example of what can happen to a superpower that was once upon a time a Christian nation!

Eight

Getting Away with Murder

GETTING AWAY WITH MURDER IN THE NAME OF RELIGION—
any religion—must end.

Who will protect the citizens of democratic nations? Shall we entrust Western media with informing us when a threat is eminent? The victims of 9/11, the London and Madrid bombings, and many others—if they could—would tell us no from their graves. We must act to protect ourselves. But how?

Many Muslims claim that the West simply misunderstands Muslim scriptures and that Islam is a religion of peace. Tell that to the three thousand Americans killed in cold blood on 9/11. Even if 90 percent of Muslims do not follow their religion's command to kill, how can they guarantee that others—however small the percentage—who consider themselves true believers will not obey the commandments? It happens all the time against people in the West. It is the duty of Western governments and democracies to protect their citizens from hate speech and calls for murder, even if such commandments are in a "religious document."

There are 35,213 Qur'an verses, hadiths, Sharia laws, and various Muslim scriptures commanding and encouraging killing, violence, war, annihilation, corporal punishment, hatred, boycott, humiliation, and subjugation aimed mainly against non-Muslims.

The majority population of non-Muslims in democratic nations must be concerned about such scriptures, and they must be protected by their governments from those who will act upon such commandments. According to the U.S. Constitution, "All men are created equal." There are no exceptions made for religious publications sold in the United States calling for the killing of U.S. citizens on the basis of religion, rejection of religion, or changing religion. It is an ethical and political commitment that is repeated in constitutions and political documents in both hemispheres.

Individual acts of terrorism have occurred many times in America by persons who act on their own as a result of a lifetime of hate indoctrination and commandments of jihad. But the U.S. government usually regards such acts as police matters and not as terror or religious hate crimes inspired by Muslim scriptures. The examples are many. The Muslim of Pakistani origin, Naveed Haq, who went on a shooting spree in 2006 at the Jewish Federation of Greater Seattle, pled "not guilty by reason of insanity" to murder and attempted murder. Our media did not report that when arrested, he said that he thought he was doing God's will. That is exactly what many Muslims think when they are killing infidels. Egyptian gunman Hesham Hadayet, in 2002, opened fire on the airport counter of Israel's El Al airline at the Los Angeles International Airport. Again, this individual terrorist act was considered a police matter and not even counted as terror or a hate crime.

Americans in general have difficulty in understanding these acts as "hate crimes," because the notion of a religion telling you to kill others is so foreign to them. In America, when a young woman in Texas drowns her children in a bathtub because "God told her to do it," or a lone gunman opens fire in a restaurant or on a college campus because "God ordered him to do it," most Americans and the legal system automatically blame mental illness. Anyone thinking God is asking him or her to kill is considered insane. They cannot comprehend that an entire religion and its culture believes God orders the killing of unbelievers.

For this reason and others perhaps having to do with political correctness, laziness, or timidity, the media has downplayed many such hate crimes by Muslims, such as instances in which Muslims with SUVs plowed into American pedestrians because they consider them their kaffir enemies. On March 3, 2006, Mohammed Reza Taheri-azar, a University of North Carolina student from Iran, was arrested for driving his SUV into a popular campus gathering spot injuring nine people. At his hearing he said he was "thankful for the opportunity to spread the will of Allah." In a similar incident in San Francisco, Omeed Aziz Popal, a native of Afghanistan, went on a rampage with his vehicle killing one pedestrian and injuring at least fourteen others.

Islamists and jihadits on the Internet encourage these lone acts of terrorism, saying that it supports the Islamic State. These Internet sites emphasize that the lone mujahid fighter does not have to physically belong to a group, since that would only compromise his mission.

The Qur'an tells Muslims that the non-Muslim victims were not really killed by them. It was Allah who did the killing by using the hands of Muslims. That is how Muslims are spared the feeling of guilt over slaying non-believers. Not only that, but Allah says that killing infidels will *heal* the breasts of believers.

Fight them, and God will punish them by your hands, cover them with shame, help you (to victory) over them, heal the breasts of Believers.[1]

Allah will afflict you with a doom from Him or at our hands [meaning: the doom afflicted on disbelievers by Allah, but at the hands of Muslims].[2]

Ye [Muslims] slew them not, but Allah slew them. And thou [Mohammed] threwest not when thou didst throw, but Allah threw.[3]

The Qur'an and Hadith command Muslims to murder Christians, Jews, Buddhists, Hindus, Bahais, Druze, Ahmediyas, and all other non-Muslims in cold blood! And to make it easier on Muslims, the following hadiths absolve them, telling those who kill non-Muslims that they will not be killed for the crime. Mohammed said:

- No Muslim should be killed for killing an unbeliever.[4]

- No Muslim should be killed for killing an infidel.[5]

- No Muslim should be killed for killing a non-Muslim.[6]

- A Muslim should not be killed for killing an infidel.[7]

- No Muslim is to be killed for killing an infidel.[8]

- A Muslim must not be killed for killing a non-Muslim.[9]

I deliberately listed several to demonstrate how such commandments permeate Muslim scriptures. These notions are not obscure or bad interpretations. They are repeated over and over again, and their meaning could not be clearer.

Not only are such verses common, but all of the above and much more have been codified into Islamic Sharia law, ensuring that a Muslim will not be put to death for the crime of murdering a non-Muslim. Here is the law: "Regard is also to be had to a difference of religion, so that a Muslim shall not be put to death for the murder of an unbeliever."[10]

All of the above is the reason that killers of Copts in Egypt are rarely arrested and never put to death for genocide against Christians. It is also the reason why many Muslims are silent in the face of terrorism not knowing what to say since their scriptures approve of the act.

How can a former Muslim like me live in peace in America when there are neighborhood mosques reading scriptures to their believers telling them to kill Muslims who left the religion? "No Umma (a member of the Muslim community) should be killed for killing a Kaffir (an infidel). . . . Whoever changes his Islamic religion, kill him."[11]

There is no peace for the apostate, not even in the West. A recent poll indicates that 36 percent of younger British Muslims believe that a Muslim who converts to another religion should be "punished by death."[12]

How can a Jew in America live in peace when the mosque next door is reciting: "The Hour Resurrection will not take place until the Muslims fight the Jews, and kill them. And the Jews will hide behind the rock and tree, and the rock and tree will say: oh Muslim, oh servant of Allah, this is a Jew behind me, come and kill him!"?[13]

How can an American Christian sleep with a feeling of peace, safety, and security while the neighborhood mosque is reciting Qur'an 9:5: "Fight and slay the pagans Christians wherever ye find them and seize them, confine them, and lie in wait for them in every place of ambush."

How can Jews, Christians, atheists, Hindus, and Buddhists in the West sleep well at night when Muslim scriptures read in a mosque built in their neighborhood by the Saudis, call for their murder and the seizure of their land and property?

How can homosexuals or lesbians live safely in America when Muslims in their neighborhood are reciting commandments by Mohammed to kill homosexuals and lesbians. The Prophet said: 1) "Kill the one who sodomizes and the one who lets it be done to him." 2) "May Allah curse him who does what Lot's people did." 3) "Lesbianism by women is adultery between them."[14] The punishment for adultery is death by stoning.

And what will a Muslim immigrant woman, who came to America to escape Sharia, do when she finds a Sharia court installed in the West giving her half the inheritance her brother gets, allowing her husband a second wife, and telling her she cannot have a divorce or custody of her children? What will happen if her husband beats her? Will the police tell her that it is his right under Sharia, so they can do nothing about it? Will she discover that Western law does not protect her? How can this woman live in peace when Muslim organizations are demanding Sharia in America and when Sharia family tribunals have functioned in Canada and Europe even on a limited scale? This is a threat too close to home.

How can an American Muslim child relate to and feel compassion for his fellow citizens when he is being told that non-Muslims are "filth" or that America is Dar al-Harb (House of War)? Qur'an 9:95: "They will swear by Allah unto you, when ye return unto them, that ye may let them be. Let them be, for lo! they are unclean, and their abode is hell." Meaning: Muslims should not let non-Muslims who pretend to believe (so they don't get killed) be, and that they are unclean and should go to hell. This kind of education is occurring in the West at a time when Muslims are still a small minority, so can you imagine what they will teach when they increase in number?

The above threat is real and will increase exponentially with the growth of the Muslim population.

In previous chapters we have examined what Sharia contains, what it does to women and to non-Muslims. We have also seen the path of no return forced on many nations across the globe. Western governments have not done enough to protect their citizens, preferring the safe, private drama of political infighting to fighting those who have their eyes on the worldwide expansion of Islam. The U.S. government has allowed Islam to operate unchecked in America for several decades as a religion. But Islam is less a religion and more a political and legal system that discriminates against non-Muslims and women and is very hostile to other religions. Furthermore, based on their scriptures, Islam sees America—and all of the West—as Dar al-Harb (House of War), which is a special designation that in the Muslim mind carries legal implications. Imam Abdul Makin, leader of an East London mosque who is in a British jail now for rape, told the BBC that he considered Britain as Dar al-Harb. British Muslim lawyer Anjem Choudary backed up the imam's position by saying that, yes, Britain is Dar al-Harb and that the whole world is now Dar al-Harb.

The threat is real for the lives of Americans, not only from large-scale jihad but also from individual acts of terror by Muslim individuals who, at a low time in their lives, might want to kill to go to heaven. Muslims are like everyone else; there are the good and bad among them. The problem sources from Muslim scriptures, which negatively impact the bad ones into doing harm to U.S. citizens. The huge amount of relentless, obsessive commandments telling poor Muslims they must fight, kill, subdue, and annihilate if they are truly good Muslims are a danger to everyone, including Muslims. Our problem thus is not and should not be with law-abiding and peace-loving Muslims but with Muslim scriptures themselves, which command them to kill non-Muslims as a guarantee to go to heaven. Even if only 10 or 15 percent of Muslims act on such scriptures and the majority are silent, the West has a huge problem on its hands. There will always be some percentage of Muslims of every generation who will take their scriptures literally, particularly with so many preachers inciting them to do so. Therefore, the source of the problem must be addressed, and Western governments must take jurisdiction over selling and buying books that order the murder of their citizens, even if such books are called holy scriptures.

Would the U.S. government allow the operation and give a tax-free status to a "religion" that practices human sacrifice? If not, why not? Such religions have existed. If the U.S. government would outlaw the practice and refuse to recognize such a group as a tax-exempt legitimate religion, then we need to also apply the same standard to *any* religion that orders its members to kill non-members.

In its war on terror, the West has been primarily concerned with individuals who actually commit or attempt to commit terror after the fact, and that is not a good solution in the long run. Penalizing Muslims who act upon what their scriptures command them to do will not solve the problem. Perhaps it is not even fair. Think of it logically. There is something intrinsically wrong with penalizing Muslims for violent acts while holding the violent parts of their scriptures in the same high esteem as the peaceful portions of their scriptures.

The legal systems in the West have too long protected the abusers instead of the abused. In Great Britain, a Saudi billionaire won a lawsuit against Dr. Rachel Ehrenfeld for offending him in her book by linking his finances to terrorist activities. So her book, according to British courts, was improper. But how could the same courts in the United Kingdom miss the libel and incitement to kill British citizens in Muslim books? British courts did not just miss libel and hate speech in Muslim scripture, but also gave protection to Muslim holy books from being sued under its religious hate speech laws.

Consider the report which aired on CNS News on July 12, 2005:

> In a victory for British Muslim campaigners, the House of Commons Monday passed a bill aimed at curbing religious hatred, despite critics' warnings that it could worsen relations between religious communities. . . . In an earlier Commons debate, a Conservative MP raised the possibility that the law, if passed, could outlaw the reading of passages of the Qur'an that called for harsh treatment against Christians and Jews. . . . Following those assertions, a delegation of prominent Muslims held talks last week with

the government minister responsible for the bill, Paul Goggins, to check whether the legislation could affect reading and quoting from the Qur'an and other Islamic texts such as the Hadith—the traditional sayings of Mohammed and other early Muslim figures. . . . The delegation suggested that it may be preferable to "totally exempt" Islamic texts from the bill. Commenting on the Muslim Council's attempt to get the Qur'an exempted from the law, the Barnabas Fund said Muslim leaders in Britain had done their best to have themselves protected by the proposed law.[15]

It is now clear that Muslims fought very hard in Britain to be exempt from having the law of religious hate apply to them simply because they know that their scriptures are full of hate speech and incitement and would not pass the test of hate speech laws, let alone orders to kill.

The legal route must be also used by the West to protect its citizens. Most Muslims are unaware of or in denial about the intrinsic problems within Islam and Sharia that create a serious threat to lives of non-Muslims, both as individuals and as nations. Non-Muslims cannot simply count on an eventual reformation of Islam because it might never happen. The starry-eyed West talks more about the reformation of Islam than Muslims themselves do. Islamic jihad is likely to continue to be a threat forever. It may go dormant when they are weak, but when they are strong, the threat reemerges. History has shown that. The West can only hope for containing the expansion and preventing the violence from spreading within its own territories.

Petition for Protection

Decades ago, the U.S. government demanded tobacco companies place a disclaimer on every cigarette box sold in America stating that cigarette smoking may cause cancer. That was done to protect the health and lives of U.S. citizens, and that was good and proper. When that was not enough, several lawsuits were filed against tobacco companies who conspired to harm the health of consumers. Muslim scriptures are no different; they are not good for the health of non-Muslim Americans.

Western governments should order the removal of all commandments, verses, and statements to kill from Muslim scriptures and from any other religion that commands its followers to kill those who do not believe in it. Yes, there is separation of church and state, but if the day arrives when the church orders the murder of non-Christians, then I will be the first one to demand the removal of such a notorious commandment from Christian literature. Accordingly, the American public will be invited to sign a petition to remove all commandments to kill non-Muslims, apostates, and gay people from Muslim scriptures bought and sold in the United States. I predict that millions of Americans will sign this petition.

The petition will hopefully be presented to Congress to be put for a vote. If this fails, then the least the U.S. government can do—and perhaps all it can properly do under our Constitution—is to require a disclaimer on all Muslim books sold in America; that includes every Qur'an, Hadith, or Sharia book and any textbook that has verses or hadiths commanding the killing of apostates or non-Muslims. The disclaimer should read something like this:

> The calls for murder and violent jihad in this book are only metaphorical and should not be acted upon against modern-day Jews, Christians, atheists, or former Muslims. Any act of violence on the basis of such scriptures will be prosecuted under the hate-crime laws of the United States of America.

Class Action Lawsuit

If this is also ignored or the matter is rejected for a vote in Congress, then I suggest a massive class action lawsuit against the U.S. government demanding protection of our lives. Every concerned American—Democrat or Republican, liberal or conservative, black or white, gay or straight, Muslim or non-Muslim—can participate in this class action suit for the removal of all calls to kill, torture, enslave, humiliate, and lie in wait to strike terror in the hearts of non-Muslims, from Muslim scriptures bought, sold, or taught in the United States. If that is not done, then the religion of Islam's right to a tax-exempt, non-profit status should be revoked. Islam should be named an ideology that is a threat to the life of U.S. citizens, to national security, and to the U.S. Constitution. Not even religion should be allowed to get away with murder.

There is no time to waste because there is a fatwa of death on the head of everyone who is not a Muslim and for Muslims who leave Islam.

It is negligence on the part of every American government official who took the oath of office if commands to kill innocent American citizens are left floating in the hands of people who think it is a holy commandment. The above disclaimer is the minimum that must be done immediately. Without such action by the U.S. government, the human rights of Americans are compromised. Human rights are not to pass the test of scriptures; it is scriptures that have to pass the litmus test of human rights.

How can we expect Muslims to assimilate in America when their religion tells them that Jews are monkeys and Christians are pigs who both should be killed? How can we put a young, vulnerable Muslim kid in jail for life if he simply follows what his religion is telling him to do? An eighteen-year-old Muslim teenager may not be mature enough to withstand the teaching of violence day in and day out in his mosque. He cannot avoid the teaching of violence simply because it is all over the Qur'an and Hadith and life and example of Mohammed. He must at least see the disclaimer on the first page of the book so he understands what behaviors are against the law in this country.

A few meek measures at stemming the teaching of violent jihad have been attempted. The U.S. Commission on International Religious Freedom issued a report on June 11, 2008, stating that the Islamic Saudi Academy in Alexandria, Virginia, uses textbooks with "extremely troubling passages that do not conform to international human rights norms." The textbooks used by the academy are filled with incitements, violence, and intolerance of other religions. The academy's 1999 class valedictorian, Ahmed Omar Abu Ali, was convicted in 2005 on charges that he joined al Qaeda and plotted to assassinate President George W. Bush. According to the commission: "The most problematic texts involve passages that are not directly from the Qur'an but rather contain the Saudi government's particular interpretation of Qur'anic and other Islamic texts." The commission's claim that the texts were not directly from the Qur'an but rather reflect the Saudi government's interpretation would imply that the commission understands the true meaning of the Qur'an better than the Saudi government! According to the commission, some passages clearly exhort the readers to commit acts of violence, as can be seen in the following two examples:

1) In a twelfth-grade *tafsir* (Qur'anic interpretation) textbook, the authors state that it is permissible for a Muslim to kill an apostate (a convert from Islam), an adulterer, or someone who has murdered a believer intentionally: "He (praised is He) prohibits killing the soul that God has forbidden (to kill) unless for just cause." *Just cause* is then defined in the text as "unbelief after belief, adultery, and killing an inviolable believer intentionally."[16]

2) A twelfth-grade *tawhid* (monotheism) textbook states that "major polytheism makes blood and wealth permissible," which in Islamic legal terms means that a Muslim can take the life and property of someone believed to be guilty of this alleged transgression with impunity.[17] Under the Saudi interpretation of Islam, "major polytheists" include Shi'a and Sufi Muslims,

who visit the shrines of their saints to ask for intercession with God on their behalf, as well as Christians, Jews, Hindus, and Buddhists.

I have news for the U.S. Commission on International Religious Freedom. What the school is teaching is the *core belief* of Islam that is found in the Qur'an and Hadith and backed up by Sharia law and is not erroneous interpretation by bad Muslim extremists from Saudi Arabia or anywhere else. These are the commandments from the Qur'an and Hadith. Again, Qur'an 9:5: "Kill those who join other gods with God wherever ye shall find them; and seize them, besiege them, and lay wait for them with every kind of ambush." Qur'an 98:6 says, "Verily, those who disbelieve from among the People of the Book and the idolaters, will be in the Fire of Hell, abiding therein. They are the worst of creatures." Hadith 9.57 states: Mohammed said, "Whoever changes his Islamic religion, kill him."

Those who take time to read the Qur'an and Hadith and want to follow the example of Mohammed cannot help but be terrorists. They must humiliate, hate, distrust, deceive, and kill non-Muslims when the situation is appropriate. This is a central doctrine of Islamic scriptures.

Not only is hate speech and anti-Semitism taught in some Islamic schools and mosques, but it is also creeping into institutions of higher learning in the United States. Listen to the words of an invited speaker at the University of California at Irvine:

We have a psychosis in the Jewish community that is unable to co-exist equally and brotherly with other human beings. You can take a Jew out of the ghetto, but you can't take the ghetto out of the Jew, and this has been demonstrated time and time again in Occupied Palestine. And now they have American diplomats and politicians and decision makers and strategists in their pocket."[18]

With the above rhetoric, American institutions of higher learn-ing are being infected with culture of the Arab Street in Gaza and West Bank. That is a clear example that the seventh-century fatwa against Jews is following them right here to America.

Quite obviously—and I cannot emphasize it enough—the causes of Islamic fanaticism, zealotry, and suicide terrorism are rooted in the Qur'an.[19] Most terrorists and their many supporters are themselves the victims of Qur'anic scripture and intense immoral teachings and indoctrination.

Most Muslims simply believe in the Qur'an with their hearts and not their minds. The majority of Muslims do not follow Qur'an and Sharia at all, and that is why they can create their own mental picture of a peaceful illusionary version of a Qur'an that does not exist and never existed in the history of Islam. Most Muslims judge Islam by their kind, tolerant Muslim grandparents who prayed five times every day. To them, that is the Islam that must be protected by any means. But those people either do not understand or totally ignore the horrific threat to the lives of non-Muslims and notorious violation of human rights in their scriptures. The danger to non-Muslims is real, and we do not want to wait until we have civil wars in the West to realize we have a major problem on our hands.

The Role of Western Media

As a journalist in Egypt in the early 1970s, I met a few American journalists who told me that "Arab media was government con-trolled." That was a fact and still is to a large extent. But having lived half my life in the Middle East and the other half in America, I am sad to say that mainstream Western media has also violated their independence. But the tables are turned. In the West, we largely have "media-controlled governments."

On September 11, 2001, a crime was committed against all U.S. citizens, and particularly against three thousand U.S. citizens and their families. The people of America were totally unprepared for such an attack and had no clue as to what hit them. Furthermore, after the shock of it began to wear off, the media went back to their previous obsessions. For weeks at a time the media served up reports on the death or drug use of an actress, on celebrity gossip and hype and juicy sex scandals of politicians, but rarely offered American citizens solid, carefully researched news and analyses as to what was going on around the world. There were rarely any reports about the nature of the threat America faced from those calling for the annihilation of America and how the safety and security of Americans are being challenged constantly in the Muslim world. Very few in America knew what was happening to Egyptian Copts or other daily-occurring atrocities in Muslim countries that do not abide by the 1948 Universal Declaration of Human Rights when it conflicts with Sharia law. Western media has failed its citizens. Americans have no idea that for decades the Muslim religious and political leaders have been threatening and cursing the West and promoting jihad against them.

The mainstream Western media, a large number of academics, and some government officials seem not to take the threat of Islamic jihad seriously. However, their lack of concern does not reflect the obvious anxiety of U.S. citizens over Islam. Those who voice concerns are too often accused of being Islamophobes. A phobia is a disease characterized by unrealistic fear. But how can such a reasonable fear be unrealistic? For a free people, *not fearing* what is in Muslim scriptures and being taught on American soil would be madness. When the American public is fully informed about Muslim beliefs and scriptures, a healthy level of fear of Islamic Sharia is only normal and actually needed for Americans to make prudent decisions. Otherwise the safety and security of American citizens is seriously threatened.

Americans could be fighting a civil war, embroiled in a Chechnya/Kosovo-style scenario in just a few decades. Leading up to 9/11, our media, on whom we depend for information, and our government, upon whom we rely for protection, failed the American public. We simply did not know anything about what is going on inside many Muslim countries that breed and prepare their youth to take over the West. The American public was kept uninformed of the magnitude of the threat awaiting them by a Muslim world hell-bent on bringing down their form of government, undermining the very foundation of Judeo-Christian society, and taking it over. "Death to America" was not only chanted by Muslims from across the ocean, but also by Muslims within the United States, such as Professor Sami Al-Arian, a former Muslim Palestinian who was professor at the University of South Florida. According to the U.S. Justice Department, Mr. Al-Arian had close ties to the Palestinian Islamic Jihad, a terror group.

There is no excuse for U.S. media to be uninformed when they have offices and reporters in various Middle East capitals. I visited Egypt for the first time in twenty years in August 2001 and returned home to the United States the night of September 10, 2001. On the flight back from Cairo, I was depressed over the conditions in the Middle East and the danger awaiting the West after what I had seen and heard during my visit. How could any reporter living in a Muslim capital miss the cries of cursing and incitement to kill the Jews, Christians, Israel, Britain, and America that occur during many Friday prayers? How could they underestimate the threat to America enforced daily by a major culture block of 1.2 billion people? How could the training of jihadists go unnoticed? How could they fail to translate the calls for jihad against the West and the praising of jihadists in Arab media, school textbooks, songs, poetry, and political speeches? How could Western journalists not report on the oft-repeated threat, "We will take over Europe and America from within through immigration" by top Muslim sheikhs? They scream it out to the world from the microphones atop the high towers of mosques on TV and in Muslim schools. The agenda of Islam has never been hidden and is clear from what taxi-cab drivers tell anyone, even Westerners, who cares to listen on the ride to the airport.

Unfortunately, Western media bureaus in Arab countries, as they did in the 1990s in Baghdad, have often agreed to stringent censorship, reporting only what was allowed by dictators such as Saddam Hussein in exchange for keeping their offices open. Thus, often it is not because the media doesn't know, but because they have allowed foreign governments to muzzle them that Americans do not get the truth. I was a journalist in Egypt for six years before moving to the U.S., and *there is no way* that the many dangerously alarming signals to the United States, and the West in general, could have been missed by any Western reporter living in Riyadh, Cairo, or Baghdad.

But beyond the issue of caving in to Arab pressure within this country and elsewhere in the West where there is no censorship, the "free" press still often fails their citizenry. Western media is practicing self-censorship when it comes to Islam or Muslims. They show little concern over the many average Americans who are reasonably afraid of the rampant anti-Americanism and anti-Semitism on college campuses and by the obsessive building and financing of mosques by Arab countries when the Muslim population in the area is not large enough to fill them.

Arab governments, especially Saudi Arabia, are building mosques at a rate of speed that should indeed raise eyebrows and make the inquiring minds of Western media and governments suspicious of their intentions. That suspicion is entitled to be expressed in public, given the regular calls by Muslim leaders, such as Sheikh Qaradawi, an Egyptian who lives in Qatar, who brags that Islam will take over Rome, Britain, and the United States. Muslims are not keeping this a secret, so why should Western media and governments not react or respond? Western officials and media rarely express suspicions or question the intentions behind the millions of dollars donated to our Western universities to start Islamic Studies and Middle East studies departments with plenty of strings attached. For too long, the "inquiring minds" of Western media and governments were dulled and distracted, leaving the American public unaware of what was going on until one day the daily calls of "May God destroy America, Britain, and Israel" that emanated from many mosques saw fruition on the morning of September 11, 2001. Was that wake-up call not sufficient? Do we still not understand?

Average Americans I talk with feel that their openness and generosity has been taken advantage of by Muslim groups who are pushing the envelope to see how far the West will bend. They see that their laws of equality are being violated and mocked, whether it's a Muslim woman who insists on taking her drivers license photo with her face covered or a Muslim taxi driver who refuses to drive American customers carrying wine from the duty-free shop. (I've never even heard of that in a moderate Muslim country. Egyptian taxis certainly do not have such a rule.)

Western media continually misses the point when reporting on individual terror acts of Muslims who go on a rampage, killing civilians in the name of Allah. The media reports them simply as criminal acts, if it is even reported at all. However, reporting on a similar act of violence by an ordinary American goes on for days, telling the public every detail about his life, family background, motivation, and whether it is a hate crime. If he happens to be a church-going Christian, this fact never goes unmentioned.

Very likely, the failure of Western media to correctly report individual jihadist attacks for what they really are has more to do with political correctness. But political correctness and timidity, for whatever reason, has proven to be the most powerful weapon for the advancement of Dar al-Islam's jihadist agenda in the West. However, the political correctness of the West is not doing Islam or its reformers a favor. Without the natural self-protective reaction by the West, Muslims do not get the message and continue with their jihad obligation from Allah.

To be taken seriously, the victim must say "ouch." But Western victims of jihad are dead, and there are few in Western media and governments who will talk for them or seem willing to take protective measures equal to the proportion of the aggression.

Muslims need to see themselves in the mirror by hearing the West boldly expose what is being said in mosques, by unabashedly showing the scriptures and linking it to the behavior of the terrorists. The jihadists themselves are certainly unabashed and straightforward when they open the scriptures and say, "*This* is why I am doing this."

Muslims are not seeing Western media (which, after all, in the eyes of Muslims is the measurement of what the West thinks) being appalled by Muslim scriptures. If the West is appalled, they must express it. Muslims do not read minds. Like anyone else, they need to hear straight talk. The West must engage at the media level with the Muslim world and not be guilty of covering up the embarrassing texts in the same way that the Arab media does.

Muslims need to be informed about what is in their scriptures simply because, believe it or not, they do not know. Take it from me: to many Muslims, the Qur'an sounds like beautiful poetry—which it is—and the contents and meaning are irrelevant. My kind and loving grandmother, who lived till she was over ninety, used to read the Qur'an regularly, and I used to watch her. She never discussed the meaning, but moved her head back and forth while reading and sounded as though she was memorizing poetry by heart or listening to music. To many, the rhythmic recitation is hypnotic and glorious even if the verse says "kill the non-believers." Believe it or not, in Arabic it sounds holy. This is no different than the way Latin sounds holy to American Catholics who loved the old-fashioned Latin mass. I must admit that when I lived as a Muslim in the Middle East and heard Qur'anic recitation all the time with words like "kill and get killed, smite necks, slay them, fight them, torment, slaughter, subdue the disbelievers," it never occurred to me that such commands were anything but holy messages from Allah. I never listened to the content of the words. Like many Muslims, I was mesmerized by the well-known Muslim beautiful rhythmic recitation and sounds of the language. The only time I felt that something was wrong was when I was at the home of a Coptic Christian friend who lived next to a mosque and we heard the Friday prayers that ended with the usual cursing of the non-believers, which included Christians of course. I was suddenly embarrassed, but my friend did not make any comment. However, she did look afraid. Only later her mother politely expressed fear of the incitement in the mosque sermons. That was when I realized that something was wrong with my religion. But Christians in Egypt, both then and now, cannot dare to complain openly.

Like living under the Mafia, they can only whisper their frustration to each other. In 2007, as I was walking between terminals in an airport in the Midwest trying to catch a connecting flight, I saw the Egyptian Coptic pope Shenouda with his large entourage. Apparently he was in the United States for medical reasons. I took that rare chance to meet Pope Shenouda in person. I greeted him with the appropriate respect and told him that I am now a Christian. As soon as I uttered those words, the Egyptian pope looked alarmed, as if he did not want to hear it. He then turned his head around with obvious fear on his face. He probably thought that Egyptian intelligence was listening to our discussion or something of the sort. Or perhaps he thought that I was a plant. He did not make any comment on what I had told him. The Egyptian pope was truly frightened for himself and his people. I walked away from this encounter in the airport with a deep feeling of sadness about the fear of Egyptian Christians—even their pope—of being accused of converting Muslims to Christianity.

Very few Americans will ever understand what I am talking about when I speak about fear of the dictatorship of Islamic Sharia. The power of fear from Islamic tyranny is tormenting

Coptic Christians in Egypt on a daily basis. And very few Muslims will ever realize how horrific their system can be and how hurtful the violent, incendiary, and disrespectful scriptures are to others.

The vast majority of Muslims do not actually act on such violent messages yet paradoxically hold them dear as Allah's commands. And that is why the majority of Muslims are silent, confused, defensive, and in denial.

A sizable portion of Muslims—some estimate as high as 15 percent—are jihadists and ready to act upon the violent commands. But here is the frightening part: to many ordinary, moderate Muslims, jihadists "may Allah bless them" are the ones who are doing Allah's work. That is how the majority feel, and that is how I once felt. Take it from me. I've been there. That is why the West and its media and institutions must firmly stand up and say *no* to Islamic jihad. Muslims simply need that firm message to bring about more understanding to the suffering Islamic jihad causes.

The Multiculturism Mistake

There is a side of the American value of multiculturism that is also playing into the hands of the jihadists. All cultures are equal only in their operational dynamics. Just as the human body in general functions the same way, cultures at the functioning level operate equally. But at the moral and human rights and happiness level, cultures can differ greatly. No culture is perfect and every culture has its challenges, but to claim that all are morally equal is a mistake.

No one can say that, to a woman, the culture of Iran or Saudi Arabia is equal to that of America, for instance. Those who advocate that cultures are all equal and neglect the basic morality of laws and institutions of cultures, cannot defend their theory to a black slave from the Sudan who violates Sharia by trying to escape to freedom from his Arab Muslim master. It is time to take the theory that all cultures are equal off its pedestal, because it promotes injustice around the world and paralyzes progress in cultures that need moral and social reform.

That, of course, is not to say that Americans should not appreciate and celebrate the cultural richness and diversity that immigrants from around the world contribute to the great American melting pot. Various immigrant cultures sharing such things as their foods, music, festivals, and art make America a great place to live. Appreciation of ethnicity is not the same as the doctrinaire multiculturism that calls all cultures "equal" and then uses it as an excuse to tolerate injustice.

By tolerating intolerance, the West is not doing Muslims or Islam a favor. Tolerance of Islamo-Fascism is not a sign of compassion; it is gross negligence. The policy of appeasement has not worked when it comes to dealing with Arab culture. America's defense of the Muslims against the Serbs and the Afghani Muslims against the Soviet Union, liberation of Kuwait from the claws of fellow Muslim Iraq, feeding the Somali Muslims starved by their own Muslim government, and even our enormous help of the many Muslim nations that suffered from the tsunami — not one has brought any appreciation of America from the Arab Street. Just the opposite — the more we try to help, the more we are despised. They simply do not want to be rescued by infidels.

Western Democracies
Need a United Strategy

The West is militarily strong but lacks the moral clarity of knowing who it is and what it wants to protect. While the Islamic militant movement has been sharpening its swords in the last three to four decades, the West has been indulging in a movement of its own: moral and cultural relativism. While Muslim children were brought up with great pride in their jihad, religion, culture, and conquest of the world for Islam, in some segments of Western society, especially in Europe, several generations of children were taught self-blame, guilt over Western success, and discouragement for taking pride in their country, flag, or way of life. Some were ridiculed for believing in their Christian or Jewish heritage and heard denials that Western culture and political institutions are based on Judeo-Christian ethics and values. What the West views as virtue, Islam views as an opportunity. While the West values assimilation, Islam values segregation. While the West values freedom of speech, Islam prohibits asking questions. While the West advocates pacifism, Islam calls for war. While the West respects all religions, Islam advocates killing or subjugating those who believe in other religions.

The two opposite cultures when put together are a clear recipe for disaster that could end in an easy takeover. Repentance, a major Christian concept, is a virtue and a healthy principle of correcting the pathologies of individuals and society. However, knowingly or not, some people in the West have taken repentance too far; in their anger over America's imperfections and mistakes that exist in all societies, they end up throwing the baby out with the bath water. Values are the basis of everything. Western institutions are supported by values of liberty, freedom, equality under the law, and justice for all. When the basic values are strong, these institutions can correct past mistakes. Where once America enslaved Africans, slavery was abolished. When that was not enough, civil rights legislation was passed. Women once did not have the right to vote. The women's suffrage movement corrected that injustice, and later laws were passed to protect women from discrimination in the workplace. Our values are something to be proud of.

Some Americans ignore the reasons why their culture is a magnet for immigration from the whole world and want to open the borders to everyone, totally undermining their country's sovereignty. They believe that since all cultures are "equal" then America is morally no better than any other nation, so why not open the borders to everyone? In an attempt to make sure our children are not arrogant or chauvinistic, or that we don't "offend" immigrants, public schools downplay the fact that Western culture has produced the most humane, fair, and equal system of government and most prosperous society ever in the history of man.

There is a certain degree of healthy secularism needed in government to allow reasonable separation of church and state, but to deny the centrality of Judeo-Christian identity in Western society is to create a vacuum. Islam and its Sharia are tailor-made to fill such a vacuum. The West is confronting Islamists who know who they are, and know what they want. Frankly, that forces the West to do the same, to identify who they are, what they want—and then stand up for it. To continue ignoring these realities will be at the risk of the demise of Western civilization.

Containing Sharia and its militant enforcers and preventing it from spilling over into Western democracies must become a priority. There must be a unified Western strategy regarding the expansion of Islam and its agenda to take over from within. The following are urgent solutions to preserve the peace, freedoms, and human rights of Western democracies. If the measures listed below are implemented, the Islamist threat and its dysfunctional ideology could be stopped in its tracks without firing a shot. If not done, a bloody confrontation with Islam will be inevitable. Here is what the West must do:

1) *Define religion and exclude any ideology from that definition that does not pass the following basic values:*

- A religion must be a personal choice.
- No religion should kill those who leave it.
- A religion must never order the killing and subjugation of those who do not choose to be its members.
- A religion must abide by basic human rights.

Islam is not just a religion; it is a political ideology, and Muslim leadership itself has referred to its similarity with Fascism and Communism. Consider for a moment what our history would be if Communism, Nazism, or other dangerous ideologies had successfully paraded as "religion" and been granted total freedom to be preached from within the United States. The scenario could have been as follows: the Soviet Union could have built thousands of Communist temples in America, imported Communist preachers who could rail against America and agitate to abolish the U.S. Constitution and impose their own set of laws. Or how about Nazi temples preaching hate from their pulpits? So how could we as a society allow imams to preach the destruction of their host country's government and rule of law and the imposition of Dark Ages punishment and desert-tribal retribution? It should be unthinkable. Even if the imams do not teach hatred and killing of non-Muslims, Muslim scriptures do. They cannot run away from it. Evil ideologies cannot simply claim to be inspired by a God and expect the West to consider it religion.

Given that Islam is in large part a political ideology, the West must understand that mosques are not only centers for prayers and worship, but also centers for political action and Sharia enforcement. Building mosques in America during Western confrontation with Islamism and the war on terror is equivalent to building Communist party centers in America during the Cold War with the Soviet Union. The West needs to closely look at the building of mosques financed by Wahabi sects from Saudi Arabia.

2) Make Sharia an illegal law and declare it not a religion but a dangerous totalitarian ideology.

What the West should know is that Muslims are not even settled among themselves about Sharia law, and there are many divisions and conflicts in Muslim society over Sharia and its application. Great Britain's top religious official, Dr. Rowan

Williams, archbishop of Canterbury, caused an uproar when he suggested, "There's a place for finding what would be a constructive accommodation with some aspects of Muslim law, as we already do with some other aspects of religious law." Immediately after this announcement, Muslims in Britain were divided over what he said. Several Muslim women's advocates were against it, and other Muslim leaders were for it. Much of the West, on both sides of the Atlantic, was mortified. And rightly so—the day the West legally allows the practice of Sharia law even at a limited level is the day they condemn themselves to the eventual status of dhimmies. Accepting Islamic Sharia, even partially, means the sacrificing of basic Western values of democracy and human rights—rights that were defined under the Universal Declaration of Human Rights by the U.N. in 1948.

The West should be clear on the nature of Sharia. It is nothing more than legal tyranny, a terminal disease that destroys the healthy functioning of society where everything is sacrificed for the sake of total control. Islam is more of a social order than a religion. This social order is based on the Sharia and the ummah (the Islamic State), which is at odds with the values and standards of Western democracies. The West must unequivocally declare that Sharia is totally incompatible with democracy and human rights and that it is "cruel and unusual punishment."

To that end, immigration forms must inform Muslims that all family matters and disputes, without exceptions, in the United States must be adjudicated according to civil law. A Muslim immigrant must be told he could be prosecuted if he demands Sharia in his divorce case, wants to marry four women, or beats his wife. It must be clear to the Muslim immigrant that Sharia law, including so-called family law, is illegal under U.S. laws, and if they cannot accept that, then Muslim immigrants who want to live under Sharia must be told they cannot immigrate to the U.S.

There will be those who cry: "Freedom of religion! You can't limit someone's practice of their religion." There is clear precedent for denying a religious group the right to practice a tenet of their faith that conflicts with our Constitution. In the nineteenth century, the Mormon faith insisted on practicing polygamy as a major aspect of their religion. But the United States government forbids it; the Mormon Church was informed that polygamy is against the law in America, period. At the time, Mormons were understandably upset and felt they were being discriminated against, even persecuted. The Mormon Church eventually went on to outlaw the practice, though some renegade sects still attempt to follow polygamy.

The U.S. justice system presses charges against those who do not obey the law, as we have seen in recent times. Similarly, Sharia directly contradicts the Bill of Rights under the U.S. Constitution. And denying the "right" of Muslims in the United States to practice religious beliefs that are clearly against the law is both proper and necessary to preserve the rights of all citizens.

3) Control immigration from the Muslim world. Forms should clearly state that the goal of immigration is assimilation into democratic society.

Western democracies have become a magnet for immigrants from all over the world. However, in today's world, immigration should be considered a national security issue. Islamist radicals with an agenda to Islamize America and change its constitution to Sharia should never be allowed inside the U.S. The ultimate goal of immigration policy should be that immigrants become part of American society. Immigration policy has a duty to produce social cohesion and assimilation. It should require that the large number of recent-arrival Muslims be carefully vetted for terrorism and jihadist backgrounds and beliefs.

Immigration needs to be alert to the following: Islam has an innate subversive element that attracts the rebel class that naturally exists in every society, especially disenfranchised youth, and perhaps minorities who might want to get back at the system that is perceived as not giving them their rights. In every society there is a segment of the population that is attracted to the violence accompanying the call for jihad. The underground religious terror groups that exist in almost all Muslim countries have started to migrate to Western democracies, creating a permanent dynamic that the West is ill prepared for, and which can quickly spread to the disenfranchised in the host country, as we are seeing inside U.S. prisons.

Furthermore, many recent arrivals from places such as Somalia, Iraq, and Pakistan come as refugees and bring with them their values of honor killing, anti-American agitation, and jihadist aspirations. It is criminal to admit these refugees without demanding some kind of training and education to assist their assimilation and understanding of the laws of the culture to which they are moving.

In early 1980, I visited a couple of mosques in California, and the message given to Muslim immigrants was to *not* assimilate in America and that their number one loyalty should belong to the Muslim world, the ummah. In 2007, after living for almost thirty years in America, I was interviewed by a representative of Al Arabiya TV station, an interview that was never aired. During the interview I was asked if my number one loyalty was to Islam, Egypt, or America. My answer was America. The disappointment and anger was clear on the interviewer's face. He then asked me another question that was completely out of line. He asked me if my husband had converted to Islam, meaning, am I an apostate and living in sin for marrying an American? Suddenly, looking at that man's face, I felt as though I was facing a death sentence. For a few seconds, I did not know if he was really a journalist or an Islamist coming to kill me. I then opened the door and told him good-bye. This kind of mentality is prevalent among Muslim immigrants in the U.S.

One could argue that anyone not ready to assimilate has no business coming here. Unwillingness to assimilate and accept the laws of a culture creates the seed of a separatist group, which later grows and with time can become a separatist movement. To the West, I say: you are importing civil war. And when all criteria are met, and a Muslim immigrant seems to genuinely want to become part of our democracy, we still must insist that these new immigrants from the Muslim world be re-educated and re-trained into life in a democracy and into respect for the equal rights of all human beings.

Gradual assimilation is the natural process in the life of an immigrant in a new country. It is also a period of discovery and even a lot of fun. But radical mosques in the West are telling Muslim immigrants not to assimilate or befriend non-Muslim Americans. A Muslim cleric in Australia said openly on camera that Muslims should not befriend non-Muslims. How could that be? Western nations are opening themselves and giving Muslims an opportunity for a better life only to be treated as if their country is inferior and unclean. It is unnatural and takes hard work for an immigrant to remain unchanged and unassimilated. I cannot imagine how hard it must be to remain "loyal" and restrict oneself mainly with one's original group, his native tongue, and the old culture and religion. What then is the point of immigrating?

4) Stop issuing religious visas to Muslim clerics imported from Muslim countries.

Many of the clerics coming from the Middle East under religious visas are educated in Islam and Sharia and little else. Most of them cannot speak the language of the Western nation they have chosen to Islamize; many of them have been ridiculed, rejected, and even jailed for inspiring assassinations and terrorist activities in their Muslim countries of origin. Such clerics have found laws to protect them under Western democracies, but instead of appreciating such democratic laws, they reject them and turn around and demand the only thing they know—Sharia law. The educational level of the majority of these immigrant Muslim leaders is embarrassingly low if compared to other religious leaders in many parts of the world. Many of those imported Muslim preachers teach the only thing they learned in the madrassas back home—cursing, inciting, and hatred. Such clerics are committed to spreading Sharia, jihad, discrimination against non-Muslims, and virulent anti-Semitism. To them the solution is always an intifada, coup d'etat, and fatwas of deaths against anyone who refuses Sharia, including their tolerant host governments.

The Muslim population in the United States is large enough to produce their own American-born, trained, and educated clerics who will reflect the values of Western democracies and better adapt to American society. Many moderate American Muslims are in fact embarrassed by these poorly educated preachers, and would, truth be known, welcome a more stringent immigration policy regarding these clerics.

5) Ban mosques and Muslim organizations that use religion to promote incitement to kill and hate speech against people of other faiths or atheists.

No religious teachings or scriptures should be allowed to violate basic human rights of U.S. citizens contrary to the U.S. Constitution within the borders of the United States. Religious institutions that insist on doing so must no longer operate in America. Mosques that advocate killing of apostates, violent jihad, Sharia, and other activities against full religious freedoms should be closed. Along the same vein, another point must be made crystal clear: advocates of violent jihad and Sharia in the West must be declared enemies of the State.

6) Add several key questions to the U.S. immigration application aimed at educating immigrants in the laws of the country to which they have chosen to immigrate.

A key question should advise prospective immigrants that to choose to live in America is to accept the *separation of Mosque and State* and that demanding Sharia law after moving to the United States will be considered a crime against the United States government, a violation of its constitution, and a violation of the immigration application requirements, which will be grounds for deportation. Such things are not unheard of. When I immigrated to the United States, which was during the Cold War, the application asked if the applicant was affiliated with any Communist organizations. That application must be changed immediately to reflect today's reality. The government of Australia has already put such a policy into effect by asking new immigrants twenty questions. The United States, as well as all Western democracies, must follow suit.

It is also a good idea to inform new Muslim immigrants that U.S. laws *do not discriminate against women*, and that women in America have the same sexual freedoms and rights as men. This could prevent honor crimes from happening in the future, saving the lives of many teenage girls and serving as a warning to Muslim fathers and brothers who bring to the United States the legal and moral sexual values that discriminate against women. By alerting Muslim men in no uncertain terms that they are moving to a totally different judicial system, they might think twice before doing physical harm to their daughters or female family members. Clear methods of informing immigrants of what is expected of them may prevent misunderstandings after immigrants are already here.

7) Demand access for access.

Trade imbalance should not be the only worry for the West. Other gross imbalances in their relationships with countries and governments around the world need to be considered. Cultural imbalance is just as vital. America has porous physical borders allowing physical penetration, but we also have a porous cultural border. Muslims have access to build mosques in the West, yet give us no access to build churches or synagogues in the Muslim world. They finance Muslim studies and Middle East studies departments in American universities but do not allow Christian or Judaism Studies departments in any Muslim country. They freely preach Islam around the world but kidnap and kill Christian preachers on their own soil. Christian missionary work is illegal in most Muslim countries.

Amazingly, some Muslims wish to extend the denial of access into their communities within Western countries, and are finding cooperation. In June 2008, British media reported a February incident in which Arthur Cunningham and Joseph Abraham, American evangelical ministers who had been living in Great Britain for years, were told by a police community support officer to "stop handing out gospel leaflets in a predominantly Muslim area of Birmingham." Cunningham said that the officer told them that they were in a Muslim area and were not allowed to spread their Christian message. "He said we were committing a hate crime by telling the youths to leave Islam and said that he was going to take us to the police station." The men also said the officer told them that if they returned, they would "get beaten up." It was not clear from media reports who would administer the beatings, the Muslims or the police. The *Investor's Business Daily* Web site cited this incident as being "another sign that much of England has given up on being England."

If Muslim governments and citizens have access to build mosques in America, then they must give the U.S. government and citizens the same access in their countries. If they have the right to proselytize in America, then Americans must have the right to proselytize in Muslim countries. If they finance Islamic Studies departments on American campuses, the same should be the right of Americans on campuses of Muslim countries. If we do not demand equal cultural access, the cultural imbalance can result in one side absorbing the other's culture, aiding and abetting the jihadist Sharia dictatorships bent on destroying the West. We cannot afford to continue tolerating intolerance while never expecting anything better from the Muslim world.

8) Stop giving petrodollars to Arab countries.

American dollars and European Euros used to buy Arab oil are financing the jihad against us. The tremendous increase in Muslim jihad and Sharia aspirations has consistently paralleled the increase in Arab wealth from petrodollars. It is reckless to subject ourselves to blackmail by Saudis and Iranians. It simply does not make any sense when the stakes are so high—the very preservation of our democracy and way of life.

How we get off Arab oil is the big question of the day. Whether it is by drilling for oil in previously off-limit areas of the United States—which I think is important—or perfecting and using more of our current coal and nuclear technologies, or speeding the development of alternative fuels—wind, solar, water, hydrogen, and yet undiscovered alternatives—or by serious conservation programs, or all of the above, that is the major debate of the day. But ending our dependency on Arab oil is a must, not years into the future, but now, in whatever way it takes. American resolve and ingenuity have solved similar difficulties in the past, and they can again. The question is, how fast can we do it, and can we do it before it is too late?

Ending our dependency on Arab oil will not end Islamic jihad, but it will certainly weaken it. Watch and see how Islamization and Arabization activities slow down when funds to do so dry up.

9) Strengthen Western Judeo-Christian roots.

One of the reasons Islam is spreading in the West, especially Europe, is due to the secularization of Europe, which resulted in a spiritual vacuum and lack of strong family ties. Any society has a need to a spiritual connection to God and a holy place to go to when times get tough. Europe is experiencing a high rate of conversions to Islam, which especially gained momentum after 9/11. Most researchers believe that the erosion of religion and family values in Western societies is causing a vacuum that is now being filled by Islam, which offers a more predictable cultural, social, and family structure. The ills of the Muslim social and family structure are not very obvious in the West, which is still protected by democratic constitutions. Western converts are often attracted to the appearance of the closeknit Muslim family and structured lifestyle of the Muslim community, which is lacking in fast-paced Western society. Many Western converts eventually leave Islam when they discover the ugly other side of the coin in Muslim life; three out of four Western converts, according to some estimates, eventually leave Islam. It is time for Europe and America to reach into their rich Judeo-Christian heritage and champion those values that made them strong and can sustain and give purpose to the youth of the West.

Whether the issue is oil, immigration policy, or anything else, the West must not rush into appeasement. Despite jihadists flexing their muscles, the Muslim world is rotting from the core. The West must stand firm, believe its values, and wait it out. It must contain the threat and demand equal access in the market-place of ideas.

Islam Without the Sword?

MUSLIMS ARE NOT CONFIDENT THAT ISLAM WILL survive without the sword and the harsh punishments of Sharia. That has been the fear of Muslims from the very beginning, even during Mohammed's time when he had to be a warrior to enforce Islam. And it was that same fear when over one hundred years after his death, Muslim caliphs had to come up with Sharia to keep their power. Sharia is Islam and Islam is Sharia, and both are for the preservation of seventh-century Arabian culture, politics, and way of life, which could not survive in this day and age except under the sword. Muslims find freedoms of the West to be very seductive, which must be fought by any means—terror, war, jihad, lies, or distortions. For them to keep their stranglehold over the population, America and all free countries must always appear evil.

The Bedouin, who succeeded in keeping his culture and surrounding cultures insulated and at a standstill for fourteen hundred years, feels the threat from the outside world all over again. But this time it is not from seventh-century Christian Egypt, Jewish tribes, Mesopotamia, and Persia. It is coming into Arabia through satellite dishes and the Internet, across seas and oceans from America, Europe, and other Western democracies. The iron curtain of Islam has been penetrated by today's technology. New ideas and ways of life are felt inside the Arabian home. The guardians of Islam are eager to acquire Western technology, but not the culture that produced it. Like his women, the Muslim male wants Western culture neither heard nor seen. The threat to Arabian and Islamic culture has been renewed once again. Thus, conquering the rest of the world to Islam is the only way it can survive. Not that the West is imposing it by force. To the contrary, it is Arabia that is imposing its culture by force. But the West, just by its mere existence is a threat to their seventh-century worldview and the cohesion of the Arabian tribal culture.

Thus, to their way of thinking, exporting Sharia to the West is the only way to preserve Islam and the culture behind it. As it was in the Arabian Peninsula in the seventh century, the mere existence of other religions is viewed as a threat. Without the jihadist sword, death sentences for apostasy, and blasphemy laws, Islam would not have grown the way it did worldwide and would have probably vanished from history's memory of religious movements. The way Islamists see it, seventh-century Sharia law must survive if Islam is to survive. That is why Muslims in the West are advocating Sharia even more stridently than in many Muslim countries. Only 10 to 15 percent of Muslims worldwide want to live under Sharia. However, in a survey in Britain, approximately 40 percent of Muslims want Sharia. The pressure on Western democracies to Islamize and Arabize is very strong. Many secular Muslims who live in the West say that mosques in the West are often more radical than the ones back home in the Middle East. After visiting the United Kingdom in 2005, the Iraq deputy prime minister said that mosques in Britain are more extreme than the ones back home. He is reported to have told a conservative MP: "I am not surprised that you British are facing so many problems with extremists after what I saw in those mosques in Blackburn. What I saw . . . would not be allowed here in Iraq. It would be illegal."

The appetite to Islamize and Arabize seems to never be satisfied. The main purpose of Islam is to annihilate all kaffir culture and replace it with Islam and Arab culture. And Sharia is the main instrument for Arabizing a culture. The Arabization of twenty-two countries and Islamization of fifty-four countries is still not enough to satisfy the march of Arabia.

This drive is only temporarily interrupted when Arabia and Muslim countries are weak. But with one hundred more years of oil reserves, Saudi Arabia is committed to expansion into every corner of the world before the oil dries up and Arabia is returned to a harsh desert life again. Arabia is in a race with time, obsessed over building mosques in every corner of the world, including every little town in America and Europe and wherever it can.

Saudia Arabia is preparing to confront a very familiar fear—fear of living under the mercy of the harsh Arabian desert again with the whole world prospering around them, while they are relying on raiding one another for survival. Such memories must go through the minds of today's wealthy Saudis, and they know that one day they might be deprived of the wealth and power that come from petrodollars. They might no longer be able to afford the air-conditioned palaces in the middle of extremely hot deserts.

It was not so long ago when things were very different. Before the discovery of oil in Arabia, Egypt, out of loyalty to the nation that produced Islam and their prophet Mohammed, used to send regular financial support annually, during the Haj, to the people of Mecca. They considered them their poor cousin. Now Egypt is their poor cousin, slipping deeper into poverty and chaos, but paradoxically producing the fiercest of jihadists to strike terror worldwide for the Saudi agenda. The rush to Islamize and Arabize the rest of the world is a reflection of Saudi fears of losing their power and wealth before bringing the rest of the world literally to its knees praying toward Mecca. Arabia is relying on an Islamized Europe and perhaps a partially Islamized America for their survival and survival of their financial investments in those societies.

That is the only guarantee that the wealth of the world will be shared with poor desert Arabians.

The Arabization is going on right now even against non-Arab Muslim countries. The "Persian" Gulf was historically named after the largest nation and civilization on the Gulf, which is Persia (today Iran). But Arabs are now shamelessly renaming it the "Arab" Gulf, depriving the Persians of their historical greatness and presence in the area. Another attempt to Arabize the world: Muslim clerics in Saudi Arabia, with the help of the Arab media, have now replaced "Greenwich Mean Time" with "Mecca Time," which will create major conflict in the airline business if there is no consistently followed mean time. Are we all going to soon be checking our Mecca Time before we travel? Even in the West, Muslim converts are told they must learn Arabic, the language of the Qur'an. And Muslim women, on whatever continent in whatever climate, are expected to adopt the covered-up robes of the desert. Arabs understand the impact of such changes on the human psyche; it is conquering the minds of the world while striking terror in their hearts from Islamic jihad, bit by bit.

Refusing to comprehend what's at stake in this conflict could be democracy's undoing. Whether ignoring the threat or giving in to it, the outcome will be the same. The victory of Sharia and triumph of Islamic jihad worldwide would be as bad for Muslims as it would be for the world. Free people ignore the threat at their own peril.

> Great nations rise and fall. The people go from bondage to spiritual truth, to great courage, from courage to liberty, from liberty to abundance, from abundance to selfishness, from selfishness to complacency, from complacency to apathy, from apathy to dependence, from dependence back again to bondage.
>
> —Author Unknown

Which stage is the West in now?

This conflict is a struggle for the soul of the world. If we value our liberty, we must protect the soul of Western civilization.

The soul of the Muslim world is also at stake. The belief that without Sharia, Islam is finished does not speak well for Muslims and shows a lack of confidence in their religion. Muslims must show respect to their own religion by allowing those who want to leave to actually leave without the threat of the sword of Sharia. Islam will reform on its own if it rejects the use of Sharia and its cruel but usual punishment to enslave its followers. With the removal of the death penalty on apostates, Islam will find a non-violent way to keep its followers in the faith. Like other religions, it will then need to compete in the realm of humanitarian religious ideas to survive. The day that the sword of Sharia is removed will be the day that a glorious Islamic reformation begins. It is up to Muslims.

In the meantime, the West needs to send a strong and firm message to Muslims everywhere. Muslims need to hear that the human right to life, liberty, and pursuit of happiness is above the right of any religion that wants to take it away. Muslims need to hear the word *no*.

The West also needs to heed this message from a very wise man:

> A strict observance of the written laws is doubtless one of the high virtues of a good citizen, but it is not the highest. The laws of necessity, of self-preservation, of saving our country when in danger, are of higher obligation.
>
> —Thomas Jefferson

Acknowledgments

I COULD NOT HAVE COMPLETED THIS PROJECT WITH-out the patience and support of my husband and children. I especially want to thank Sharia expert Mr. Hasan Mahmud, director of Sharia Law of Muslim Canadian Congress whose writings and docu-movie helped me immensely with my research of this book. Mr Mahmud is one of the frontliners in the successful movement against Toronto Sharia Court.

I am also appreciative of the daily translation and reporting of the Middle East Media Research Institute (MEMRI) who keep us all informed with what is going on in the Arabic Media world.

I am grateful to my agent, Lynne Rabinoff, and to accomplished writer Elizabeth Black who was my editor and helped me immensely along the way.

And last but not least, I want to thank my publisher, Thomas Nelson, its dedicated staff, and especially the very talented editor Thom Chittom.

Notes

A Warning to the West

1. Sayyid Abul Ala Maududi, *Jihad in Islam* (Beirut: Holy Koran Publishing House, 1980), 9.

2. "American Muslim leader urges faithful to spread Islam's message," *The Argus* (Fremont, CA), July 4, 1998.

3. Sayyid Abul Ala Maududi, *Islamic Law and Its Introduction* (Pakistan, 1983), 13-14.

4. Sayyid Abul Ala Maududi, *Towards Understanding Islam*, trans. Zafar Ishaque Ansari (Leicestershire, UK: Islamic Foundation, 1995), 131.

5. Maududi, *Jihad in Islam*, 28.

6. Sean O'Neill, "Muslim students 'being taught to despise unbelievers as filth'," *Times of London*, April 20, 2006.

7. Qur'an 19:83.

8. Qur'an 3:28, trans. Abdullah Yusuf Ali (London: Wordsworth Editions, 2000).

9. "Ellison Speaks to Radical Groups," Little Green Footballs, December 26, 2006, http://littlegreenfootballs.com/weblog/?entry=23784_Ellison_Speaks_to_Radical_Groups_in_Dearborn&only.

10. Paul Marshall, "Muzzling in the Name of Islam," *Washington Post*, Sept 29, 2007.

11. Pamela Geller, "The Islamists Day Parade," Atlas Shrugs, September 9, 2007, http://atlasshrugs2000.typepad.com/atlas_shrugs/2007/09/the-islamists-d.html.

12. "Shootings at the Jewish Federation," SeattlePI.com, July 28, 2006, http://seattlepi.nwsource.com/specials/jewishfederationshootings.

13. Michael Adrian, "Ontario Bans Sharia Arbitration," Library Boy, February 17, 2006, http://micheladrien.blogspot.com/2006/02/ontario-bans-sharia-arbitration.html.
   Daniel Pipes, "Is Islamic Law Enforced in Canada?" *New York Sun*, September 27, 2005, http://www.nysun.com/foreign/is-islamic-law-enforced-in-canada/20630.

14. Qur'an 4:91, trans. Thomas Irving (Brattleboro, VT: Amana Books, 1979).

15. Qur'an 4:56, Irving.

16. Qur'an 4:76, Irving.

17. Qur'an 8:12, 17, Yusuf Ali.

18. Qur'an 8:60, Yusuf Ali.

19. Qur'an 47:4, Yusuf Ali.

20. Syed Kamran Mirza, "Qur'an is the Primary Manual of Islamic Suicide Terrorism," Islam Watch, April 21, 2006, http://www.islamwatch.org/SyedKamranMirza/TerrorManual.htm.

21. Islam Kamal, "Why are we afraid of terrorism when the Quran demanded it from us?" *Rose El Yusef*, January 30, 2006.

One

1. Sahih Bukhari 1:4:149, trans. M. Muhsin Khan (Alexandria, VA: Al Saadawi Publications, 1996).

2. Sahih Bukhari 1:4:162, Muhsin Khan.

3. Sunaan Abu Dawud 1:67, trans. Ahmad Hasan (Lahore: Sh. M. Ashraf, 1984).

4. Sahih Muslim 4:1062, trans. Abdul Hamid Siddiqui (India: Kitab Bhavan, 2000).

5. Quran 3:104, 110.

6. Sahih Muslim 41:6985, Siddiqui.

7. Sayyid Abul Ala Maududi, *Towards Understanding Islam*, trans. Zafar Ishaque Ansari, commentary 2:144 with respect to verse 2:143, http://www.tafheem.net/main.html.

8. Qur'an 37:48-49, 55:54-59, 55:70-77, 78:31-34.

9. Qur'an 44:51-55, 52:17-20, 52:24, 56:17, 76:19.

10. Codified Islamic Law, vol. 3, no. 914.

Two

1. Qur'an 66:5, trans. Thomas Irving (Brattleboro, VT: Amana Books, 1979).

2. Abd ar-Rahman al-Gaziri, *al-Fiqh 'ala al-Mazahib al-Arba'a*, (Beirut: Dar al-Kutub al- 'Elmeyah, 1990), 4:8.

3. Ahmad ibn Naqib al-Misri, *Reliance of the Traveller*, trans. Nuh Ha Mim Keller (Beltsville, Maryland: Amana Publications, 1991), m8.10, 535.

4. Ibn Kathir, *Tasfir ibn Kathir*, (Dar Ussalam Publishers, 2000), comment Q. 4:24

5. Ibn Abdullah Tabrizi, Sheikh Wali-ud-Din Muahmmad. 'Mishkat-ul-Masabih', 2:57 trans. Abdul Hameed Siddiqui, Kitab Bhavan (New Delhi: 1990). Reported from Abu Daud, also reported by Ahmad.

6. *Reliance of the Traveller*, al-Misri, m8.6, 534.

7. Abu Hamid Al-Ghazali, "Book of Etiquette of Marriage," *Ehya Ulum Al Deen* (Beirut: Dar al-Kotob al-'Elmeyah, year), 2:64.

8. Al-Ghazali, "Book on the Etiquette of Marriage," chapter 2.

9. Al-Ghazali, "Book on the Etiquette of Marriage," 33.

10. Sahih Bukhari 7:62:10, trans. M. Muhsin Khan (Alexandria, VA: Al Saadawi Publications, 1996).

11. Kitab Al-Talaq Law no. 1537 and 1538. *Reliance of the Traveller*, al-Misri, n1.2 and n1.3.

12. Sunaan Abu Dawud 12:2173, trans. Ahmad Hasan (Lahore: Sh. M. Ashraf, 1984).

13. Qazi Khan, Mishkat al-Masabih, 1:15n.

14. *The Hedaya: Or Guide, a Commentary on the Musselman Laws*, trans. Charles Hamilton (Delhi, India: Kitab Bhavan, 1988), 523.

15. *Reliance of the Traveller*, al-Misri, m7.4, 532.

16. Ibid., n7.1, 564.

17. Ibid., n5.0, 562.

18. Al-Gaziri, 4:522.

19. Ibid., 4:523.

20. Ibid., 4:488.

21. Ibid., 4:495-497.

22. Ibid., 4:498.

23. Ibid., 4:497-498.

24. Ibid., 4:497-499.

25. Sayyid Qutb, In the shadow of the Quran, (Cairo: Dar el Shurouk, 1972), 654.

26. The Australian Minaret, (Australian Federation of the Islamic Councils, 1980), 10. And also quoted in M. Rafiqul-Haqq and P. Newton, *The Place of Women in Pure Islam.*

27. Khan, Mishkat al-Masabih, 1:60.

28. Sunaan Abu Dawud 11:2142, Hasan.

29. "Violence against Women Highlighted" *Guardian Weekly*, Dec. 23, 1990.

30. Sayyed Qutb, *In the shadow of the Quran*, (Cairo: Dar el Shurouk, 1972) 654.

31. Qur'an 4:128, Irving.

32. Sahih Bukhari 7:62:81.

33. Sahih Bukhari 7:62:16.

34. Al-Ghazali, "Book on the Etiquette of Marriage," 1:235.

35. *Reliance of the Traveller*, al-Misri, e13.5.

36. Al-Ghazali, "Book on the Etiquette of Marriage," 2:311.

37. Khan, Mishkat al-Masabih, 1:138, 40.

38. Sahih Muslim 2:3367, trans. Abdul Hamid Siddiqui (India: Kitab Bhavan, 2000).

39. Sahih Bukhari 4:54:460, Muhsin Khan. Sahih Muslim 2:3368, Siddiqui.

40. Kanz-al-Ummal 22:868, trans. al-Hindi (Hyderabad: 1314). Copy at Birmingham University, UK

41. Mishkat Al-Masabih 1:1:2 Tabrizi.

42. Ibid., 1:2:60.

43. Ibid., 2:691.

44. Al-Ghazali, "The Revival of the Religious Sciences," Ascha, 41.

45. Al-Ghazali, Ihy'a 'Uloum ed-Din, Dar al-Kotob al-'Elmeyah, *Beirut*, vol. II, Kitab Adab al-Nikah, 34.

46. Ibid., 2:37.

47. Abd ar-Rahman al-Gaziri, al-Fiqh 'ala al-Mazahib al-Arba'a, Dar al-Kutub al-'Elmeyah, 1990, vol. 4, 89.

48. Qortobi, *Tafsir Al Qortobi*, commenting on Q. 4:3.

49. Mishkat al-Masabih, 1:62, Tabrizi.

50. Ibid., 1:62n.

51. Qur'an 44:51-54, Irving.

52. Qur'an 55:56-58, Irving.

53. Qur'an 55:70-72, Irving.

54. Qur'an 78:31-34, Irving.

55. Ibn-Kathir, comment on Q. 56:35-37.

56. Sahih Muslim 40:6793, Siddiqui.

57. Ayatollah Khomeini, *Tahrirolvasyleh* (Gom, Iran: Darol Elm, 1990), 4:#. Bear in mind, the revered status of Ayatollah Khomeini, considered one of the greatest imams and saints of Shiite Islam in the whole world, is responsible for the spread of radicalism across the Muslim world after the Iranian revolution.

58. Khomeini, *Tahrirolvasyleh*, 241, 12.

59. Sahih Bukhari 3:48:805.

60. Khomeini, "The Little Green Book: sayings of the Ayatollah Khomeini", Bantam Books, 1985.

61. Recently in Egypt, a graduate of Al Azhar Islamic University wrote a booklet on how a Muslim should have sex with his wife the Sharia way. The booklet, "Islamic Love-making Manual," which sold millions of copies in Egypt and elsewhere, provides details for both men and women on what to do before, during, and after sex. For instance, a man must say a prayer during orgasm. In a modern revision of the manual, at the end, it does not miss the opportunity to blame the Zionists for certain misinformation about sex that Muslims should look out for and ignore.

Three

1. Sunaan Abu Dawud 2:11:2142, trans. Ahmad Hasan (Lahore: Sh. M. Ashraf, 1984).

2. Out of embarrassment, some Muslims try to misinterpret this verse, saying that "Allah is forgiving" was meant for the slave girl not for the slave owner. But how could that be, when the verse is clearly addressing men and not the slave girl? Also, how can Allah forgive the slave girl for something she has no control over?

3. Sunaan Abu Dawud 2:11:2150, Hasan.

4. Codified Islamic Law o5.4.

5. MEMRI.org http://memri.org/bin/latestnews.cgi?ID=IA35507. May 25, 2007.

6. Sahih Muslim book 008, number 3428

7. Muhammad al-Mussayar, Panorama show, Al-Arabiya TV, February 12, 2007.

8. Ahmad ibn Hanbal d.855 http://raceandculture.blogspot. com/2008/07/essay-on-women-in-islam.html

9. Kanz-el-'Ummal 22:858, Abu Hamid Al-Ghazali, "Book of Etiquette of Marriage," *Ehya Ulum Al Deen* (Beirut: Dar al-Kotob al-'Elmeyah), 2:65.

10. Al-Ghazali, 2:65. Reported by Tirmizi as a true and good Ahadith. (This hadith is classed as *sahih*, "sound" or "faultless.")

11. Ibid.

12. Sadaf Farooqi, "How to Guard Your Husband's Honor as a Muslim Wife," How To Do Things, http://www.howtodothings. com/religion-spirituality/how-to-guard-your-husbands-honor-as-a-muslim-wife.

13. Sahih Muslim 24.5310, trans. Abdul Hamid Siddiqui (India: Kitab Bhavan, 2000).

14. Julie Henry and Laura Donnelly, "Female Muslims 'disobey hygiene rules'," *The Telegraph* (London), February 4, 2008.

15. Al-Ghazali, 2:5.

16. Ibid.

17. Sahih Bukhari 7:62:33, trans. M. Muhsin Khan (Alexandria, VA: Al Saadawi Publications, 1996).

18. Kanz-el-'Ummal 21:825, al Hindi.

19. Sahih Bukhari 1:6:301, Muhsin Khan.

20. Rasha Al-Disuqi, http://www.youtube.com/watch?v=FEcNaVkQUx 4&feature=related

21. Sahih Bukhari 7:26:126, Muhsin Khan.

22. Sahih Bukhari 5:59:709, Muhsin Khan.

23. Sahih Muslim 8:3240, Siddiqui.

24. Sahih Muslim 36:6603, Siddiqui.

25. Codified Islamic Law m10.4

26. Al-Ghazali, 2:311.

27. Tabari 9:112-114.

28. Tabari 3:367.

29. Sahih Bukhari 7:62:113, Muhsin Khan.
30. Al-Ghazali, 2:51.
31. Sahih Bukhari 1:6:301, Muhsin Khan.
32. "God's Warriors," interviewed by Christiane Amanpour, CNN, 2007.
33. Halide Edib, quoted in Phillip Mansel, *Constantinople: City of the World's Desire 1453-1924* (New York: St. Martin's Griffin, 1998).
34. memritv.org, "Polygamy in Egypt," clip # 796 31 July 2005, http://www.memritv.org/clip/en/796.htm

Four

1. Felix Doligosa Jr., "Saudi gets long sentence; Man was convicted of sexual assaults on housekeeper," *Rocky Mountain News*, September 1, 2006.
2. Saleh Al-Fawzan, quoted in Daniel Pipes, "Saudi Religious Leader Calls for Slavery's Legalization," Daniel Pipes Blog, 7 November 2003, http://www.danielpipes.org/blog/2003/11/saudi-religious-leader-calls-for-slaverys.html.
3. Sahih Muslim 2.3471, trans. Abdul Hamid Siddiqui (India: Kitab Bhavan, 2000).
4. Thomas Patrick Hughes, *Dictionary of Islam* (Chicago: Kazi Publications, Inc., 1994), 675,
5. Hughes, *Dictionary of Islam*, 675-6.
6. Sahih Bukhari 7:62:115, trans. M. Muhsin Khan (Alexandria, VA: Al Saadawi Publications, 1996).
7. Al-Hilyah 7:332. Al-Silsilat al-Sahihah 1446.
8. Sahih Bukhari 7:62:126, Muhsin Khan.
9. Qur'an 8:12, trans. Thomas Irving (Brattleboro, VT: Amana Books, 1979).
10. Qur'an 9:5, Irving.
11. Sunaan Abu Dawud 38:4348, trans. Ahmad Hasan (Lahore: Sh. M. Ashraf, 1984).
12. Qur'an 9:38-39, Irving.
13. Qur'an 61:10-12, Irving.
14. Sahih Bukhari 4:52:50, Muhsin Khan.
15. Sahih Bukhari 4:52:53, Muhsin Khan.
16. Sahih Bukhari 4:52:73, Muhsin Khan.

17. Sahih Bukhari 4:52:801, Muhsin Khan.

18. Sahih Bukhari 9:89:282, Muhsin Khan.

Five

1. "Report: Non-Muslims Deserve to Be Punished," FoxNews.com, April 1, 2008.

2. Ahmad ibn Naqib al-Misri, *Reliance of the Traveller*, o.24.3 (3), 636. Hanafi Law, 361.

3. Penal Law of Islam, 47.

4. Hanafi Law, 362.

5. *Reliance of the Traveller*, al-Misri, 04.9.

6. *Wall Street Journal*, April 9, 2002.

7. *Reliance of the Traveller*, al-Misri, o1.2.

8. Penal Law of Islam, 149.

9. *Reliance of the Traveller*, al-Misri, w52.0 (384).

10. Ibid., w52.0.

11. Ibid., w59.2.

12. Sahih Bukhari 9:91:368, trans. M. Muhsin Khan (Alexandria, VA: Al Saadawi Publications, 1996). Ibn Kathir, Kasasul Ambia 3, 112.

13. Ehud R. Toledano, *The Ottoman Slave Trade and it's Suppression* (Princeton: Princeton University Press, c1982), 93.

14. R. W. Beachey, *The Slave Trade of Eastern Africa* (London: Collins, 1976), 157, 262.

15. Qur'an 5:101-102, trans. Thomas Irving (Brattleboro, VT: Amana Books, 1979).

16. Sahih Bukhari 4:54:496, Muhsin Khan.

17. *Reliance of the Traveller*, trans. al-Misri, o5.4.

18. Codified Islamic Law 1:1:13.

19. *Reliance of the Traveller*, trans. al-Misri, w59.2.

20. Sunaan Abu Dawud 38:349, trans. Ahmad Hasan (Lahore: Sh. M. Ashraf, 1984).

21. Qur'an 2:178-179, Irving.

22. Sunaan Abu Dawud, trans. Hasan.

23. This hadith is found in the four *Sunan* works and in *Musnad Ahmad*. Some scholars declared it to be authentic or at least good, including al-Tirmidhî, al-Hakim, al-Dhahabi, Ibn Taymiyah, al-Shâtibî, and Ibn Hajar al-`Asqalânî.

24. Ali Gum'a, *Relgion and Life: Modern Everyday Fatwas* (Cairo: Azhar, 2006). Also http://sweetness-light.com/archive/uproar-over-fatwa-on-drinking-prophets-urine

25. Quran 113:5, Irving.

26. Sahih Muslim 26:5427 trans. Abdul Hamid Siddiqui (India: Kitab Bhavan, 2000).

27. Sunaan Ibn Majah 5:3506:3507.

28. Qur'an 114:2-5.

29. Qur'an 72.

30. Sahih Bukhari 3:30:113, Muhsin Khan.

31. Sahih Bukhari 4:52:183-184, Muhsin Khan.

32. Sahih Bukhari 4:53:409, Muhsin Khan.

33. Sahih Bukhari 4:52:182-184, Muhsin Khan.

34. Sahih Bukhari 5:59:297, Muhsin Khan.

35. Sahih Muslim 4:30:6297, Siddiqui.

36. Hadith Malik 511:1588.

37. Sayyıd Abul Ala Maududı, *Towards Understanding Islam*, trans. Zafar Ishaque Ansari (Lahore, Pakistan: Kazi Publications, 1958), 54.

38. That show was later translated into English and was posted on the Internet by www.memri.org.

39. Codified Islamic Law, vol. 2. no. 575n.

40. Codified Islamic Law, vol. 2, no. 17n.

41. Sahih Bukhari 4:53:386, Muhsin Khan.

42. Sahih Bukhari 4:52:177.

43. Abd Al-Hamid Al-Ansari, "How the Arabs Explain the Terror Phenomenon," *Al-Raya* (Qatar) June 15, 2007.

44. *Reliance of the Traveller*, o8.4

45. Hanafi Law, 362.

46. *Reliance of the Traveller*, L1.0.

47. Ibid., m7.4.

48. Ibid., o8.0.

49. Ibid., o8.7.

50. Maulana Abdur Rahman, *History of Hadith-Compilation*, 94. Muhiuddin Khan, *Qur'anic Tafsir*, 743, 256.

51. *Reliance of the Traveller*, o8.7 (18).

Six

1. Sayyid Abul Ala Maududi, *Islamic Law and Constitution*, trans. Kurshid Ahmad. (Kazi Pubns Inc, 1955), 262.

2. Qur'an 2:30, trans. Thomas Irving (Brattleboro, VT: Amana Books, 1979).

3. Sahih Bukhari 4:52:203, trans. M. Muhsin Khan (Alexandria, VA: Al Saadawi Publications, 1996).

4. Hanafi Law, 188. Codified Islamic Law, vol. 3, no. 914c.

5. Ibn Hajar Haytami, "List of Enormities," w52, 317-1.

6. Sayyid Abul Ala Maududi, *A Short History of the Revivalist Movement in Islam* (Kuala Lumpur:Islamic Book Trust, 2002), 65n.

7. Shafii Law o25.0 to o25.9. Also see: http://www.usc.edu/dept/MSA/ politics/khalifa.html lectures on Muslim Khilafa by Gharm Allah Al-Ghamdy at USC between 11-91 and 12-92

8. Ibn Ishaq, *Life of Allah's Messenger*, trans Guillaume (Oxford University 1955), 243.

9. Sahih Muslim 20:4565, trans. Abdul Hamid Siddiqui (India: Kitab Bhavan, 2000).

10. Mohammed Abduh, Mufti of Egypt, 1903.

11. Sayyid Abul A'la Maududi, *Jihad fi Sabilillah (Jihad in Islam)*, trans. Prof. Kurshid Ahmad. (Birmingham: UK Islamic Mission Dawah Centre, 1997 [1939]), 14.

12. Qur'an 9.111, Irving.

13. Ahmad ibn Naqib al-Misri, *Reliance of the Traveller*, trans. al-Misri, w52.1 (377), 987.

14. Majid Khadduri, *War and Peace in the Law of Islam*, (Baltimore: Johns Hopkins Press, 1955), 64.

15. Sahih Bukhari 9:87:127, Muhsin Khan.

16. Sahih Bukhari 4:52:220, Muhsin Khan.

17. Sahih Bukhari 9:88:178, Muhsin Khan.

18. Maher Hathout (address, MPAC Jerusalem Day Rally, Washington DC, October 28, 2000), http://www.youtube.com/ watch?v=n6_LwJ4Dd_o.

19. Sahih Bukhari 4:52:267-68, Muhsin Khan.

20. Sahih Muslim 19:4329, Siddiqui.

21. Ahmad ibn Yahya al-Baladhuri, (2002), 109. Also Q:41

22. Bill Warner, "The Study of Political Islam," FrontPageMag.com, February 05, 2007.

23. Qur'an 21:44, Irving.
24. Qur'an 28:58, Irving.
25. Qur'an 13:41, Irving.
26. Qur'an 46:27, Irving.
27. Qur'an 33:27, Irving.
28. Qur'an 59:2, Irving.

Seven

1. Sayyid Qutb, *Milestones* (India: Islamic Book Service, 2006), 130-131.
2. Qur'an 9:14, trans. Thomas Irving (Brattleboro, VT: Amana Books, 1979).
3. Sahih Muslim 2:234, trans. Abdul Hamid Siddiqui (India: Kitab Bhavan, 2000).
4. David G. Littman, "Human Rights and Human Wrongs," National Review Online, January 19, 2003.
5. "Almaydan," (Cairo, Egypt), April 15, 2004.

Eight

1. Qur'an 9:14, trans. Thomas Irving (Brattleboro, VT: Amana Books, 1979).
2. Qur'an 9:52, Irving.
3. Qur'an 8:17, Irving.
4. Sahih Bukhari 1:3:11.
5. Sahih Bukhari 4:52:283.
6. Sahih Bukhari 9:83:50.
7. Sunaan Abu Dawud 39:4491.
8. Sunaan Abu Dawud 39:4515.
9. Sunaan ibn Majah 4:2658, 2659.
10. Penal Law of Islam, 149. Ahmad ibn Naqib al-Misri, *Reliance of the Traveller*, trans. o1.2, 583-584.
11. Sahih Bukhari 9:84:57, trans. M. Muhsin Khan (Alexandria, VA: Al Saadawi Publications, 1996).
12. Graeme Wilson, "Young, British Muslims 'getting more radical'," *The Telegraph* (London) January 30, 2007, http://www.telegraph.co.uk/news/uknews/1540895/Young,-British-Muslims-'getting-more-radical'.html.

13. Sahih Bukhari 4:52:177, Muhsin Khan.

14. *Reliance on the Traveller*, 17.3, 664.

15. Patrick Goodenough, "Religious Hate Law Aimed At Protecting Muslims Passes UK Vote," CNS News, July 12, 2005.

16. US Commission on International Religious Freedom, June 11,2008 http://www.uscirf.gov/index.php?option=com_content&task=view&id=2206&Itemid=1

17. Ibid.

18. Imam Muhammed Al-Asi, (lecture, University of California, Irvine, February 21, 2001).

19. Qur'an 3:169, 4:74, 4:95, 9:111.